COLORADO
Wildlife

NUMBER SIX **COLORADO** geographic series JEFF RENNICKE

Falcon Press

Dedication

To my daughter Katelyn and the wildlife that will still roam in her future.

Acknowledgments

The Colorado Division of Wildlife supported and encouraged this project from the very beginning. Special thanks go to Bob Hernbrode, who spearheaded this project as Watchable Wildlife Coordinator for the division, and to all the CDOW employees who graciously and diligently read and commented on the text. Special thanks also go to Dr. Jim Benedict of the Center for Mountain Archaeology, who freely shared his thoughts on the early relationship between humans and wildlife.

About the author

Jeff Rennicke is the author of the first two books in the Colorado Geographic Series, *Colorado Mountain Ranges* and *The Rivers of Colorado*.

Copyright © 1990 by Falcon Press Publishing Co., Inc., Helena and Billings, Montana

Text copyright © 1990 by the Colorado Division of Wildlife

Published in cooperation with the Colorado Division of Wildlife

Design, typesetting, and other prepress work by Falcon Press, Helena, Montana. Printed in Korea.

Library of Congress Number 90-84866

ISBN 1-56044-036-8

Title page photo

Coyote at sunrise, Sage Prairie W. PERRY CONWAY

Contents

From high mountain meadows—such as this one at Schofield Pass on Gunnison National Forest—to vast prairie grasslands and even urban backyards, Colorado contains a variety of habitats for an astonishing array of wild creatures. In many ways, wildlife forms an integral part of the state's natural beauty and heritage. WILLARD CLAY

Foreword

It's easy to see wildlife in Colorado. Even without specific knowledge about where, when, and how to observe wild animals, people see wildlife every day—often without thinking about it. We see sparrows, starlings, and rock doves everywhere in our cities. Many people would feel their day was not complete without seeing deer or Canada geese.

But with a little specific information, wildlife can become significantly more accessible to us. We can see sage grouse on remote leks, learn to enjoy the infinite variety of songbirds in parks, open spaces, and backyards of our cities, listen to bugling elk, see and understand social interaction in a herd of bighorn sheep on a crisp fall day, and much, much more. All we need is a little information and help.

That is part of the purpose of this publication—to help you find new places and different wildlife to enjoy throughout Colorado. This book was also written to help you better understand and appreciate our great natural heritage—our wildlife.

Enjoy.

Bob Hernbrode
Watchable Wildlife Coordinator
Colorado Division of Wildlife

Natives of Colorado's mountains, bighorn sheep such as this ram symbolize the state's rich wildlife heritage. Bighorns are found in more than 75 locations across the state, from easily accessible roadside areas to remote wilderness. They are Colorado's official state animal. D. ROBERT FRANZ

The Heartbeat of the Land
Colorado's Watchable Wildlife

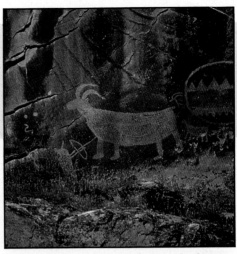

A petroglyph of a bighorn sheep and a hunter with a bow and arrow adorns a rock wall in Dinosaur National Monument's Echo Park. Early rock art often featured wildlife, an indication of the importance of wild animals to early cultures. WENDY SHATTIL / BOB ROZINSKI

The forest is quiet and cold. In the moments just before dawn, the soft light among the aspens is the color of ice. The songbirds have migrated, taking their music with them. Marmots and ground squirrels have curled up to hibernate. Trout hang motionless in the deep ice-free pools of the creek. In the silence of late autumn, the land seems barren.

Then, as the sun rises, a string of tracks becomes visible on the frosty ground. A small herd of elk has moved along the ridge sometime during the night, working slowly downhill to the creek. The first tentative chirps of a mountain chickadee crack the morning silence. A small vole stirs the reeds at the edge of the trail. The new day seems suddenly charged with life.

Wildlife is the heartbeat of the land. The sight of deer grazing in a high meadow, a red-tailed hawk circling in the sky, or a set of coyote tracks stretching across the snow can make the Colorado landscape come to life. It is the bighorn sheep and the ptarmigan that make the high country more than just rock and ice. It is the cloud of dust behind a running herd of pronghorns that makes the prairie more than empty horizons. And it is the song of the canyon wren that makes the canyons more than silent walls.

Colorado has one of the most varied landscapes in the United States. It encompasses 104,247 square miles, with a low point of 3,300 feet along the Arkansas River and a high point of 14,433 feet atop the summit of Mount Elbert—nearly two vertical miles from head to toe. The state holds 53 of the 67 U.S. peaks higher than 14,000 feet, and the Continental Divide runs through its center. Yet it also contains 40,000 square miles of high plains to the east and vast expanses of canyon country to the west. Through it all flow more than 100 rivers, from major waterways such as the Colorado and the Platte to lesser known streams such as the Purgatoire and the Mancos.

The variety of climate, topography, and soil types results in a wide array of habitats. Within its boundaries, Colorado holds ponderosa pine forests, alpine tundra, shortgrass prairie, pinyon stands, glacial valleys, sagebrush flats, sweeping subalpine forests, meadows of wildflowers, sand dunes, high mountain parks, bristlecone groves, willow thickets, and more. Each weaves a unique thread into the tapestry of the Colorado landscape. Each creates a different set of conditions for wildlife, poses a different set of challenges, and offers the wildlife watcher a different viewing opportunity.

Colorado contains some of the most pristine and unbroken wildlife habitat on the continent. Much of this habitat lies on 23 million acres of public land administered by the state of Colorado, the U.S. Forest Service, the Bureau of Land Management, the National Park Service, and the U.S. Fish and Wildlife Service. Here you can find the great wildlife spectacles: a bugling elk on a misty autumn morning, a flock of waterfowl rising from a prairie marsh, bighorn sheep clashing horns on a cliffside, a mountain lion sunning in a box canyon.

Yet the wildlands are not the only home to wildlife. While many species have suffered at the hand of man, some have adapted to the human presence with surprising success. The establishment of city parks and greenways, even the growing number of backyard bird feeders, has helped to make a place for wildlife in our urban areas. Wherever you are in Colorado, you are not far from a place to watch wildlife.

Wildlife-watching is not a new activity. Man's relationship with wildlife in Colorado dates back at least 16,500 years, to when pre-Clovis men tracked camels, bison, deer, and pronghorns. Wildlife meant life or death to these early cultures. Hides were used for clothing and shelters, bones were made into awls and needles, horns were fashioned into dippers or tools, meat was a dietary staple. Our long tradition of hunting and fishing in Colorado has been well-documented.

But evidence suggests that early cultures saw other value in wildlife. On canyon walls, primitive rock art—petroglyphs and pictographs of elk, deer,

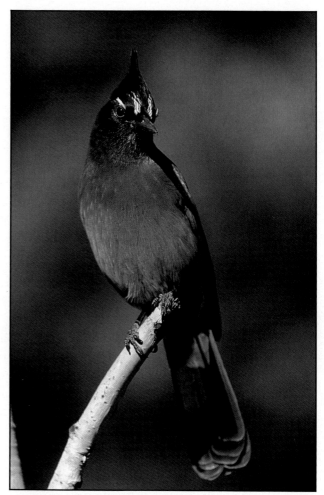

Found in coniferous and pine-oak forests, the Steller's jay is Colorado's most widely distributed jay. It is readily identified by its black and blue colors and its distinctive crest. Steller's jays frequently visit campsites where they sit quietly in treetops before gliding down in search of food. WENDY SHATTIL / BOB ROZINSKI

bighorns, bison, eagles, lizards, snakes, and wolves —speaks of long hours spent studying wildlife. No one can say with scientific certainty what meaning these pictographs and petroglyphs held for their creators, but the sheer beauty of the work attests to a recognition of wildlife as something more than just a resource to be used and discarded.

The influence of wildlife can be found in many early Colorado cultures. Some of the dances of the Plains Indians mimic the strutting displays of sage grouse. A ceremonial headdress of flicker feathers and another made from the hide of a mule deer have been unearthed in a cave alongside the Yampa River. A 4,000-year-old, split-twig figurine of an animal

Wildlife cannot exist without good habitat, and Colorado contains some of the best wildlife habitat in the United States. This view of Snowdon Peak in the San Juan Mountains shows three types of habitat: alpine, the areas above tree line; subalpine, the forested sections and adjacent meadows; and riparian, the wet area around the pond. Each supports a variety of wildlife. LARRY ULRICH

was found in a desert cave in southwestern Colorado. There are frogs carved in turquoise, vessels shaped like birds, and images of lizards on pottery made by the Anasazi of Mesa Verde.

All show that animals were studied, celebrated, and enjoyed long before the advent of field guides and spotting scopes. Humans have acknowledged for thousands of years that they share the earth with a wide variety of living things.

Today that recognition remains. Although we no longer depend on hunting or fishing for our survival, wildlife remains an important part of our lives. The bighorn sheep is a symbol of our state, the bald eagle a symbol of our nation. Colorado hunters and

fishermen annually spend about 40 million dollars on license fees. More than six million dollars has been raised for nongame wildlife programs through a checkoff on state income-tax forms.

More and more people are getting out to enjoy Colorado's wildlife, making wildlife-watching one of the fastest-growing outdoor activities in the state. Recent research indicates that more than 85 percent of Colorado residents participate in some kind of wildlife-related activity other than hunting or fishing. People from across the world are drawn here by the many opportunities available to bird-watchers, photographers, artists, and those who just wish to observe wildlife in its natural habitat. More than 25

Comfortably content, a black-tailed prairie dog suns itself near its burrow. Prairie dogs are common and conspicuous residents of Colorado's eastern plains. Their colonies, or towns, often include hundreds of prairie dogs and attract a variety of other animals. These sites make excellent locations for watching wildlife. WELDON LEE

percent of the almost 14 million annual visitors to Colorado specifically note wildlife-viewing among their reasons for traveling here. Many others enjoy it as a bonus.

Wildlife-viewing can be as casual as glancing out a car window at a kestrel on a telephone pole or sitting quietly in an open field to watch deer feed. It can also be a very serious endeavor. In much the same way that some people set out to climb all the 14,000-foot peaks in the state, serious wildlife watchers strive to see all of Colorado's 439 bird species or to track down rare species such as the wood frog. Some set out specifically to view certain behaviors, such as bighorn rams clashing in the mountains.

Watching wildlife can be educational, enjoyable, exciting, and even humbling. To see a mountain goat is to marvel at its ability to survive in conditions that an unprepared human would find life-threatening.

To witness a peregrine falcon swoop from the sky for a kill can send chills up your spine. To discover the rainbow of colors shimmering in the feathers of a broad-tailed hummingbird can lend new meaning to the word enchantment.

We cannot fully understand a landscape until we come to know the creatures that inhabit it. Mammals, birds, reptiles, and amphibians are products of their environment. They reflect a landscape—its moods, demands, beauties, and perils—as clearly as a still pond reflects the mountains.

Colorado is home to more than 900 species of wildlife. Of these, about 750 species are classified as nongame, meaning they are not hunted or fished. Some species, such as river otter, black bear, and mountain lion, are secretive and rarely seen. Others, such as mule deer, yellow warbler, mallard, eastern fox squirrel, and tiger salamander, are common and abundant.

This book is an introduction to Colorado's watchable wildlife. It will provide information on the habits and habitats of some of the state's wildlife species and offer hints on where and how to view them.

Still, no book can replace the experience of moving personally into the world of wildlife. It is a world of mountain goats climbing to dizzying heights, golden eagles riding on rising air currents, pheasants bursting out of cornfields, marmots scurrying against the first cold winds of winter, Canada geese winging through a brilliant autumn sky.

This is the world of Colorado's wildlife. This is the heartbeat of the land. ■

A young bull elk pauses in the middle of a stream. Colorado contains about 175,000 elk, the largest population of any state. Their abundance, size, and interesting behavior make elk one of the most commonly observed large animals in the state. They are found from the foothills to the tallest peaks and may be seen throughout the year. CHASE SWIFT

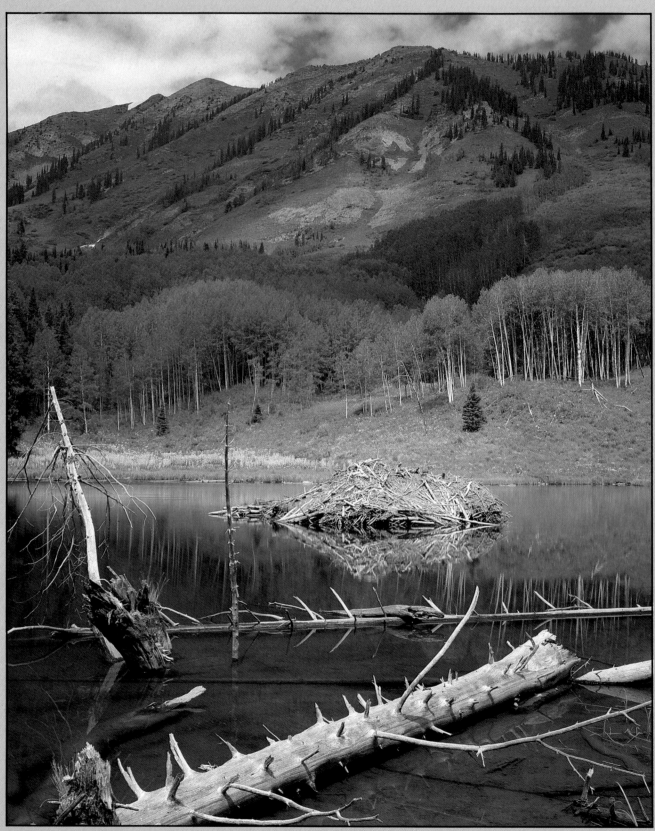

A beaver pond—complete with a beaver lodge made of sticks and mud—fills a valley in the West Elk Mountains on Gunnison National Forest near Aspen. Beavers range throughout Colorado along tree-lined waterways. Largely nocturnal, beavers may be seen by patient observers at dawn and dusk. Wildlife viewers also should look for beaver sign such as dams, lodges, fallen trees, gnawed sticks, and distinctive five-toed, webbed tracks. WILLARD CLAY

The Search

The Search
Observing Colorado's Wildlife

Bright as a summer sky, a mountain bluebird holds a feather used to line its nest in an aspen tree. For bluebirds, woodpeckers, flickers, and other cavity-nesting birds, standing dead trees provide critical nesting locations. Bluebirds readily adapt to nest boxes placed in appropriate sites, such as fence posts in open areas. CHASE SWIFT

I n the darkest hour of the night, owls are calling and raccoons are prowling in the riverside reeds. On the coldest day of winter, mule deer are gathering in the thick brush and flocks of rosy finches are chirping from the branches of pine trees. Under the hottest summer sun, rattlesnakes are coiling in the shade of sagebrush and golden eagles are soaring on rising air currents.

No matter what the season or time of day, wildlife-watching opportunities abound in Colorado. Still, successful and enjoyable wildlife-viewing requires some information, planning, and the right equipment.

Gearing up

Wildlife-watching is one of the simplest of outdoor activities. It does not require a lot of complicated and expensive equipment to get started. But there are a few things that can make it easier, safer, and more enjoyable.

Because of the size of Colorado and its complex topography, maps should be an integral part of any outing. Maps of specific wildlife-viewing areas are often available from the Colorado Division of Wildlife. General topographic maps, available from the U.S. Geological Survey and from many sporting goods stores, can also be helpful. The more you know about an area, the better your chance of being in the right spot to view wildlife and the less likely you are to trespass on private land.

Wildlife must have carefully honed senses in order to survive in the wild, so it is often difficult to get close to wild animals without being detected. The use of binoculars, spotting scopes, or cameras with telephoto lenses can provide a good look without disturbing the wildlife.

Views are often fleeting. A good field guide can

Tracks tell tales for observant wildlife watchers. In the top photo, an eagle has landed in the snow at the Rocky Mountain Arsenal and walked away, perhaps to investigate a winter-killed carcass. In the bottom photo, the large tracks of a great blue heron mark the mud along the Platte River. In any season, learning to see and interpret the signs of animals—a process called ''reading the landscape''—can add information and enjoyment to wildlife-watching trips.
WENDY SHATTIL / BOB ROZINSKI

explain the marks that help identify a species at a glance. Checklists are often provided in field guides to keep track of sightings. Journals are used to record more in-depth observations about behavior, conditions, and unusual occurrences.

A day of wildlife-watching in some areas requires little besides a guidebook, a map, and binoculars or a spotting scope. Of course, any time you venture into the wilderness, you should also be prepared for bad weather, insects, and wilderness emergencies.

Reading the landscape

The landscape is not a blank page. Every creature that passes leaves some clue to its movements: tracks in the snow, calls from the darkness, scat, a nest, flattened day beds in the grass, signs of feeding, game trails. Learning to observe and decipher signs of wildlife can help in wildlife-watching.

Reading the landscape requires the use of all the senses, as well as patience and a keen sense of observation. Travel slowly. Look around. Listen. Some of the most obvious and useful wildlife signs are bird songs. Birds sing most often early in the morning and in the evening, most commonly in the spring. Bird songs are used both to attract mates and to define breeding territories. The notes of most songs are like tracks in the air. With a little practice, a wildlife watcher can identify a species without even seeing it.

But birds are not the only wildlife species that can be identified by sounds. The bugling of bull elk in autumn, the warning calls of prairie dogs, the yipping of coyotes, the buzzing of a rattlesnake, the chattering of the chickaree can all be audible evidence of wildlife. In wildlife-watching, good listening skills are as important as good eyesight.

Tracks are the signatures of wildlife. A single set of clear tracks can enable a knowledgeable tracker to identify a species, tell how long ago it passed, guess as to its age, sex, and weight, and provide insight into its behavior. Tracks are easiest to find in places such as valley bottoms, along riverbanks, in the snow, on low passes, or on known game trails.

Not all signs of wildlife are as clear as tracks in the snow. Close observation can yield other readable clues. Aspen trees are often scarred by deer or elk rubbing the velvet off their antlers or by the claw

The red light of dawn silhouettes a mallard hen stretching her wings. Many animals are most active in the low-light periods of morning and evening, making these times rewarding for wildlife watchers who are willing to rise early and stay late.   KEN ARCHER

marks of bears. Mounds of vegetation piled under boulders in alpine areas can be a sign of pika. Seed husks littering the snow beneath a ponderosa pine tree can be a sign of Abert's squirrels. Prairie fields pockmarked by digging may mean badgers have been at work. A flattened place in the sagebrush may be a strutting area or "lek" for sage grouse. Tufts of white fur strung on alpine vegetation may indicate the passage of mountain goats shedding in the spring.

Field guides are available to identify signs of wildlife. To the knowledgeable watcher, the landscape is an open book, and the stories of its creatures unfold with every page.

Sunshine and moonlight

Wildlife is not ruled by the clock. Sunlight and darkness govern the activity of most species. So time of day can be a key factor in wildlife-watching.

The activity patterns of wildlife can be divided into three categories. Those species which, like humans, are most active during the day and which rest at night are called "diurnal." Unfortunately for wildlife watchers, few species fit into this category.

Mountain goats, because of their precarious habitat, are mostly diurnal. Vultures, hawks, and eagles soar on air currents heated by the sun. Many songbirds, although active, are much less conspicuous at midday. Most amphibians and reptiles are creatures of the night or twilight hours, but some, like the bull snake, the collared lizard, the coachwhip, the side-blotched lizard, and a few others are diurnal except during the hottest weather. Prairie dogs, too, are most likely to be spotted during the day.

9

A sure sign of spring, sandhill cranes migrate over the San Luis Valley on their way to northern nesting areas. Each February, more than 17,000 sandhill cranes pass through Colorado and provide one of the state's most inspiring wildlife-watching spectacles. Many wildlife events are seasonal, making a knowledge of when to watch wildlife as useful as knowing where to watch.
WENDY SHATTIL / BOB ROZINSKI

Still, the heart of the day is barren and empty compared to the hours of dusk and dawn—the best times to view wildlife. The creatures most active during these times are called "crepuscular."

Mornings and evenings are usually heralded by an increase in bird songs. Great blue herons hunt the edges of ponds and marshes. Mule deer move out from cover toward feeding areas as night comes, then back as dawn approaches. Species such as western box turtles and rattlesnakes are most likely to be active in the low-light hours.

Although darkness poses difficulties for wildlife watchers, it is popular with wildlife. The night is the most lively time of day. Nearly 80 percent of the world's mammals are crepuscular or "nocturnal," which means most active at night. More than 60 percent of the world's carnivores do their hunting at night. After dark, owls replace hawks in the sky. Raccoons, striped skunks, most species of bats, longnose snakes, bobcats, pine martens, snowshoe hares, and many other Colorado species are mostly nocturnal.

These boundaries of light and dark are not sacred. Black bears, coyotes, and badgers are active at any time of day. When migrating, many bird species will spend the day feeding and resting and save the night for flying. In cool weather, reptiles and amphibians may be most active during the day, while in hot weather they are more active at night. Sage grouse may dance on their leks all night under a full moon. At any moment, the land may come alive with wildlife.

The seasons of wildlife

Just as wildlife-watching spans the clock, it also spans the seasons. And each season offers unique viewing opportunities.

Spring is a time of awakening. Life begins pouring back into Colorado in waves. With parts of both the Central and Pacific flyways passing through Colorado, the state is a kind of crossroads for migratory waterfowl. Many of these birds stop here to nest; others move through to breeding grounds in the northern states and Canada.

The migration of the sandhill crane creates one of the most inspiring wildlife spectacles in the state. Each year, beginning in February, more than 17,000 sandhill cranes alight in and around the Monte Vista and Alamosa national wildlife refuges in the San Luis Valley. There they feed, rest, and begin their courtship dances before moving on to mating grounds farther north.

Many species of songbirds—mountain bluebirds, lark buntings, yellow warblers, and others—move back into the state in spring. Birds that wintered in low areas of the state, such as chickadees, pine siskins, nuthatches, and rosy finches, head back up the mountainsides.

With so many birds on the move, with the foliage not yet leafed out to obscure the view, and with the birds in full song as they stake out their territories, spring is a prime season for bird-watching.

Spring ends the long sleep of hibernating species. Black bears, marmots, ground squirrels, and some

Two bull elk engage in a mild sparring contest during an early winter snowfall. Elk, deer, bald eagles, and many other animals remain highly visible through the winter, a season often overlooked by people who like to watch wildlife. Care should always be taken to avoid adding stress to wintering animals. GEORGE M. HAGER of the bat species reappear. Other species, such as mice, voles, prairie dogs, pikas, and beavers, which do not hibernate but spend much of the winter underground or beneath the snow, also begin to emerge. Deer and elk begin the move to their summer ranges in high country.

Few of the 64 reptile and amphibian species in Colorado are active all winter. Spring represents a new beginning for these creatures as well. Large congregations of rattlesnakes leave their dens in April. Many western box turtles are visible along roadsides. Nights are filled with the calls of the northern leopard frog, and warm rains trigger the calls of the canyon tree frog.

By early summer, the flocks and herds have broken up. But if the opportunity for viewing huge congregations of wildlife has passed, new opportunities have arisen.

Summer is the season of accessibility. The high country thaws, making possible the viewing of alpine species. Bighorn sheep and mountain goats are most easily seen in summer. Deer and elk spend a good deal of time above timberline at this time of year and can be highly visible. In early summer, the ptarmigan, still wearing some of its white winter plumage, can be easily seen against the tundra.

Summer is the time of rearing young. One of the best places to look for bird nests is among large stands of dead trees. Some 85 species of North American birds nest in cavities found in these dead trees, called "snags." The cavities offer protection from predators, safe havens from the weather, and stability in the wind. In Colorado, a prime snag may afford nesting sites to several species of birds at once—hairy woodpeckers, mountain bluebirds, pygmy nuthatches, saw-whet owls, house wrens, tree swallows, red-naped sapsuckers. With the logging of old-growth forests, the number of cavity sites has been greatly reduced, creating intense competition among species for prime locations. Allowing these trees to stand can be an important factor in the breeding success of many Colorado birds.

Another prime site for summer wildlife watching is the prairie dog town. In addition to the prairie dogs excavating their burrows and chattering from the lips of their tunnels, more than 100 other species of wildlife have been recorded in association with these sites. Rattlesnakes, burrowing owls, coyotes, badgers, golden eagles, and others can be found around the towns in the summer.

Autumn in Colorado brings the turning of the aspen trees. Flocks of waterfowl begin to fill the sky again. Swainson's hawks can sometimes be seen in flocks of more than one hundred birds on the eastern plains. Blackbirds, starlings, and grackles gather in great roosts. From midsummer until late September, Franklin's gulls can often be seen covering fields on the eastern plains, flying over cities, or following farmers' plows looking for insects. Townsend's and Tennessee warblers pass through the state. The songbirds come down from the mountains; the blue grouse move up. Ptarmigan begin to molt, donning their white winter plumage.

Black bears often extend their normal home ranges in the fall to search out food sources such as acorns and berry patches to supplement their diet and help them lay on the layers of fat needed to get them through the winter. Abert's squirrels and chickarees busily stock their stores for the winter. By September, earless lizards are spending long hours trying to capture the warmth of the autumn sun. The king snake and the garter snake, the western rattlesnake and the bull snake are returning to dens, where they may gather with hundreds of their fellows into a slithering ball.

But the most distinctive wildlife event of the autumn is the rut. By September, bull elk are in prime condition, their antlers shed of velvet and shined. Mule deer bucks reach their peak in December. Because the males of both species can cover large distances in their search for mates, and because the bugling of elk and the clatter of antlers can help to pinpoint the animals' whereabouts, the rutting season can be a good time to view deer and elk.

With the coming of the snow, most people put away their binoculars and field guides. They are missing some splendid and unique viewing opportunities. In winter, common goldeneyes can be seen along waterways. Rough-legged hawks replace Swainson's hawks in the skies. Large numbers of mallards decorate the reservoirs.

One of the grandest wildlife sights in Colorado is visible only in winter. From December until the

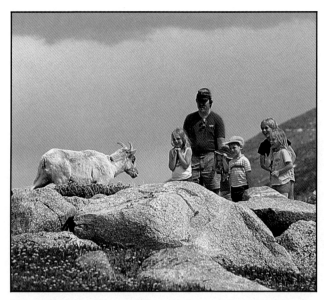

The thrill of watching wildlife starts at an early age, as shown by these youngsters meeting a bighorn sheep at Summit Lake, along the Mount Evans Highway south of Idaho Springs. Mount Evans is one of the easiest places in Colorado to view high country species such as bighorn sheep, mountain goats, marmots, pikas, and white-tailed ptarmigan. Wherever wildlife is being watched, viewers should avoid harassing or disturbing the animals. CECILIA T. ARMBRUST

spring thaw, some 200 to 300 bald eagles gather in the San Luis Valley. As many as 68 eagles have been seen perched in a single tree along the Rio Grande River. By summer, when most wildlife watchers are out, the eagles will be gone.

During the winter, elk and deer congregate in large herds and move down from the high country into areas more accessible to wildlife viewers. Tracks are more visible in the snow. With few leaves on the trees, bird-watching is easier. Many bird species come more readily to feeders in winter, when food is not as abundant. Where there are open streams, the American dipper may still be found. Geese and ducks sometimes winter on the state's ice-free lakes and reservoirs.

The art of wildlife-watching

Against the shortness of the breeding season, the difficulties of finding prey or forage, the need for long migrations, the battles for mates, and other natural hazards, many wildlife species walk a fine line to survive. Wildlife watchers should follow a few simple rules to keep from forcing creatures over that line and into danger.

Never approach any animal too closely. Each species of wildlife, and even individuals within a species, has a different level of tolerance. Some nesting birds will allow photographers to move in closely with no sign of disturbance, while others, such as Swainson's hawks, may abandon their nests at even the slightest provocation. If pressed too closely, young may be forced to leave the nest or burrow before they are ready, increasing their chances of starving and making them more vulnerable to predators.

The best wildlife-viewing occurs when the viewer does not disturb the animal. Move slowly and quietly. Use binoculars, spotting scopes, or telephoto lenses for close-up views. Watch for signs of disturbance such as agitation, aggressive behavior, warning calls, or distraction displays (the broken-wing act of some birds), and move away at the first sign. Never stay at a nest or burrow longer than a .few minutes, and never handle the young or eggs of any species. Never cut or destroy vegetation around nests or burrows in order to get closer or to compose photographs.

Although one part of the landscape may look much like another to us, wildlife species have favorite feeding, breeding, calving, and wintering areas that can be vital to their survival. Never repeatedly flush any species out of one area. This may deprive them of needed resources. Repeated harassment can also stress an animal, which makes species such as bighorn sheep more susceptible to disease. In the winter, repeated disturbances can burn up energy that an animal needs for survival in the cold.

Sometimes in national parks, where large congregations of animals may be seen near roads or buildings, the creatures can seem tame. But they are still wild animals. You should never feed wildlife or use bait to lure them closer. Some species, even golden-mantled ground squirrels, can be dangerous if surprised, fed, or confronted too closely.

Some wildlife refuges, national forests, and national parks contain private land. Honor the rights of land-owners by obeying "no trespassing" signs, closing gates where trails cross fence lines, removing litter, and leaving outbuildings or other facilities undisturbed.

Wildlife-viewing in Colorado is a privilege. If we engage in it carefully and respectfully, we can help to ensure that our wildlife legacy will remain intact for generations to come. ■

Striking symbol of the plains, a pronghorn buck depends on sight and speed to survive in the "kingdom of space and light." Although known for its mountains, Colorado contains nearly 40,000 square miles of high plains from the slopes of the Rockies to the eastern border. Despite their sometimes barren appearance, the plains form one of Colorado's richest and most varied wildlife habitats. PAT POWELL

A Kingdom of Space and Light

A Kingdom of Space and Light
The Plains

A vividly marked kestrel perches on a cottonwood stump on Colorado's eastern plains. Also called sparrow hawks, kestrels have actually increased in numbers since the arrival of settlers. They use cottonwood trees planted as windbreaks and telephone poles for convenient perches when they look for small prey such as mice, insects, lizards, and snakes. GEORGE M. HAGER

T he rising moon is the color of old bones. Its pale light flows out across the eastern plains, which rise and fall as softly as the chest of a sleeping man. Somewhere off in the dark, a coyote yips—once, twice, with a sound as sharp as the stars. Then the night falls silent.

Despite its reputation for mountains, Colorado is more than rock and ice. About 40 percent of the state, from the foothills of the Rockies to the eastern border, is high plains—almost 40,000 square miles of wind and sky and space.

The plains are a different world than the mountains, but many of the same forces are at work: harsh winds, brutal sun in the summer, and hard cold in the winter. But unlike the mountains, the plains get little precipitation. An average of less than 20 inches falls annually, and some places receive much less. Stephen Long, namesake of the mountain that looks out over the plains, called the region "The Great American Desert" on maps of his 1820 expedition. It is not a desert, but it shares many of the desert's beauties and hardships.

From the window of a car—the way most people first see them—the plains look rugged, barren, and lifeless. On foot, away from the highway, the prairie is clearly a delicate ecosystem, knitted together in a fragile balance.

The vegetation of the plains is much more varied than it may appear at first glance. The sharp spines of yucca, the dry stems of blue grama and buffalo grass, the delicate and short-lived blossoms of prickly pear cactus—all can be found here. Although the plains plant species can seem fragile, hanging onto life by a thin edge, many are perennials. They often have deep roots both to seek moisture and to serve as anchors against the constant wind.

Out on broad flats or in areas of specific soil types, single plant species can dominate, covering hundreds of

A variety of wildflowers and the sharp spines of yucca plants decorate part of Colorado's eastern plains. These vast open spaces support a surprising number of plants and animals, including a wide array of birds. One of the best times to visit the plains is the spring, when birds are establishing territories, nesting, or migrating through the area.
WENDY SHATTIL / BOB ROZINSKI

acres. Nearer the mountains, along creeks and rivers, or in places where conditions vary because of buttes and mesas, there can be scores of plant species within a short distance's walk.

The landscape is not as monotonous as it may look from a car window. True, in some places the land is smooth and awash in clear, unbroken light. But in other places it rolls and swells like an earth-bound ocean. In still other places, the smooth lines are suddenly broken by mesas, buttes, or canyon walls or pocked with marshes, lakes, and ponds. The plains also are cut by two great river systems: the South Platte and the Arkansas.

With this subtle diversity comes a wide variety of habitat for wildlife. You may walk for hours and see nothing but your own shadow, then suddenly come across a herd of pronghorns, a meadowlark spilling forth its song, or a western hognose snake strung out on the prairie floor. In the vast solitude of the plains, the sudden sight of wildlife draws the eye like lightning.

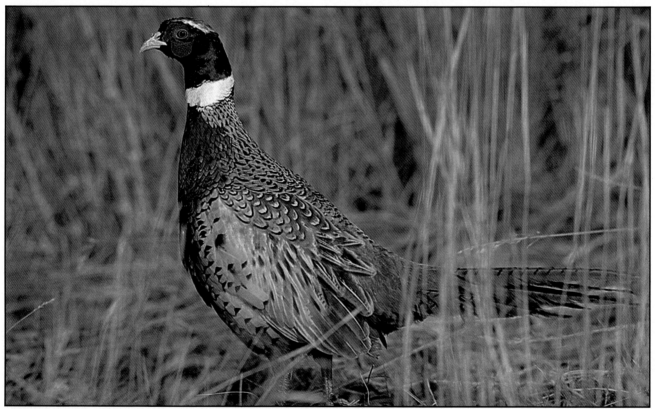

Colorful exotics, ring-necked pheasants were first released in Colorado as game birds in the 1800s. Today, there are self-sustaining populations in agricultural areas throughout the eastern plains and in the vicinity of Montrose, Delta, Grand Junction, and the San Luis Valley. They are commonly seen along roads throughout the year. DENNIS & MARIA HENRY

A Kingdom of Space and Light

Close to the ground and even below it are a wide variety of species: snakes, such as the the western rattler and the eastern yellow-bellied racer; badgers that dig deep dens or burrow after prey; prairie dogs with their elaborate tunnel mazes; rodents, including the kangaroo rat, the plains harvest mouse, and the silky pocket mouse; even burrowing owls. In a land with so little ground cover, many species go underground to find protection, den sites, and food.

Above ground, the plains do not harbor the diversity of wildlife found in lusher ecosystems. But in some cases, what is lacking in diversity is made up in sheer numbers. Bison once roamed the prairies of Colorado by the millions, raising clouds of dust that could be seen for miles. The bison are gone. But pronghorns still are a common sight. Black-tailed jackrabbits proliferate. Prairie-dog towns still cover hundreds of acres. Foxes and coyotes still flourish.

Although mule deer are more abundant in other ecosystems, they can be found on the plains where there is cover. Beaver and white-tailed deer also may be found near rivers and streams.

Of all the wildlife of the plains, the birds are the most abundant and varied. Colorado's state bird, the lark bunting, soars above the grasslands; the fluid notes of the meadowlark spill through the prairie air. There are mountain plovers, mourning doves, grasshopper sparrows, and eastern and western kingbirds. Prairie chickens strut on the flats; sharp-tailed grouse dance their ancient dance among the scrub oak on the rimrocks. Overhead, the prairie sky is home to golden eagles, prairie falcons, kestrels, and a trio of hawks: Swainson's, red-tailed, and ferruginous.

Small pothole lakes and marshes attract flocks of migrating and nesting waterfowl. Grebes, sandpipers, gulls, sandhill cranes, terns, and other species use them as stopovers on their migration journeys. Others—including piping plovers, least terns, and avocets—nest here. Where vegetation grows thickly around the ponds, there are yellow-headed blackbirds, herons, egrets, bitterns, and wrens. Irrigation and manmade reservoirs provide additional habitat.

The effect of human development on the plains has not always been so beneficial to wildlife. The drought of the 1930s hit portions of eastern and southeastern Colorado very hard, destroying the habitat of many wildlife species. Waterfowl suffered. White-tailed deer became scarce. There is evidence that the canyon tree frog vanished from Mesa de Maya, and the western ribbon snake disappeared from places such as Furnish Canyon.

Parts of the plains are still recovering; other parts may never be the same again. The growing of crops, the grazing of livestock, the building of roads and reservoirs, all have shown us that the plains are not as endless as they first seem. Development has slowly eaten away at them until certain prairie ecosystems can now be found only in thin strips along railroad beds or highway rights-of-way or in cemeteries or other tiny protected areas.

Homesteading laws that encouraged ranching and farming left relatively little of the prairie ecosystems in public land. Yet many good areas for watching wildlife still remain. Like a pair of stone ships tacking into the wind, the Pawnee Buttes are the centerpieces of Pawnee National Grassland, which contains vast examples of shortgrass prairie. Comanche National Grassland, in the southeastern part of the state, protects southern-prairie habitat. Barr Lake State Park, northeast of Denver, provides an example of how irrigation can benefit wildlife. More than three hundred species of birds have been recorded at the manmade lake.

At first glance the plains may seem empty of all but the low moaning of the wind. But this is not a landscape that can be appreciated with a single glance. It is a place that makes us slow down, look closely, and rethink our definition of Colorado as a land of soaring mountains. The plains force you to add to that definition the chorus of birds in the marshes, space for species that need long horizons, and the far-reaching light of the rising moon. ■

Western Meadowlark

Scientific name: Sturnella neglecta
Range: Statewide in lower elevations
Habitat: Open fields, prairie, mountain parks
Size: 8 to 10 inches long
Identifying traits: Yellow underbelly and black bib, fluid song, white sides to tail

Few sounds announce spring as clearly as the fluid song of a western meadowlark. Common throughout Colorado's plains, meadowlarks are frequently observed singing from fence posts, tall vegetation, and convenient signs, such as this one near Cherry Creek Reservoir. WENDY SHATTIL / BOB ROZINSKI

If melting ice made a sound, it would be just like the song of the meadowlark on a spring morning.

The western meadowlark is a year-round Colorado resident. But for much of the year, it goes unnoticed; its plumage is drab, and it is relatively silent. In the winter, it forages in solitude or in small flocks along the edges of fields.

Then, in spring and summer, as the state awakens from winter, the meadowlark seems to come to life. It dons its bright summer plumage—throat and underbelly as yellow as the sun; breast draped with a black, V-shaped bib; sides brightened by white feathers.

Most often the meadowlark can be seen perched atop a fence post or old snag, its head thrown back and its bill parted widely in song. The melodious singing is meant to do more than fill a summer morning. Like all bird song, its beauty is also functional. The sweet call announces the male bird's presence to prospective mates and rivals.

The notes lay down a kind of song line, claiming a breeding area and warning others out of the territory of its nest.

The meadowlark nests on the ground, the woven nest hidden in the deep grasses. The female lays from three to seven eggs between May and June and then spends two weeks incubating them. When the meadowlark sits on its nest, it blends in well with its surroundings and refuses to flush until pressed closely. The female rears the young, while the male stays close by and provides food. Meadowlarks feed on seeds and insects.

White-tailed Jackrabbit

Scientific name: Lepus townsendii
Range: Statewide
Habitat: Open country from plains to above timberline
Size: 21 to 24 inches long, 4 to 10 pounds
Identifying traits: Long ears, large size

The two species of Colorado jackrabbits—white-tailed and black-tailed—can be distinguished, as their names suggest, by the color of their tails. That is convenient

A white-tailed jackrabbit's large ears serve as an early-warning system to detect predators, of which it has many. Both the white-tailed and black-tailed jackrabbits are hunted by eagles, hawks, coyotes, foxes, and other predators. Frequently seen along rural roads, jackrabbits usually sit quietly before sprinting away in a sudden burst of speed. SHERM SPOELSTRA

A Kingdom of Space and Light

for wildlife watchers, as jackrabbits most often are seen from behind as they race away. The animal's long ears pick up distant sounds and, when pressed, the jackrabbit can reach speeds of up to 40 miles an hour.

The jackrabbit is actually a hare, not a rabbit. Its young are born with hair and open eyes. Breeding takes place from March to August. A single litter of one to 11 young (the average is five) is born after a gestation of six weeks. The young grow quickly and are soon weaned. The nest is merely a shallow depression under cover.

In summer, jackrabbits eat mostly green plants, such as clover, western wheatgrass, and blue grama, and flowers, such as dandelions and Indian paintbrush. In winter, they rely more on shrubs, such as winterfat, Parry's rabbitbrush, and fringed sage.

Just as the jackrabbit's diet changes with the season, so does its pelage. In summer, the fur is a mottled gray and brown. In winter, it becomes almost pure white in northern areas of the state, while to the south it gets paler but still holds tinges of brown and gray.

Although jackrabbits are not nearly as prolific as cottontails, their populations sometimes skyrocket. Their fur is not very valuable, but the animals historically have been heavily trapped and shot. Unskinned jackrabbits once were marketed for the making of felt and sold as food to mink farms. In earlier days, more than 65,000 carcasses were sold annually at Colorado markets.

In the late 1800s, the jackrabbit's abundance was seen as a possible solution to the hunger problem of Colorado's indigent population. On December 22, 1894, a mass hunt involving 101 people was organized in Prowers and Los Animas counties. The day's kill was 5,142 jackrabbits, and many ended up on the Christmas dinner tables of the poor. Between 1893 and 1895, several similar hunts took an estimated 32,000 jackrabbits, which were distributed through churches to the poor.

Besides humans, predators of jackrabbits include coyotes, foxes, hawks, and bobcats. To survive, the hares rely first on their keen sense of hearing and then on their camouflage coloring. If all else fails, they will flush suddenly from hiding and race off in a cloud of dust, taunting pursuers with their white or black tails.

Western Box Turtle

Scientific name: Terrapene ornata
Range: Eastern Colorado to 5,500 feet
Habitat: Prairie grasslands—sandy soils

Size: Four to six inches long
Identifying trait: Yellow radiating lines on shell

You have to look closely to see it, a small, slow-moving piece of the prairie. In the vast space of the eastern plains, the western box turtle can move frustratingly slowly. But with a lifespan of more than 50 years, it has no need to rush.

About the only time the western box turtle seems to quicken its pace is during its unusual courtship ritual. The male will rise up and hurl itself atop the female's shell repeatedly until mating occurs. The female lays two to eight eggs, which hatch in 10 weeks. The young are vulnerable to predation by many species, such as coyotes, badgers, and hawks. Such dangers keep them underground for a time before venturing out to hunt.

Even adults spend much of their time burrowed into the ground to rest or cool off during the heat of the day. They will also cool off in ponds but spend little time in the water. Adult turtles will hunt insects, caterpillars, and earthworms. They will also eat vegetation and even

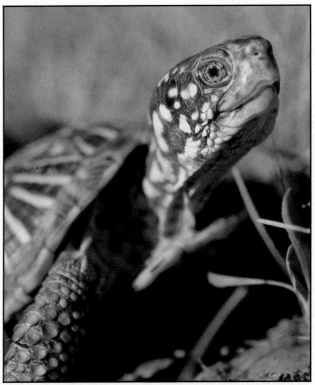

One's first sight of a western box turtle often seems odd—a slowly moving shell on the dry, flat expanse of eastern plains. But western box turtles prefer such terrain, having adapted to life on the grasslands. They are often seen along roads, especially in sandy areas. Colorado has five species of turtles. All are associated with water except the western box turtle. WELDON LEE carrion. In winter, the turtles hibernate in burrows.

Once the turtle reaches adulthood, its shell provides a measure of protection. The shell is "hinged" so that the turtle can completely withdraw its legs and head. But the shell is no protection against automobiles, and during the spring many dead turtles are seen along the highways of eastern Colorado.

Against its natural predators, the turtle's best protection seems to be its coloration. The shell of an adult is dark brown or black and streaked with yellow lines and spots. The turtle is almost impossible to detect against the prairie floor, whether it is moving or not. And the western box turtle is not in any hurry to move.

Lark Bunting

Scientific name: Calamospiza melanocorys
Range: Eastern Colorado to foothills
Habitat: Shortgrass prairie
Size: 7 inches
Identifying traits: White wing patches

It is spring on the plains. In the distance a small bird, black with white wing patches, rises high into the sky and then plummets, singing a clear, fluid song. The lark bunting is back, performing its aerial courtship dance.

The spectacular dance and the song, which has been described as "the glory that was and the everlasting joy that is living in Colorado," were two of the reasons the lark bunting was designated the state bird of Colorado in 1931. A more practical reason tendered by another supporter was that its black and white plumage were "best and most economically adaptable to trademark and letterhead use." Following a rousing debate in which school children from Fort Collins lobbied for the lark bunting before the state legislature, the bird of the plains beat out the meadowlark, the mountain bluebird, and the horned lark.

Only a summer resident, the lark bunting arrives at its nesting grounds on the eastern plains in early spring. There the male stakes out its territory, challenging intruders with his song. A nest is built on the ground, sometimes in the protective shadow of cactus or yucca. Both the male and the less colorful female care for the greenish-blue eggs.

When the young are grown, the lark buntings gather again in large flocks, sweeping across the plains and feeding on insects such as grasshoppers and ants. By

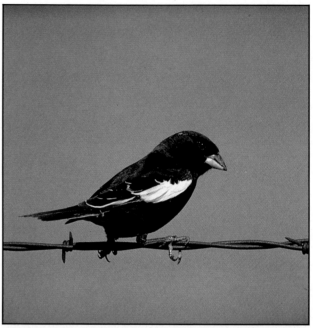

The beauty of the lark bunting—Colorado's state bird—lies in its spectacular mating flight and song as well as its black and white plumage. In April and early May, look for these mating displays in areas of native grasslands such as Pawnee National Grassland, Comanche National Grassland, and near Barr Lake. WENDY SHATTIL / BOB ROZINSKI

the first cold winds of late September, the flocks have headed south to their wintering grounds in Arizona, Texas, and Mexico.

Badger

Scientific name: Taxidea taxus
Range: Statewide
Habitat: Open parklands and prairie
Size: 10 to 20 pounds, 24 to 30 inches long including short tail
Identifying traits: Low profile, grizzled fur, white stripe

Just ahead of the stopped jeep, a short, squat animal stands its ground in a barrage of snarls and hisses. Despite the fact that it is barely two feet long and weighs less than most dogs, this member of the weasel family has few predators. None would dare attack an animal that stands up to a jeep.

From a distance, a hunting badger can look like a dust devil on the prairie. With powerful forelegs and stout claws up to two inches long, it can rip up a 10-square-yard patch of ground in minutes searching

A Kingdom of Space and Light

Short, squat, and seemingly fearless, badgers prowl open country throughout Colorado. With powerful front legs, long claws, and fierce determination, badgers hunt by digging up prairie dogs, ground squirrels, and mice. In fact, one's first sight of a badger will often be clouds of dirt flying in the air. Their name derives from the distinctive "badges" on their faces. WENDY SHATTIL / BOB ROZINSKI

Pronghorn

Scientific name: Antilocapra americana
Range: Eastern Plains, northwestern corner, parklands
Habitat: Grassland, pinyon-juniper, sagebrush
Size: 4 feet long, 3½ feet tall at the shoulder, 110 pounds (male), 85 pounds (female)

for prairie dogs or ground squirrels. The aftermath can look like an accident site.

The badger spends its life within a few inches of the ground, above it and below it. The animal is born in March or April in a large den dug into a hillside. When it grows old enough to venture out of the den, it learns to dig for rodents or to capture nesting pheasants and other birds. By winter, it is weaned. It returns to the burrow on the harshest winter days to wait out the cold.

The number of badgers in Colorado has declined during the past century, primarily due to loss of habitat. As native grasslands disappeared under cities, roads, farms, and intensive livestock grazing, so did the number of badgers. In addition, for many years badgers were killed as varmints by ranchers whose livestock had been crippled in badger holes, and badgers suffered inadvertently when they ate poisoned meat intended to control the numbers of coyotes, wolves, mountain lions, and bears.

Despite its ferocious displays, the badger is reclusive and mostly nocturnal. It will turn away from humans if given the chance, or it will dig furiously in loose soil, burying itself completely within minutes.

One moment they stand motionless, almost invisible against the dry brown grasses of autumn. Then, with a flash of white rumps, they are gone, moving across the skyline like the prairie wind.

Speed is the essence of the pronghorns' survival. They are built to move; they are streamlined, light-boned, and equipped with the large efficient hearts of runners. Frightened pronghorns have been clocked at 84 miles an hour. Forty- to 50-mile-an-hour bursts are common. In fact, the pronghorn is the fastest mammal in North America. Its motion, according to one early observer, is "like the flight of a great bird," and its sky is the great expanse of the Colorado prairie.

The pronghorn, also called antelope, is a purely North American species. Although it looks much like a deer and its scientific name translates to "American goat-antelope," it is not related to any other creature in the world. Fossil evidence shows that it is the only modern hoofed mammal to have evolved in North America. It has roamed the plains since the late Cenozoic period, five to 10 million years ago, when it ran from dire wolves and prehistoric cheetahs.

The pronghorn escaped its predators often enough that once it numbered more than 20 million, making it nearly as abundant as the bison. It ranged across much of North America. In Colorado, it could be found from the plains to the high meadows and was abundant in such places as South Park and the San Luis Valley. When the George Frederick Ruxton Expedition entered the San Luis Valley in 1839, it saw, "...innumerable herds of antelope." Thirty years later, J.B. Pond, on a train ride from Denver to Cheyenne, Wyoming, saw so many pronghorns that "their numbers changed the color of the country." He wrote, "For 10 or 12 miles in the Cache la Poudre valley and all the way west of the trail, about three quarters to one half mile away, was one long band of Antelope, twenty to forty rods wide, practically continuous and huddled together for warmth."

The only enemy the pronghorn could not outrun was the bullet. Its numbers dwindled fast as Indians and early explorers hunted it for its meat, particularly as the bison

Herds of pronghorns may be viewed at any time of the year. They are often seen from Limon to Kit Carson on U.S. Highways 40 and 287, in the San Luis Valley from Poncha Pass to Saguache on U.S. 285, from Craig to Elk Springs on U.S. 40, from Craig to Baggs, Wyo., on Colorado 13, and, during the winter, east and west of Kremmling on U.S. 40. DENNIS HENRY

disappeared. The coming of fences that sliced up the land and restricted herd movement also cut deeply into the population. By 1918, there were only about 1,000 pronghorns in Colorado. By 1920, an estimated 13,000 remained in North America. The great herds that had survived Ice Ages and saber-toothed tigers had dwindled to almost nothing.

Today, thanks to conservation efforts, about 60,000 pronghorns make Colorado their home. Large herds inhabit much of the eastern third of the state, as well as the extreme northwestern corner. Smaller populations are scattered through North Park, Middle Park, South Park, and the San Luis Valley.

Millions of years on the plains have given the pronghorn more than speed. The animal's eyesight is keen—equal, it is said, to an eight-power lens. Its coat of brittle, hollow fur is colored like its surroundings—reddish brown on the back with broad bars across the chest and neck and a prominent white rump patch. Both sexes have horns, but the male's are usually larger.

In summer, pronghorns browse on forbs, shrubs, and a wide variety of plants, including the fruit of cactus. Researchers have found cactus spines embedded in the animal's stomach lining, where they apparently have caused little or no harm. In winter, large herds congregate on vital wintering grounds. Sagebrush makes up an important winter food source.

Pronghorns mate in September, and a pair of fawns is usually born in May. Each weighs about seven pounds. For their first few days, young pronghorns must rely upon their camouflage coloring rather than speed for protection. They are also born with very little scent, making them nearly undetectable to predators. Within a few days, the young can outrun a man.

Today the speed of the pronghorn seems to be something of a relic, an echo of a distant time. The dire wolves are gone. The prairie wolf and plains grizzly no longer roam the grassland. Modern predators such as the coyote have no hope of overtaking a pronghorn at full speed. Yet the pronghorn still runs, raising dust clouds on the horizon as it has for millions of years, outracing everything but the wind on the Colorado prairie.

Black-tailed prairie dogs live in large colonies, or towns, that form fascinating wildlife-viewing areas on Colorado's eastern plains. Besides prairie dogs, the towns attract burrowing owls, coyotes, hawks, and foxes. Many prairie-dog towns are accessible by car, and vehicles function as effective blinds from which to watch the town activity. WENDY SHATTIL /BOB ROZINSKI

Black-tailed Prairie Dog

Scientific name: Cynomys ludovicianus
Range: Eastern Colorado
Habitat: Shortgrass and mixed-grass prairies, fallow fields
Size: 12 to 16 inches long, one to three pounds
Identifying traits: Black-tipped tail, larger size

As the shadow of a hawk darkens the ground, a sharp bark-like call cuts the air. There is a sudden scurry for cover, a flicking of tails. While the hawk passes, nothing moves in the prairie-dog town but the slowly settling wisps of dust.

This scene has played for thousands of years on the plains. Colorado is home to three of the five North American subspecies of prairie dogs, which are close relatives of ground squirrels and marmots. The largest, most common, and most widespread is the black-tailed prairie dog, which is found all across the plains. The Gunnison's prairie dog is found in mountain parks, the San Luis Valley, and the southwestern part of the state. The white-tailed prairie dog is restricted to the northwestern corner, Grand Valley, and along western rivers.

In earlier days, Indians caught prairie dogs with nets and traps and ate their meat. Both the Pike and Long expeditions noted huge towns covering many square acres. Ruxton, one of the first explorers to observe the creatures without killing them, saw huge towns in the San Luis Valley. ''No animals in these Western regions interested me so much as the prairie dogs,'' he wrote.

The coming of settlers did not spell the immediate demise of the prairie dog. In fact, settlement actually increased habitat, for a time at least. Land was opened by grazing and cleared by fires. Agriculture provided huge new food sources. By the 1920s, when prairie-dog numbers peaked, their towns covered more than 100 million acres in 12 states.

But then the settlers began to fear plague and

23

The Plains

tularemia, both of which can be carried by prairie dogs, especially the Gunnison's. The diseases posed serious health risks not only to humans, but to the prairie dogs themselves. From 1945 to 1949, plague wiped out 95 percent of the Gunnison's prairie dogs in a town in Park County.

Prairie-dog towns have been destroyed to make room for airports, subdivisions, highways, and reservoirs. But the real inroads into the animals' numbers have been made on behalf of the livestock industry. Ranchers worried that their stock would step into the burrows and be crippled and that the prairie dogs would compete with the livestock for forage. So, in a program unequaled in wildlife history, towns were flooded with soapy water, fumigated, and bulldozed. Grain soaked in strychnine and cyanide flakes were scattered around burrows. In 1947, a drug called 1080 was used on 1.21 million acres of prairie-dog towns in Colorado. The Civilian Conservation Corps, the U.S. Fish and Wildlife Service, and the Biological Survey all were involved in the eradication effort.

Yet today, 75 to 90 percent of the three Colorado prairie-dog species remain. South Park, once covered with prairie-dog towns, is all but empty.

But even this marginal success had its price. Untold numbers of golden eagles, magpies, ravens, hawks, bobcats, badgers, and other predators were killed when they consumed poisoned prairie dogs. The black-footed ferret, dependent upon prairie dogs for its diet, is today considered one of the most endangered animals on earth, a result of early prairie-dog eradication efforts. And still there are prairie dogs. Although their numbers were greatly reduced, prairie dogs have recovered and may be seen in many places in Colorado today.

We are starting to see prairie dogs in a new light. The towns, vital components of the prairie ecosystem, have become tourist attractions. They also attract more than 100 other species of wildlife, which feed on the prairie dogs or use their burrows. One researcher collected more than 800 rattlesnakes in three years around a prairie-dog town near Platteville. The snakes both dine on a few of the young prairie dogs and use the burrows for dens. Burrowing owls, jackrabbits, cottontails, deer mice, coyotes, foxes, and badgers also have been associated with prairie-dog towns.

Prairie dogs spend a good deal of their time digging and repairing their complex system of tunnels and packing the dirt mounds around the tunnel openings. In their burrows, they bear litters of three to eight young, usually in April. They sleep in their burrows at night and appear early in the morning to feed on forbs and grasses such as western wheatgrass, blue grama, and buffalo grass.

In winter, although they do not hibernate, they stay deep in their tunnels during the worst weather, venturing out a few at a time to feed.

Burrowing Owl

Scientific name: Athene cunicularia
Range: Statewide
Habitat: Plains, shrublands, often in association with prairie-dog towns
Size: 9 to 11 inches long
Identifying traits: Small size, seen on the ground, long legs, sandy color

From a weathered fence post, the yellow eyes of a burrowing owl stare out at the winged shadow of a hawk crossing the field, following it until it is out of sight. The pigeon-sized bird retreats to its nearby burrow when the hunting hawk reappears.

The small, long-legged burrowing owl is one of the strangest sights of the eastern plains. Unlike other owls, it is often seen during the day, and it spends much of its time on the ground. It hunts insects and mice and hisses like a rattlesnake when cornered.

This unusual bird was first recorded on the plains around Pikes Peak by the men of the 1820 Long Expedition. It was a common sight across Colorado then, nesting in abandoned prairie-dog burrows or fox dens or excavating its own sites with powerful backward kicks. Efforts to control the prairie-dog population have also reduced the numbers of burrowing owls by limiting their nesting sites.

The bird is a summer resident, arriving in Colorado with the spring. Although it lives in the vicinity of rattlesnakes and prairie dogs, the coexistence is not always peaceful. The owls will prey on an occasional young prairie dog, along with grasshoppers, beetles, lizards, and snakes, including young rattlesnakes. Adult rattlesnakes will take young owls. Still, besides sharing the ready-made dens and the food supply of the prairie dogs, the owls may benefit from the warning signals so often given by the rodents, which are the victims of many of the same predators as the owls.

Burrowing owls lay six to 12 eggs beginning in May. The young, covered with fine down, appear at the mouth of the burrow by early summer to yawn, stretch, and play in the sun while waiting for their parents to return with food.

Ever curious, a burrowing owl turns its head for a better look. Although most often associated with the plains, burrowing owls may be found in open areas throughout Colorado. Popular viewing areas are prairie-dog towns at the Rocky Mountain Arsenal, Chatfield Reservoir, and Cherry Creek Reservoir. CHASE SWIFT

By October, burrowing owls have begun moving to wintering grounds as far south as Argentina. The dark shadow of the hawk passes again over the fence post, but there are only the eyes of the prairie dog to follow it. The owls' burrows sit empty until the birds return to the area to breed in the spring.

Swainson's Hawk

Scientific name: Buteo swainsoni
Range: Plains to foothills
Habitat: Grasslands, open fields, foothill parks
Size: 19 to 22 inches long, 50- to 56-inch wingspan
Identifying traits: Black and white wing pattern, black band and bars on tail

Wildcat Creek more often contains dust clouds than water. But the creek just south of Pawnee National Grasslands waters a few old cottonwoods surrounded by the rolling horizons of the prairie—a perfect place for the Swainson's hawk.

Moving into Colorado in spring from wintering grounds in South America, the Swainson's hawk is particularly conspicuous because it often migrates in large flocks. The sight can be spectacular, reaching its peak in mid-April.

The Swainson's hawk is a buteo, a broad-winged, broad-tailed, rodent-eating hawk. Other Colorado buteos include the red-tailed hawk, which can be found in almost every part of Colorado; the rough-legged hawk, which is a winter resident; and the ferruginous hawk, which is the largest buteo in the state.

Even experts can have difficulty telling one buteo from another. But the Swainson's hawk has a distinctive black and white pattern on its underwing. It also has a terminal band on its tail, unlike the red-tailed and ferruginous hawks, and the tail is more obviously barred than that of the rough-legged hawk. All four of the Colorado buteos exhibit a dark phase known as "melanism." Adults in the dark phase can be very difficult to identify.

As with the other buteos and many birds of prey, the female Swainson's hawk is larger than its mate. This size difference, called "reverse sexual size dimorphism," is not fully understood. One theory holds that her greater size enables the female to better protect her young. Or perhaps the size difference allows males and females to hunt different prey and so not compete with one another. Or perhaps the female needs large reserves of fat to withstand the long incubation period.

The Swainson's hawk can be bold and easy to approach in the fall before its migration, but it is shy and secretive during nesting. It often builds its nest in the branches of the cottonwoods, sometimes constructing it right over an abandoned magpie nest. The female lays from two to four eggs. If disturbed, the hawk will leave the nest and circle nearby or even abandon the site if the disturbance continues.

Although for generations all birds of prey have been indiscriminately shot on sight by many ranchers and hunters because of an ingrained hatred of predators, the Swainson's hawk is today considered a very beneficial species. It eats large quantities of insects, such as crop-destroying grasshoppers, as well as small mammals and rodents.

From perches high in the cottonwoods along Wildcat Creek, the Swainson's hawk uses its highly evolved eyesight to watch for movement. When it spies a potential meal, it leaves the branches to soar in slow

Colorado's plains support a variety of birds of prey, including Swainson's hawks like the one shown here. A migratory species, Swainson's hawks often gather in flocks of 100 to 200 birds before leaving for wintering grounds in South America. Wildlife watchers should look for these flocks on freshly tilled fields in mid-September. W. PERRY CONWAY

circles before diving on its prey.

By early October, it leaves the branches for good and gathers in flocks to move south to its wintering grounds. As the Swainson's hawk departs, the first of the rough-legged hawks begin to move into the state from the north, taking their cousins' place on the branches of the old cottonwoods along the creek.

Northern Harrier

Scientific name: Circus cyaneus
Range: Statewide
Habitat: Marshlands, fields
Size: 17 to 22 inches long
Identifying traits: White rump patch, long tail

On a windy day, a northern harrier glides over the grasslands surrounding Barr Lake, rising and falling slowly as if on the swells of an ocean. Also known as a marsh hawk, this bird is most often seen patroling the marshlands and grasslands. It is the only harrier found in North America.

Despite the long wings, long tail, and white rump patch, the harrier is not always easy to identify. As with the kestrel and merlin, the harrier exhibits different plumage depending upon its sex: the male is blue or gray above and white below with faint red bars, while the female is a cinnamon brown. Like owls, harriers have disk-shaped faces edged in feathers that direct sound to their ears and help them to locate their prey: voles, frogs, small birds, small snakes, and grasshoppers.

Although a few harriers winter in the state, most migrate northward into Colorado in the spring. The male does an elegant aerial courtship dance, rolling, swooping, dipping, and stalling. Nests are just bundles of sticks set on the ground. The larger female lays five to nine eggs; a month-long incubation begins with the laying of the first egg.

After fledging their young, harriers wander over much of Colorado, even venturing above timberline to hunt for prey. They may often be seen hovering or flying low over cultivated fields or along the grassy rights-of-way beside highways.

The draining of wetlands has reduced available nesting and hunting grounds for the harrier, and the use of pesticides such as DDT has resulted in eggshell thinning and a higher mortality rate among the young. Although DDT has been banned in the United States, a good part of the harrier population winters in South America, where the use of pesticides continues. As a result, fewer harriers ride the spring winds over the Colorado meadows.

Mountain Plover

Scientific name: Charadrius montanus
Range: Eastern plains to mountain parks
Habitat: Shortgrass prairie, sagebrush
Size: 8 to 9 inches
Identifying traits: White wing strips, black banded tail with white border

Three speckled green eggs lie behind a cactus in a shallow scrape in the ground. Against the huge dome of the prairie sky, darkened with thunderclouds and streaked by a racing wind, the nest of a mountain plover seems frail and vulnerable, a tiny island of life in the midst of nearly endless space. The wind rattles in the

A Kingdom of Space and Light

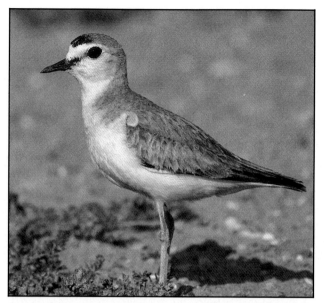

Despite their name, mountain plovers prefer the grasslands of the eastern plains. One of seven plovers in Colorado, the mountain plover may be distinguished by its plain white throat and breast, thin white wing stripes, and dark tail band. They are often seen foraging for insects in open grassland areas such as Pawnee and Comanche national grasslands.
WENDY SHATTIL / BOB ROZINSKI

grasses. The first drops of rain splatter the dust nearby.

The mountain plover is a bird with a poorly chosen name. Although it does occasionally nest in mountain parks, it is much more common on the shortgrass prairie. Unlike most other plovers, the mountain plover is most often found away from water in the open or in large flocks skirting across the plains. It is one of seven plovers in Colorado. Of the others, only the snowy and the killdeer nest regularly in the state. The semipalmated, piping, American golden, and black-bellied plovers are much less common nesters or are infrequent migrants passing through Colorado.

The mountain plover arrives in Colorado in April from wintering grounds in northern Mexico and southern Baja. As with many birds of the open spaces, plovers exhibit a flight dance when courting, whirling and spiraling through the spring skies. Their nests are little more than depressions in the soil sparsely lined with roots, leaves, even chips of cow manure. The very well-camouflaged eggs are laid in May.

Like some other shorebirds, the females may mate with more than one male, creating a second brood so rapidly after the first that the male must incubate one set of eggs while the female sits on the other. Soon after the young are fledged, flocks of mountain plovers gather to feed for the rest of the summer.

The mountain plover is a ground bird and a fast runner when pressed. It rarely flies more than a few hundred yards when flushed. On the ground, it hunts for grasshoppers, flies, and beetles. But its territory is shrinking as more and more of the prairie succumbs to the plow.

The primary enemies of the mountain plover are most threatening at nesting time: wind and rain, snakes, coyotes, badgers, as well as cattle and horses that step on the nests. When a predator comes too close, the adult birds are experts at feigning broken wings to draw it away. They will even sometimes fly at the enemy to distract it.

Against the harsh weather of the prairie, there is little the plover can do. Although its name comes from the Latin word for rain, the plover cannot distract a thunderstorm or lead it away with its broken-wing act. It can only nestle softly on its eggs and wait it out.

Colorado Checkered Whiptail

Scientific name: Cnemidophorus tesselatus
Range: Southeastern Colorado
Habitat: Gullies, canyons, bluffs
Size: 12 to 16 inches including tail
Identifying traits: Long tail, checkered pattern

Lying on a rock in the hot sun, a Colorado checkered whiptail jerks its head nervously. Its long tongue slashes

Swift resident of gullies, canyons, and bluffs in southeastern Colorado, a Colorado checkered whiptail suns itself before dashing off in pursuit of insects. One of the few wildlife species that is exclusively diurnal, it is often seen—or heard—rummaging for insects under dry leaves and grasses.
GEOFF TISCHBEIN

the air once, twice, and then the reptile vanishes among the grasses.

The Colorado checkered whiptail is one of four species of whiptails to inhabit the state. It is a daylight creature, moving out with the morning sun and then retreating at sunset into a small burrow that it defends against all others. From October to April, it stays below ground. During the months that it is active, it spends most of its time searching for insects in a home range of as much as a quarter of an acre.

The Colorado checkered whiptail has adapted an unusual asexual reproductive strategy. The population is almost entirely female. Eggs develop without the presence of male sperm in a process known as "parthenogenesis."

The female digs a nesting burrow in loose soil and lays two to four eggs. She stays with the eggs for a day or two and defends the nest for a short time after that. The young emerge in fall and may return to the site at night for a time before moving off. As a result of this strange reproductive process, as many as 40 whiptails can occupy an acre of quality habitat.

Coyote

Scientific name: Canis latrans
Range: Throughout Colorado
Habitat: All habitat types
Size: 24 to 28 inches at shoulder, 42 to 46 inches long, 20 to 45 pounds
Identifying traits: Doglike appearance, yipping

In 1968, a driver along U.S. Highway 71 near Limon came upon a gruesome sight: five dead coyotes strung up on a fence, beer bottles jammed into their mouths. The incident was but a single skirmish in a long, bitter battle that man has waged against the coyote, a battle that, despite the odds, the coyote seems to be winning.

Like many other predators, the coyote has alienated mankind by preying on livestock and domestic fowl. Government officials across the country have responded by putting bounties on its head. From 1915 to 1947, bounties were paid on 1,884,897 coyotes in the United States, 294,000 in 1946 alone. The animal has been shot from airplanes, injected with chemicals such as M-44, trapped, run down with snowmobiles, and buried alive in its den.

The result of this extermination effort is surprising.

Coyotes have actually expanded their range in North America. In Colorado, coyotes are probably more abundant today than they were before the arrival of the first settlers. The animal's success has frustrated and infuriated some, leading to scenes such as that along Highway 71. But its success can be attributed to the decline of the wolf population and to its own uncanny ability to adapt.

The coyote can be found in every habitat type in Colorado—from hunting mice at the edges of marshes on the eastern plains to snatching ptarmigans from the slopes of the alpine tundra. It inhabits the deepest wilderness and suburban Denver.

Like that of most successful creatures, the coyote's diet is varied. It includes mice, beaver, rabbits, birds, carrion, insects, and vegetation. The coyote will hunt alone but is also capable of complex teamwork. It will scavenge along highways for road kills and follow ski trails looking for deer or elk stranded in deep snows. It is one of the few animals smart enough to kill a porcupine without being imbedded in quills, and it readily eats the fruit of prickly pear cactus.

In the mythologies of native cultures, the coyote is at once a trickster, helpful spirit, creator, and troublemaker. Its name comes from the Aztec word "coyotl," the barking dog.

Coyotes breed from January to March, and pairs often stay together for several years. The young, from four to six in a litter, are born 60 days later, blind and hairless. They will stay in one of several dens prepared for birthing for more than two months, and the family will often hunt together through the fall.

Few large predators have stood up well to the growing human population in the United States. The coyote is an exception. But perhaps that was to be expected. A myth of one western Indian culture says that the coyote and the black bear will walk the earth long after the wolf and the grizzly are gone. In Colorado at least, that prediction may already have come true.

Other Common Wildlife of the Plains

BIRDS: turkey vulture, red-tailed hawk, common crow, golden eagle, prairie falcon, greater prairie chicken, lesser prairie chicken, scaled quail, long-billed curlew, American goldfinch, burrowing owl, red-headed woodpecker, brown thrasher, Say's phoebe, western

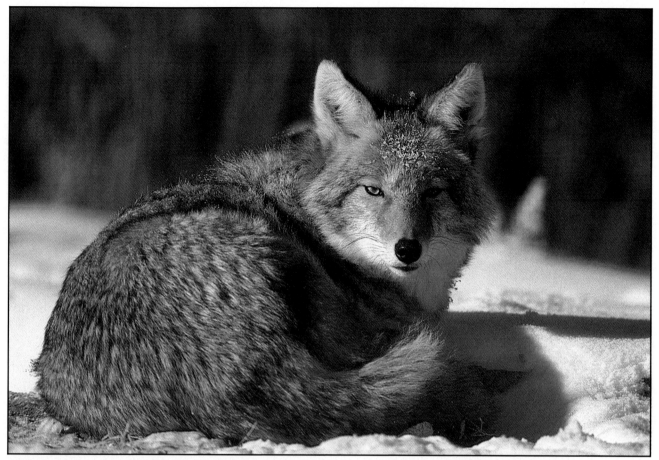

Coyotes range throughout Colorado from the lowest to the highest points, from wilderness areas to settled suburbs. One key to the coyote's adaptability is its varied diet. It feeds on virtually anything from large animals to fruit. Although not easily seen, coyotes often reveal their presence by yipping and barking at night. JUDD COONEY

kingbird, horned lark, ferruginous hawk, yellow warbler, orange-crowned warbler, yellow-rumped warbler, Wilson's warbler, lazuli bunting, chipping sparrow, Brewer's sparrow, lark sparrow, mourning dove, song sparrow, Lapland longspur, and northern flicker.

MAMMALS: big brown bat, desert cottontail, black-tailed jackrabbit, thirteen-lined ground squirrel, rock squirrel, fox squirrel, Ord's kangaroo rat, deer mouse, porcupine, red fox, long-tailed weasel, bobcat, and mule deer.

AMPHIBIANS / REPTILES: Woodhouse's toad, leopard frog, plains spadefoot, eastern fence lizard, northern earless lizard, short-horned lizard, bullsnake, western plains garter snake, and prairie rattlesnake.

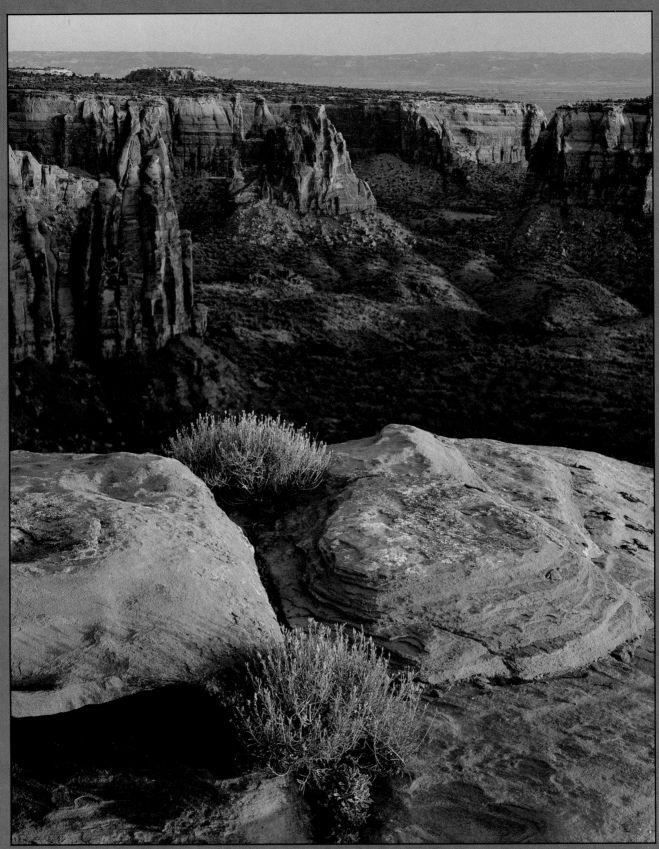

Neither mountains nor plains, Colorado's foothills and canyonlands contain important areas for wildlife. Shown here is Monument Canyon in Colorado National Monument near Grand Junction. Other types of "the lands between" are sagebrush flats, juniper-covered hillsides, and oak-filled valleys. Together, these lands sustain some of Colorado's most life-filled ecosystems. LARRY ULRICH

The Lands Between

The Lands Between
Foothill Shrublands & Woodlands

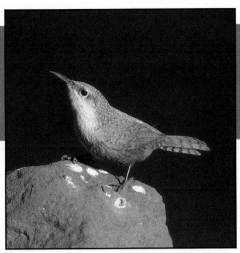

A small bird with a big song, the canyon wren graces rock cliffs and canyons below 8,000 feet throughout Colorado. Its loud, bright call has been described as a gushing cadence of clear notes tripping down a scale "like a stone skipping down a well." The small bird—less than six inches long—is one of eight wrens found in Colorado. WENDY SHATTIL / BOB ROZINSKI

If the Colorado landscape were a tapestry, the most intricate and complex patterns, the most profuse blends of color and texture would be found in the foothills. To the south and west in Colorado are the dark greens of pinyon pine and juniper. Just a bit lower on the flats of the west and northwest is the gray-green of sagebrush. On the higher flanks of the foothills, in wetter areas as far east as the Front Range and as far north as Mount Evans, are the autumn browns and oranges of Gambel oaks. Higher still, ponderosa pines sometimes add their furrowed bark and vanilla-like scent to the mixture. From below, the grasslands creep upward.

The places where ecosystems meet, called "ecotones," are often diverse, as plants and animals from several habitats overlap. In such places, the land comes alive, and the Colorado foothills are no exception. Neither mountains, plains, nor desert, these lands between are one of the most life-filled ecosystems of the state.

Although the boundaries between these shrublands are, in places, indistinct, each has its own very distinctive characteristics. The sagebrush flats are the lowest and driest. Sagebrush dominates huge tracts of the west slope and mountain parks. It is found less abundantly on the east slope. A classic symbol of the West, it is of more than symbolic importance to wildlife.

Pronghorn feed heavily on sagebrush year-round. To deer, it is an important winter forage. To the sage grouse, this plant is the staff of life, providing nesting material, winter food, and year-round cover. It also outlines strutting areas for the bird's mating dance. In areas with few large trees, sagebrush, which can grow to more than six feet high and which averages two feet, provides vital cover, shelter, and nesting sites for many species. The importance of the vegetation is reflected in the names of some of the species found here: sage

31

thrasher, sage sparrow, sage grouse, scrub jay. There are also western rattlesnakes, Great Basin gopher snakes, short-horned lizards, white-tailed jackrabbits, Brewer's sparrows, striped skunks, and chipmunks.

The wide horizons of the sagebrush flats are lost at elevations between 5,000 and 7,000 feet. Here the pinyon-juniper woodlands appear, and the trees can grow taller than 30 feet. The trees are usually well-spaced and broad-branched, offering important cover and nesting sites.

But the main feature of these forests is something hardly bigger than a thumbnail: the pinyon nut. Larger and heavier than most other pine nuts, pinyon nuts are said to contain as many calories pound-for-pound as chocolates and as much protein as beef.

Their nutritional value and abundance makes them one of the most important wildlife foods in the West.

Patches of pinyon trees seem to be cyclical in nut production, rarely producing bumper crops two years in a row. Yet, somewhere each fall, the nuts are abundant, drawing wildlife from far and wide to the bounty. Pinyon jays, Clark's nutcrackers, scrub jays, and Steller's jays, all make use of the sweet, nutritious pinyon nut, as does the pinyon mouse. Abert's squirrels, so closely tied to the ponderosa pine forests, will move into an area of pinyon forest in times of a good crop. Black bears, rock squirrels, and other wildlife species consume the nuts in season. The nuts were once the staple of life for early Indian cultures as well.

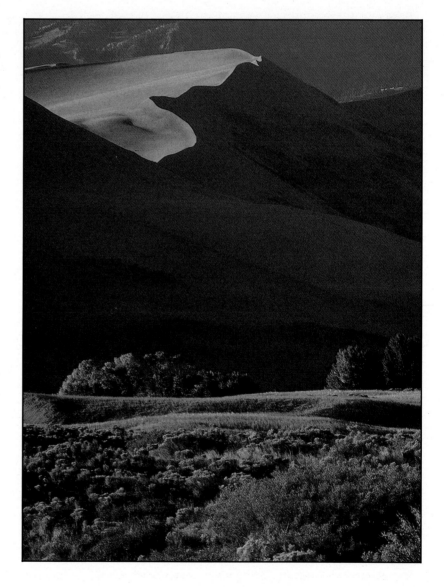

Huge dunes loom above grasslands and shrublands at Great Sand Dunes National Monument adjoining the Rio Grande National Forest. The dunes themselves host only a few wildlife species, but the adjacent hills support coyotes, mule deer, jackrabbits, and many other animals. WENDY SHATTIL / BOB ROZINSKI

With the abundance of life drawn to the woodlands by the pinyon nut come predators as well. Mountain lions, badgers, coyotes, red-tailed hawks, longtail weasels, rattlesnakes, golden eagles, and great horned owls all live in this habitat.

Observing any wildlife in the thick tangles of Gambel oak can be difficult. Oak brush grows in areas of slightly higher elevation (7,000 to 8,500 feet) and more precipitation than the pinyon-juniper forests. Most stands are six to 10 feet high, not as tall as pinyons or junipers, but the branches interweave, forming an almost impenetrable wall of vegetation.

This maze of branches can be the bane of hikers and horseback riders, but it provides vital cover to mammals such as mule deer, black bears, mountain lions, gray foxes, weasels, chipmunks, and wood rats. Townsend's big-eared bats have also been known to lurk in the dark, shadowy recesses of the thick groves.

Birdlife also takes advantage of the cover, including such species as Virginia's warblers, lazuli buntings, scrub jays, towhees, and band-tailed pigeons. Oak brush is a favorite haunt of wild turkeys.

Like the pinyon, the oak brush also provides an important food supply. Many species move into the oak brush in fall for the acorn crop, the black bear perhaps most notable among them. A foraging black bear can consume more than 20,000 calories a day on an acorn diet as it lays on fat for its long winter's sleep. Deer and elk browse the branches and twigs. Mountain mahogany, another important browse species, often is found in association with oak brush.

Because these lands lie between the good farming soils of the bottomlands and the stands of harvestable

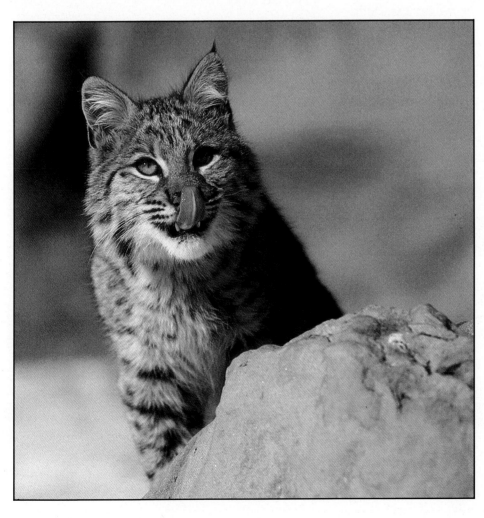

Because of their secretive nature, bobcats are seldom seen, but they range throughout Colorado in virtually every habitat below 10,000 feet. Bobcats mainly prey on rabbits, squirrels, and other small animals, but given the right opportunity (such as deep snow), they are capable of taking larger animals such as deer. Wildlife watchers looking for bobcats usually must be content with tracks on the ground or in the snow. The sharp calls of bobcats are sometimes heard during the mating season in March and April. W. PERRY CONWAY timber on the upper slopes, they have been less developed by humans. But cattle grazing has had a big influence on the shrublands. Large expanses of sagebrush have been ripped up to induce the growth of grass. Pinyon woodlands and oak-brush stands have also been heavily grazed, causing erosion and disruptions in the makeup of the understory vegetation.

These may not be the most dramatic lands in the state; there are few deep canyons or high summits. But good wildlife habitat is not always good scenery. The value of our shrublands slowly is being recognized. The expansion in 1980 of the boundaries of the West Elk Wilderness Area took in large areas of oak brush for their wildlife values. Expanses of pinyon-juniper woodlands are found in such places as Dinosaur National Monument, Mesa Verde National Park, and many of the Bureau of Land Management areas currently under study for possible wilderness designation. Sagebrush has received little protection by national parks or wilderness. Still, examples of this habitat type can be seen in places such as Uncompahgre and Grand Mesa national forests, and Arapahoe National Wildlife Refuge.

At times you must look closely to see the beauty of the shrublands. Their value is subtle: the sky-blue juniper berries, the pattern of shadows in the oak brush, the fragrance of the wind in the sage. But perhaps the beauty of this area is best reflected in the many species of wildlife that call it home. ■

Sage Grouse

Scientific name: Centrocercus urophasianus
Range: Northern and western mountains
Habitat: Sagebrush, shrublands from 7,000 to 8,000 feet
Size: 22 to 30 inches long, four to six pounds (male)
Identifying traits: Size, black belly, pointed tail

The light of the full moon reflects silver off the sagebrush of North Park. A gurgling sound, like running water, whispers quietly. It is April and the dancing has begun—the dancing of the sage grouse.

The sage grouse is the largest of the six Colorado grouse species, which include the ptarmigan, blue grouse, sharp-tailed grouse, and two species of prairie chicken. In mid-March the males, their plumage in full color, gather on

A male sage grouse displays on a ''lek,'' or dancing ground, during the spring breeding season. Colorado has numerous leks available for public viewing, including several locations in North Park near Walden. The Colorado Division of Wildlife provides information and directions to viewing sites, but be prepared for an early day—sage grouse dance at dawn. CLAUDE STEELMAN

traditional grounds known as ''leks.'' Some of these leks, which can be half a mile long and 400 yards wide, have been used for centuries. Arrowheads and awls made from grouse bones, dating back thousands of years, have been found near areas still in use today.

Dominant males dance in the center of the lek. Their movements are elaborate and stylized. Their feet shuffle, their tail feathers spread, their wings droop. With a jerking motion of its head, each male inflates a pair of sacs on its breast to enormous size and then deflates them with a popping noise that can be heard for a long distance.

The males dance at dusk. They dance at dawn. And on nights when the full moon shines, they dance all night. The drab-colored females move in, cautiously at first and then boldly. Most gather near the dominate males, which initiate most of the mating.

Though mating ends in late April, the males will dance until May, even after the females have moved off alone to nesting sites in the sage. Each female lays six to nine eggs in a ground nest lined with feathers and sage leaves. Now the coloration of the female, so drab next to that of the males on the dancing grounds, allows it to become almost invisible on the nest.

The eggs hatch after 25 days—if the nest is not destroyed by ground squirrels, skunks, or badgers, which take a heavy toll. The young grow quickly. Within 10 days, they fly short distances to feed on insects and flowers, such as dandelions and clover.

Sage grouse once abounded in Colorado. A.J. Wallahan, a Colorado wildlife photographer of the mid-1800s, wrote of a flock numbering more than 1,000 that came to a watering hole where he had set up a blind to photograph pronghorns. Early residents of Walden in North Park told of the skies filling with flocks. During the early part of this century, thousands of the birds were killed in mass hunts to feed the crowds at the annual "Sage Hen Days" in Craig.

In fact, sage grouse were so abundant that they were all but left out of early game laws. When some measure of protection was finally given them in 1905, the bag limit was set at 25 birds and the possession limit at 50. Today the limits are more reasonable and are based on extensive research.

Recent studies of sage grouse in such places as North Park, Moffat County, and the Gunnison River basin have shown that controlled hunting does not significantly affect the bird's population. But the destruction of its habitat does. Few wildlife species are so closely tied to a vegetation type as the sage grouse, which depends upon sage for its nesting sites, shelter, and most of its winter diet.

Once, undisturbed sagebrush habitat covered more than 35,000 square miles of Colorado. But agricultural practices, livestock grazing, highway development, mining, and chemical pesticides have drastically reduced the habitat and, as a result, the sage grouse population.

Today, the population has stabilized thanks to hunting regulations, habitat protection, and a better understanding of the bird. Still, sagebrush habitat is not inexhaustible in Colorado. Proper land-use planning and other measures must be instituted to ensure that the sage grouse will continue to dance under the light of the Colorado moon for generations to come.

Wild Turkey

Scientific name: Meleagris gallopavo
Range: Scattered, highest density in southern Colorado
Habitat: Ponderosa pine, woodlands, 5,500 to 9,000 feet
Size: 35 to 50 inches long, 20 pounds, five-foot wingspan
Identifying traits: Naked head, wattle, fanlike tail

The barnyard turkey brings to mind a large, flightless, overstuffed bird that belongs more on the dinner table than in the woods. But the wild turkey conveys a very different image.

Honed by life in the wild, the wild turkey is slimmer than its domestic relative. Its flight is a burst of power, and although it usually prefers to run for cover, its flight speed can be surprising. As turkey hunters or photographers can attest, the wild turkey is elusive and cunning in ways the barnyard variety could never imagine.

Once, the turkey was common in Colorado. It could be found along most of the waterways of the southern mountains, north along the foothills, and west into the mountains. The Indians of Mesa Verde in southwestern Colorado had domesticated the bird as early as A.D. 700. They wove its feathers into blankets and clothing for warmth and used the strong, sharp bones of its lower legs to make awls and picks. At archaeological sites near Chimney Rock along the Piedra River, there is evidence of "turkey pens." Early Utes of that area constructed hunting platforms in oak trees near watering sites. Evidence of some of the platforms was still visible early in this century.

The first recorded sighting of a turkey in Colorado was perhaps an omen of things to come. "Killed a turkey," reads the Pike Expedition journal entry for November 13, 1806, when the group was camped along the Arkansas River, "the first we have seen since we left Pawnee."

Hunting pressure, combined with habitat loss and diseases transmitted by domestic fowl, brought the bird almost to extinction by the early 1900s. Some wildlife historians believe the Colorado population may have dipped as low as 250 birds. But reintroduction and conservation programs, begun as early as 1940, have stabilized the population today.

The turkey prefers thick cover near water and clearings. It roosts high in the branches of ponderosa pines and often also can be spotted in stands of scrub oak or pinyon. In May, the males begin wild, exuberant dances designed to attract mates. Nests are simple depressions scratched in the ground and lined with leaves and grass. They are usually built next to stumps or brush for cover. The female leads her young away from the nest soon after they hatch.

The diet of the wild turkey varies with the season. In summer, the bird eats grasshoppers, other insects, clover, grasses, seeds, and leaves. In fall, it amends its diet to include juniper berries, gooseberries, kinnikinnick, and nuts such as pinyons and acorns. Through the year, its diet is composed of about 90 percent vegetation and 10 percent animal matter.

The turkey's association with Thanksgiving and the barnyard has earned it a comical and frivolous reputation. But perched in a ponderosa pine, strutting its dance in spring, or bursting for cover through the brush, the wild turkey has proved itself to be a magnificent bird very much at home in the forests of Colorado.

Common Raven

Scientific name: Corvus corax
Range: Central to western Colorado
Habitat: Mountains, canyons, plateaus
Size: 21 to 26 inches long
Identifying traits: Uniform black plumage, croaking call

In full strut for an admiring hen, a male turkey displays its magnificent feathers and brilliant red and white head. Natives of Colorado, wild turkeys are found throughout southwestern Colorado, in foothill country along the Front Range from Fort Collins south to the New Mexico border, and on the eastern plains along the Arkansas River and Bonny Reservoir.
SHERM SPOELSTRA

The Lands Between

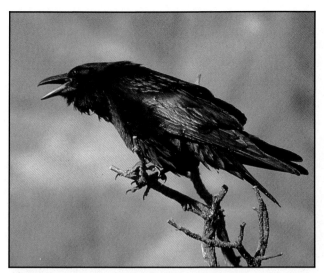

Colorado contains two species of big, black birds—ravens and crows. Ravens, such as the one shown here, can be distinguished by their larger size, heavier beak, wedge-shaped tail in flight, and shaggy throat feathers. Both birds may be seen in urban areas, but ravens are more common than crows in wild areas. R. E. BARBER

In the mountain air, a pair of ravens toss and whirl in flight. They veer suddenly away and then dive nearer. Against the white clouds of a summer day, they are as black as wind-blown ashes.

Colorado's largest songbird, the raven is a graceful, acrobatic flier. Pairs sometimes fly close together, as if dancing in the air. Their wingtips lightly touch.

The raven is easily identified both by its gun-barrel black coloration and its unmistakable calls—one a raspy croak and the other a bell-like tone often sounded in flight. In the air, it can be distinguished from the crow by its wedge-shaped tail, slow wingbeats, and frequent soaring.

Colorado is home to two species of ravens, the common raven and the Chihuahuan raven. The latter is a bird of the plains. When huge herds of bison wandered eastern Colorado, it was common there, too. Zebulon Pike probably referred to a Chihuahuan raven in his journal— the first written record of the species in the state. In mid-November 1806, after an unsuccessful bid to climb Pike's Peak, Pike wrote that, for several days, he and his men had eaten only "one partridge and a piece of deer's ribs the ravens had left us."

Although capable of killing small game such as squirrels, mice and some birds, the Chihuahuan raven dines primarily on insects and carrion. With the passing of the large bison herds, the bird has all but disappeared from the plains. It is now known to nest only in the southeastern counties of Colorado.

The common raven, as its name implies, is much more abundant in the state. A bird of the mountains and canyons it is also found in the high parks—North, South, and Middle parks, and the San Luis Valley. Unlike the crow, which is often seen in the city, the common raven is rarely found in or around places inhabited by man.

The common raven nests on inaccessible ledges deep in the mountains. It lines its thick, sturdy nest with bark, fur, and hair. The same nest will be repaired and used year after year. Any nesting material that falls from the nest is not recovered and reused. As a result, the ground below a raven's nest is often littered with sticks and debris.

The female lays four to six greenish-brown eggs. As she incubates them for the next three weeks, the male brings her food. After successful fledging, the ravens often gather in large flocks to roost.

Ravens have long been considered highly intelligent creatures. One ornithologist referred to them as "the dolphins of the avian world."

Of all the Colorado birds, none has been as deeply entwined in the mythology of the area. The sight of ravens was once considered good fortune, because they led hunters to the bison herds. The sight of a pair wheeling over the mountains in the spring courtship dance was a sign of benevolence. Even today, it can seem like the sight of a spirit dancing with the sky.

Golden Eagle

Scientific name: Aquila chrysaetos
Range: Throughout Colorado
Habitat: Plains, canyons, mountainsides
Size: 30 to 42 inches long, eight to 10 pounds
Identifying traits: Large size, soars with level wings, uniform coloring

Even from a distance, the silhouette of the golden eagle soaring against the storm clouds above Pawnee National Grassland is unmistakable—straight-winged, broad, finger-like feathers at the wingtips.

Like the sky in which it soars, the history of the golden eagle in Colorado was stormy from the start. The first written record of the bird was made in 1843 by Rufus B. Sage, who noted the carcasses of 36 golden and bald eagles at a camp along the North Saint Vrain River. Arapaho Indians had trapped the birds for their feathers, which were used to make ceremonial clothing. Eagle "traps," simple enclosures of stone in which hunters would lie in wait with rabbit carcasses for bait, were said

Regal in appearance, this golden eagle shows two reasons why it is a formidable winged hunter—keen eyes and powerful beak. It also displays the reason for its name—the golden-brown feathers on its neck. Year-round residents, golden eagles soar throughout Colorado. Pawnee National Grassland and the Rocky Mountain Arsenal are two good viewing areas.   W. PERRY CONWAY

to have been constructed atop several high Colorado mountains, including Longs Peak and Mount Blanca, as well as on ridges near the edge of western Colorado plateaus.

More recently, the golden eagle has been shot by ranchers worried about their stock, electrocuted by high-voltage power towers, and poisoned by carcasses left by predator-control officers. The pesticide DDT has entered the eagle's food chain and rendered many of its eggs too thin-shelled to hatch successfully. Today, the golden eagle is protected nationally, and it still flies over Colorado.

With a wingspan of five to 7.5 feet, the golden eagle is one of the largest birds in the West. It is a year-round resident of Colorado and can be seen over almost any habitat type—mountains, canyons, and plains. It hunts jackrabbits, prairie dogs, snakes, grouse, and lambs of both bighorn sheep and mountain goats at the higher elevations. It also eats carrion when it is available. It has even been known to attack deer floundering in mountain snow and pronghorns out on the plains.

Eagle nests can be huge. Golden eagles mate for life, which can be a long time, and pairs often use the same nest year after year. Each season, beginning in December or January, the eagles reinforce their nest with whatever materials are available. In Colorado, nests have been constructed with deer antlers, the bones of cattle, barbed wire, newspaper, burlap bags, and stockings. More often, the birds use new branches, yucca spears, and fresh green spruce boughs.

Sometime in February or March, the female lays four mottled eggs. Both parents incubate them and provide the hatched chicks with food. Since the family stays at the nest until June or longer, the area below it is often strewn with bones.

Young golden eagles are covered with fine down at first. The dark flight feathers begin to show through in a few weeks. By June, the surviving young are standing at the lip of the nest, feeling the first movements of air beneath their wings.

Immature golden eagles have streaks of white in their feathers and, at a distance, resemble young bald eagles. In fact, the difficulty in distinguishing between the two was part of the reason for protecting golden eagles—perhaps some young bald eagles would inadvertently be

The Lands Between

saved as well. By their fourth year, the birds have taken on the gold-streaked plumage of adults.

Like the bald eagle, the golden eagle has suffered greatly at the hands of humans. And it has natural enemies as well. In 1925, C.H.E. Aiken logged an unusual observation of 23 golden eagles on a frigid March morning in Colorado. A sleet storm during the night had coated the birds' wings with layers of ice so that they could not fly. They perched on fence posts and stood idly on the ground, waiting for the morning sun to thaw them out. Within a few hours, the day had warmed. The eagles unfurled their wings a few times to dry them and then returned to their rightful place in the Colorado sky, backlit by the last clouds of the storm as it moved away.

Turkey Vulture

Scientific name: Cathartes aura
Range: Statewide
Habitat: Open areas, canyons, cliffs, plains
Size: 26 to 32 inches long, 72-inch wingspan
Identifying traits: Naked red head, lighter undersurface on the trailing edge of the wings

They circle down from the sky as if out of a nightmare. To many Indian cultures, they were messengers of the gods, appearing from out of nowhere to mark the spot of death. In movies and television shows, they are harbingers of doom. But in reality, turkey vultures are simply a species that fills a valuable ecological niche, cleaning carcasses from the face of the land.

The turkey vulture is one of the largest birds in North America. In Colorado, it is most often seen turning slow circles in the summer sky over the canyons and mountains. Even from a long distance, it can be distinguished from the golden eagle and other soaring species by the lighter undersurface of its primary feathers and the V-shaped profile of its wings in flight.

With its relatively weak talons and beak, the turkey vulture does not kill its own prey. Instead it scavenges for the carcasses of almost any creature. Its featherless head enables it to feed without becoming caked in gore.

With its scavenging ways, the vulture has both suffered and prospered at the hand of humans. During the predator-control programs of the early 1900s, the bird was often an unwitting victim of poisoned carcasses meant to destroy wolves or mountain lions. On the other hand, man has presented it with a new food source—the thousands of

When they soar in the Colorado sky, turkey vultures appear as large, dark, eagle-like birds. But vultures soar with their wings curved upwards in a V-shaped pattern while eagles hold their wings nearly straight across. Turkey vultures are most common along the Western Slope and in southeastern Colorado. Their naked, red heads are noticeable only at close range. WENDY SHATTIL / BOB ROZINSKI

animals killed by automobiles each year in the state.

The eyesight of the vulture is amazing by human standards. Some experts believe that a soaring vulture can spot a three-foot-long carcass, such as that of a jackrabbit, at a distance of four miles. It can spot a gathering of other vultures, a sure sign of a dead animal, from as far away as eight miles. The vulture also has a particularly good sense of smell, another aid in finding food.

The turkey vulture is a warm-weather species, since snowfall makes it more difficult to find food. It usually arrives in Colorado in April. Although it is a fairly common summer resident, few of its nests have been observed. They are usually set in remote, inaccessible terrain. Nesting sites include rock caves, hollow logs, cliffs, and old snags. Usually the nest is just a small depression rather than a structure of twigs and sticks.

The female lays one to three large eggs, which she incubates for six weeks. After hatching, the young are covered with fine white down. Within nine weeks, they seek out the thermal updrafts near their nest so that they can rise into the summer sky with their parents. By October, when the first snows dust the land, the vultures move south, following the sun and searching out the dead.

Western Rattlesnake

Scientific name: Crotalus viridis
Range: Throughout Colorado to 9,500 feet
Habitat: Grasslands, shrublands, rocky areas, pinyon-juniper
  forests, open coniferous forests
Size: 15 to 65 inches long including rattle
Identifying traits: Rattle at tip of tail, triangular skull

Deep in the slickrock canyons of Dinosaur National Monument, there is a rock wall dotted with pictographs, drawings done by the Fremont Indians nearly a thousand years ago. Among them is a figure instantly recognizable, so clear even after all this time that you can almost hear the echo of its buzz—a rattlesnake.

For as long as humans have walked the West, the buzzing of the rattlesnake has inspired strong emotions. Some early cultures strung necklaces with rattles and wore skins on ceremonial garb to garner the reptile's power. The snake has been depicted on pottery and spoken of with awe around the campfire, and yet all too often it

is killed on sight, a victim of ignorance and fear.

Contrary to popular belief, the western diamondback rattlesnake does not occur in Colorado. Only two of the 17 U.S. members of the viper family can be found here—the western rattlesnake and the massasauga. The most common is the western rattlesnake, which has two subspecies in the state. A western subspecies, the faded midget rattler, is found mostly in the west-central canyons, while the more widespread prairie rattler occurs below 9,500 feet throughout much of the rest of the state.

The western rattlesnake has a heat-sensitive pore called a loreal pit on each side of its head. These help it to locate prey. They are so sensitive that the snake can sense the heat given off by a fist-sized mouse from a foot away.

The snake kills its prey by injecting venom through hollow fangs that snap downward and forward as it strikes. The prey does not die instantly. So the snake uses another tool called a Jacobson's organ to track the scent trail of the victim until the poison takes effect.

The rattlesnake preys on lizards, prairie dogs, nesting birds, young rabbits, ground squirrels, and mice. Its jaws are loosely hinged and can pull back almost 180 degrees. Its ribs are not attached to its spine, so that it can swallow large prey whole and head-first.

Despite widespread belief, the venom of a young rattlesnake is no more deadly than that of an adult. In fact, mature snakes inject greater quantities of venom and so pose a greater danger. Potency of the venom varies between the subspecies. The venom of the faded midget rattlesnake is 10 to 30 times more deadly than that of the prairie rattler.

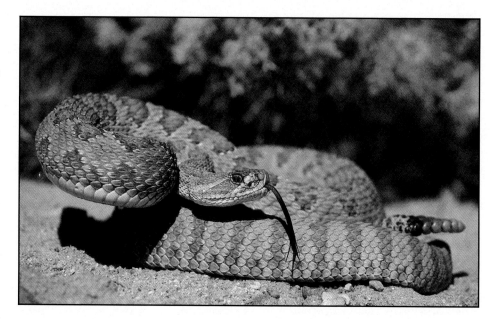

Coiled and cautious, a western rattlesnake tastes the air with its wet, forked tongue. Scents in the air and heat sensed through pores in their heads help rattlesnakes detect prey. To avoid an unexpected encounter with a rattlesnake, exercise caution around prairie-dog towns and rocky areas, especially in the mornings, evenings, and after summer thunderstorms.
JUDD COONEY

Rattlesnakes account for up to 90 percent of all venomous snake bites in North America annually—more than coral snakes, copperheads, and cottonmouths combined. Although the bite is painful and can cause infection and illness, there have been few documented reports of fatalities among bitten adults. According to the Colorado Department of Health, only four people (two children and two adults) died from snakebites in the state between 1970 and 1987.

As many stories are told about the snake's rattle as about its fangs. The rattle evolved as a first-line defense mechanism, an audible warning that gives humans or other predators the option of avoiding a fight. Rattles are added each time the snake sheds its skin, but since this may occur two to four times a year—and since rattles may also be lost—it is not possible to tell the age of a snake by counting its rattles.

The activity pattern of the rattler depends upon the elevation at which it is found. Usually it emerges in April or May from dens in rock crevices or burrows sometimes shared by great numbers of snakes. In 1937, at least 1,500 rattlesnakes were crushed by automobiles on U.S. Highway 81 in northern Colorado as the snakes made their way en masse to their dens. Until September, the snake hunts during the cooler parts of the days, seeking the shade. Female rattlers older than two years give birth to between four and 16 young in the fall before returning to the den.

Young and mature snakes are preyed upon by red-tailed hawks, badgers, coyotes, golden eagles, other snakes, and humans, the most deadly predator of all. Despite mounting scientific evidence of the value of the rattlesnake to its environment and the limited threat it poses to humans, the buzz of the rattlesnake continues to strike fear into the hearts of many.

Mountain Lion

Scientific name: Felis concolor
Range: Eastern foothills to Utah line
Habitat: All forested ecosystems but prefers rocky canyons and
*   foothills*
Size: Seven to nine feet long, 150 to 200 pounds (male); five
*   to seven feet long, 80 to 150 pounds (female)*
Identifying traits: Large size; long, cylindrical tail

Broken cliffs where the wind blows strong, shadowed canyons thick with the scent of mule deer and elk, rocky mesas, hillsides of pinyon and juniper, silent places with room to roam—these are cougar country. The mountain lion has a taste for long horizons.

Once, the mountain lion had all the space it needed. Before the United States was settled, the big cat ranged from the high mountains of British Columbia to the southern tip of South America and east and west across much of the continent. That range made it the most widely distributed native mammal in the western hemisphere, and it accounts for the cat's many names. Depending upon where in the New World you live, the cat is called cougar, puma, panther, catamount, painter, or mountain lion.

As settlers pushed west, the mountain lion's horizons began to shrink. Today, except for small populations in southern Florida, the mountain lion is a western species seeking out the last remnants of quiet land, of rough country where it can move unseen and silent. In Colorado, populations of mountain lion also are known to exist on the fringes of cities along the Front Range, such as Boulder.

The mountain lion moves so stealthily that less is known about the big cat than about any other large mammal in the West. Guides, packers, ranchers, wildlife managers, and others who spend time in the backwoods can travel for years in cougar country and see only tracks or a few deer bones bleaching in the sun. Even in areas of known populations, the mountain lion is like a phantom, hunting mostly at night, staying near cover. Its secrecy has helped it to survive in the face of encroachment upon its habitat, but a lack of scientific information has also resulted in myths and misinformation about the cat.

The mountain lion has been branded a stock killer. In fact, the scientific name of the subspecies found here in the central Rockies—*hippolestes*—translates to "the horsethief." That reputation led the 1929 Colorado legislature to put a $50 bounty on mountain lions. Between 1929 and 1965, bounty hunters collected the fee on 807 carcasses, although there is reason to believe that some of the animals may have been killed in bordering states without bounties and brought into Colorado.

Although early records are not reliable, there were only three confirmed cases of mountain lions harming livestock in Colorado between 1945 and 1965. Obviously, a predator with the stalking skill and killing power of the mountain lion is capable of taking livestock, but its reputation may outreach reality.

The bounty was finally lifted July 1, 1965, and the mountain lion was reclassified as a big-game species. It became the last animal on which bounties were offered in the state.

The mountain lion's main prey in Colorado is the mule

A mountain lion mother tends her two kittens. Mountain lions are fairly abundant in Colorado but rarely seen, hunting mainly at night and usually avoiding people. They are most common in areas with abundant mule deer, their favorite prey. To many Coloradoans, mountain lions are striking symbols of wild areas. W. PERRY CONWAY

deer. Although the cat will take elk, porcupines, bighorn sheep, and smaller mammals when the opportunity arises, it seems designed to hunt deer. It is a stalker, taking advantage of cover such as trees and boulders to move up close to its quarry before pouncing. Because of its small lungs, it is not able to outrun a deer over a long distance, and so it relies upon stealth and its powerful jaws and forepaws to make a quick kill. Leaping onto the deer's back, the lion attempts to crush the vertebrae with its jaws while snapping the head back with its forepaws. Of the lion kills investigated, almost all reveal a broken neck or strangulation as the cause of death.

Once its prey is down, the mountain lion often drags it into cover before eating it. The digestive system of the lion is designed for a feast-or-famine lifestyle and can hold as much as 20 or 30 pounds of meat at a time. When a lion has eaten its fill, it covers the remains of the prey with sticks and leaves and returns to the site frequently until the entire carcass is consumed or until the meat begins to spoil.

Predation by the mountain lion does not jeopardize mule deer populations. A male lion in winter, when it is more dependent upon larger game, will take a deer every 10 to 14 days, killing perhaps 15 to 25 a year. The numbers could be slightly higher for a female with kittens to feed. In fact, the mountain lion population seems to depend upon the mule deer population rather than vice versa. When deer are abundant, so are lions. When deer populations decline because of severe winters or lack of forage, the number of lions also declines. Also, some theories suggest that the presence of a mountain lion in the range of a deer herd keeps the animals on the move, preventing them from depleting the forage of any particular area.

Mountain lions mate anytime during the year but most often in late winter or early spring. After a three-month gestation, the female gives birth to one to four kittens in a hollow log or cave. They are blind and weigh less than a pound. The young nurse exclusively for only about a month, after which meat is gradually added to their diet.

The Lands Between

The young grow quickly, reaching 10 pounds by their second month and as much as 50 pounds by the end of a year. As with most predators, the young stay with their mother for an extended period of time—as long as two years—while she teaches them hunting skills. She also protects them from male lions, which have been known to kill and feed upon the kittens.

Although the lion is strong and powerful, it does not always have the upper hand when hunting deer and elk twice its size. Mountain lions have been found trampled by the sharp hooves of scattering herds. The hides of many lions show the scars of being gored by antlers. In 1985, in Rocky Mountain National Park, a mountain lion was found dead beneath the carcass of a bull elk it had attacked, apparently crushed when the dying animal fell upon it. Even hunting smaller prey has its dangers. In 1973, a Division of Wildlife employee was attacked by a lion near Spanish Peaks. The lion was killed and its throat was found to be full of porcupine quills.

By the time a lion is two years old, its hunting lessons are over. It is almost as large as an adult, and it has long since taken on the adult's coloration, losing the spots that identify kittens up to six months old. It ventures off to find its own home range.

The task may not be easy. Each male has a territory of 25 to 40 square miles, which it fiercely protects from intrusion by other males. It marks the boundaries with scent and urine. In areas where prey species are scarce, the range may spread more than 100 square miles. Although males' territories do not overlap, they may cross into the smaller (15- to 30-square-mile) ranges of females.

It is often the two-year-old lions searching for a range that wander into developed areas. In April 1959, a lion was killed within the city limits of Pueblo. Another was found in 1975 on the grounds of the East Street Elementary School in Trinidad. A growing number of mountain lions are spotted each year around the cities of the Front Range.

Because the mountain lion is protected as a game animal and because much of its range has been designated as wilderness or national park, its population is stable and secure in Colorado. But threats do remain. Developments encroaching farther into the foothills, high-altitude reservoirs flooding canyons, and recreationists moving into the high country in increasing numbers all could potentially hurt the mountain lion.

Good mountain lion habitat can be found in the foothills that surround the San Luis Valley, in the deep canyons of the Dolores River country in southwestern Colorado, and on the empty flats of the Uncompahgre Plateau. If left alone, the lion heads for rugged terrain, uncut by roads. It is a creature of the untamed places, the unbroken lands where it can stalk the herds unmolested and stop and drink at a canyon sinkhole. The mountain lion has become a symbol of the Colorado wilderness.

Brazilian Free-tailed Bat

Scientific name: Tadarida brasiliensis
Range: Southern Colorado
Habitat: Caves, mine shafts, old buildings
Size: Four inches long, up to 12-inch wingspan
Identifying traits: Brown color, long tail

At first there are just a few black specks against the last light of day. The specks increase until they look like a column of black smoke rising out of the ground. As darkness falls, the sky above the San Luis Valley is stirred by wings. A roost of more than a hundred thousand Brazilian free-tailed bats, one of the largest aggregations of the males of the species north of Mexico, pours out of an abandoned mine shaft to begin its nightly rounds.

Creatures of the night, silent, mysterious, bats fly out of their roosts and into the dark depths of the human heart and mind. They carry our nightmares on their wings.

But fear of bats is unwarranted. The 17 species that occur in Colorado are all insect eaters, beneficial to humans in the vast quantities of bugs they consume. A single little brown bat can capture 150 insects in under 15 minutes and will consume as many as 3,000 mosquitoes in a single night. The vast flock of free-tailed bats over the San Luis Valley can eat over a ton of insects in a night.

Bats do not, as old wive's tales suggest, swoop down and get tangled in your hair. Vampire bats, which are not found in Colorado, are the only bats that drink the blood of large mammals. And though there have been cases of rabies transmitted by bats, fewer than a dozen people in the United States have died in the past four decades as a result. More people have died from bee stings and power-mower accidents in that time.

To most people, a bat is a bat. But the bats of Colorado are varied in habit and habitat. Unlike the huge colonies in the San Luis Valley, other species prefer to roost singly or in small groups—the red bat in deciduous trees along rivers such as the South Platte and the Arkansas, the hoary bat in the branches of conifers all the way to timberline. Some species, such as the long-

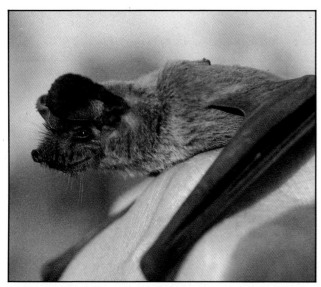

In hand, a Brazilian free-tailed bat appears less fearsome and more oddly interesting than indicated by bat legend and lore. Flocks of more than 100,000 Brazilian free-tailed bats inhabit abandoned mine shafts in the San Luis Valley, where they gobble up more than a ton of insects each night. The Brazilian free-tailed bat is one of 20 bat species in Colorado.
W. PERRY CONWAY

legged myotis, leave their roosts before dark and are a common sight in the evening skies over places such as Aspen. Others move only in the full darkness of midnight, such as the Townsend's big-eared bat, and so they are rarely seen.

Little is known about some bat species because of their nocturnal habits, but others have been widely studied, revealing some amazing adaptations.

Bats are the only true flying mammals, and some are acrobatic in flight. The little brown bat can travel 50 miles in a night in search of food. Some of the insect-eating bats can fly at great speeds, as much as 40 miles an hour for short spurts, turning and diving with incredible agility. Most bats skim low above the ground or over water to find concentrations of insects and then swat the flying bugs with their wings or scoop them up in the flap of skin between their legs. Then they transfer the prey to their mouths, consume them in flight, and move on in search of more.

How insect-eating bats locate their prey is perhaps their most striking adaptation. Unlike the old saying, bats are not blind. Most have at least rudimentary vision, but it is their hearing that guides them more so than their eyes. In a method known as "echolocation," bats emit a series of ultrasonic sounds from their noses or mouths and then listen for the echoes bouncing off objects before them. A bat in the open will emit about five calls per second.

Once it locks onto a target, the rate can increase to 200 calls per second. The bat rapidly computes the time lapse between the returning echoes to measure the distance to an object. Some scientists even believe it draws a mental image from the echoes, a kind of sound shadow. The method is complex, not yet fully understood, and even more effective than the most modern radar devices.

The life cycle of Colorado bats is still only vaguely understood. Most of the species in the state breed in the fall. Yet, ovulation, fertilization, and gestation do not occur until early spring. Often, as is the case with the fringed myotis and the big brown bat, the pregnant females gather in large rearing colonies. A single offspring, sometimes two, is usually born in early summer. Because they are mammals, bats bear live young, which they nurse for the first few weeks after birth. The young are weaned in about six to eight weeks, depending upon species, and can fly within a month.

Most bats shun the light and roost in caves, rock crevices, spaces under loose bark, attics, or old mine shafts during the day. As the sun sets, they begin to stir, different species moving out to feed at different times. Often there are two periods of activity a night and then, with the growing light, a return to the roost.

Some bat species live in Colorado year-round: the small-footed myotis, the western pipestrelle, the big brown bat, the pallid bat. Others, such as the red bat, the hoary bat, and the Yuma myotis, migrate out of state in winter and appear in Colorado again with the warm months of spring.

Bat populations seem to have declined in many areas and among many of the 850 species worldwide. Natural disease has taken its toll. Although some species live as long as 30 years, bats are slow breeders, each having only a single litter a year. The survival rate among the young is as low as 50 percent. Bats are also preyed upon by raccoons, snakes, hawks, owls, and weasels.

But the main cause of the bat's decline has been humans. The use of pesticides such as DDT to control pests has both lessened the food supply and caused toxic build-up in the insect-eating species. And a deep-seated fear of bats remains. Roosts have been bulldozed shut. Entire colonies have been killed when their roosts were flooded with fire hoses or poison gas.

Humans have long been afraid of the dark, a fear that is embodied in the bat. Only the light of knowledge, acquired through more in-depth scientific study of bats, will help us to come to grips with our fears and begin to understand and perhaps even respect these creatures of the night.

Kit Fox

Scientific name: Vulpes macrotis
Range: Western Colorado
Habitat: Pinyon-juniper stands, canyons, sagebrush
Size: Three to six pounds, 20 to 30 inches including long tail
Identifying traits: Small size, black-tipped tail, black patches
  on snout

Against the slickrock of the canyon floor, its furred feet are silent. At dawn, returning from the night's hunt, it moves without a shadow in the soft light, its coat the same dusty brown as the canyon walls.

The kit fox and its close relative the swift fox of the eastern plains are Colorado's smallest foxes. The swift fox lives in the remote parts of the canyon country and is active all year. It has adapted to life in the hot, dry canyons in several ways. Its ears are large, two times as large proportionally as those of the gray fox. As a result, the fox both has a sharp sense of hearing and a means of radiating heat away from its body. Hair lines the ears to direct sound and filter out blowing sand. The swift fox is mostly nocturnal, spending the hot part of the day in a cool den, hunting by night for its prey of kangaroo rats, ground squirrels, mice, jackrabbits, lizards, birds, and insects.

Swift fox pairs often mate for life. Breeding takes place in January or February. The female bears two to seven furred, blind pups in the den about two months later. They will spend the first three weeks in the den while the male hunts. By fall they will be on their own.

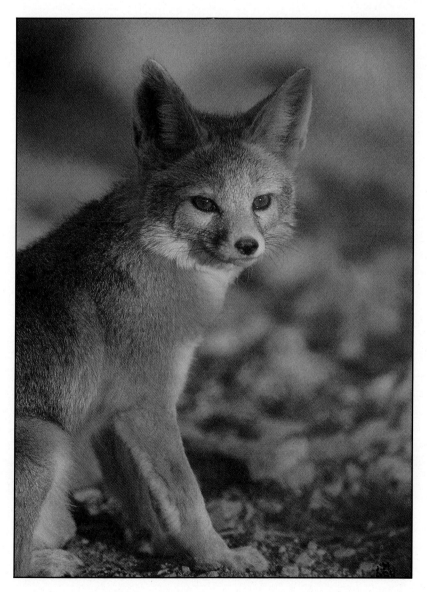

Large ears mark the kit fox, a small, slender predator about the size of a house cat. Never abundant in Colorado, the kit fox population appears to be increasing in protected canyon and desert habitat on Colorado's west slope. JUDD COONEY

Foxes have suffered in Colorado because of predator-control programs aimed at coyotes, wolves, mountain lions, and bears. The kit fox has never been an abundant species in the state, but some biologists believe that it has made something of a comeback in recent years with the preservation of canyon and desert habitats on Colorado's Western Slope.

The canyons hunted by the kit fox are often filled with the howling of the coyote. Although the two belong to the same family, the Canidae, the kit fox is quieter and less noticeable. It communicates with soft barks and whimpers more fitting to such a tiny, inconspicuous predator. While the coyote calls at the break of day, the kit fox just twitches its ears once toward the sound and disappears into its den.

Pinyon Jay

Scientific name: Gymnorhinus cyanocephalus
Range: Statewide
Habitat: Pinyon-juniper forests
Size: Nine to 11 inches long
Identifying traits: Gray-blue plumage; thin, sharp beak; short tail

Step quickly over a rise into a draw filled with pinyon pines, and the ground below the trees can suddenly explode with birds. The pinyon jay, a common year-round resident of the pinyon-juniper stands, is so fond of the pinyon nut that an area with a good crop can be crowded with birds. Although it will eat ponderosa pine seeds, caterpillars, beetles, ants, and grasshoppers, the pinyon jay prefers the pinyon nut over all other foods. A good crop can stimulate breeding; a poor one can mean hard times.

The pinyon jay is not a flashy bird, and it is usually noticed when it congregates in large and noisy flocks. Its plumage is gray tinged with blue. Its call is distinct but not very musical. Locally, it is sometimes called the "blue crow," and bird books describe it as "crow-like in its feathers and habits." It spends a good deal of time on the ground, pecking for nuts that have fallen from the trees. Not only does it depend upon the pinyon for nuts, but it often builds its nest in the branches, using yucca fibers, fur, and soft vegetation. It usually breeds in loose colonies.

The relationship between the jay and the pinyon forest may not be all one-sided. In years of bumper crops of nuts, the jay often stashes nuts in cracks or along the ground. When not all the stashes are collected, the seeds of a new generation of trees are sown, trees which will be the staff of life to a coming generation of pinyon jays.

Canyon Wren

Scientific name: Catherpes mexicanus
Range: Throughout Colorado below 8,000 feet
Habitat: Canyons, cliffs
Size: Five to six inches long
Identifying traits: Upturned tail, distinctive call

To anyone who has floated the rivers or hiked the maze of side canyons in western Colorado, the song is the backdrop of fond memories. In the still, bright air, it is sharp and clear—seven to 12 notes descending like a stone skipping down the canyon walls. It rings throughout the canyons and rock cliffs all over Colorado. Behind the huge song is the small canyon wren.

Compared to the size of its song, which can sometimes be heard as far as half a mile away, the bird itself is tiny, no bigger than a handful of sand. Its habits keep it close to the rocks, taking short flights, creeping slowly, probing the cracks for insects with its sharp beak.

You can look directly at the canyon wren and not see it. Its colors are taken directly from its canyon habitat. Its upper parts are a sandy brown, its head the gray of river stones, its tail as reddish-brown as sandstone. Only its white throat and upper breast give it away, and as soon as you see it, it is gone.

The canyon wren nests in some of the most inaccessible terrain in the canyons. The cup-sized nest is usually jammed into a crack or crevice or pushed up under a rock. The female does most of the nest-building, using strips of bark, spider webs, and feathers to line the nest before laying five to seven whitish, speckled eggs in May. The female does most of the incubating, but the male stays close by.

Much of the life of the canyon wren is private, lost among the immensity of the cliffs. Yet its song gives a voice to the Colorado canyon country.

Collared Lizard

Scientific name: Crotaphytus collaris
Range: Southern Colorado
Habitat: Rocky areas, canyons below 6,000 feet
Size: Three- to four-inch-long body, 14 inches long including tail
Identifying traits: Black rings around neck

Heat rises off the rocks in waves. Beyond the heat waves rise the waves of Snaggletooth Rapid on the Dolores River. A long line of kayakers and rafters are along the trail to scout the rapid, but few eyes are on the water. They are, instead, watching a collared lizard.

The collared lizard is one of the most recognizable and conspicuous reptiles in the state. The black rings around its neck, often set against a backdrop of yellow, are readily identifiable. It inhabits rocky canyons and shrublands, sometimes along waterways such as the Arkansas River in the southeastern part of the state and the Dolores River in the southwest.

Like all 10 species of lizards in Colorado, the collared lizard is carnivorous. It searches along the ground or scouts from favorite perches on high rocks, looking for grasshoppers, beetles, and even other small lizards. In turn, it is preyed upon by large birds and some snakes.

The collared lizard is a summer creature; it spends the cold months from September to April in an underground den. In spring, it emerges to claim a territory that it will defend vigorously. It uses a bobbing motion to signal its agitation and to threaten potential invaders. If that is unsuccessful, it chases its challengers and may engage in short fights.

Breeding takes place in early summer. Clutches vary greatly in size, with from one to 12 hatchlings having been recorded. In Colorado, hatchlings appear in August. They seem to stay active longer than adults and may sometimes be observed as late as October.

Startled by the ring of river runners, the collared lizard bobs three times as a threat and then scurries off into the rocks. The paddlers turn back to the business of scouting a route through the waves of Snaggletooth Rapid.

Other Wildlife of the Transition Zone

BIRDS: sharp-shinned hawk, kestral, red-tailed hawk,

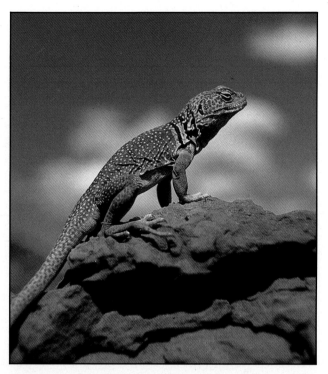

Once seen, the vividly marked collared lizard is never forgotten. One of ten species of lizards in Colorado, the collared lizard inhabits rocky canyons and shrublands in southern areas of the state. Its characteristic bobbing motion when perched on a rock serves as a sign of agitation and as a threat against predators and other lizards. SHERM SPOELSTRA

peregrine falcon, house wren, band-tailed pigeon, great horned owl, common nighthawk, white-throated swift, broad-tailed hummingbird, Lewis woodpecker, western wood-pewee, western kingbird, violet-green swallow, Steller's jay, rufous-sided towhee, black-billed magpie, scrub jay, mountain chickadee, rock wren, dark-eyed junco, evening grosbeak, ruby-crowned kinglet, mountain bluebird, robin, sage thrasher, loggerhead shrike, Wilson warbler, yellow-rumped warbler, black-throated gray warbler, western tanager, black-headed grosbeak, lazuli bunting, western bluebird, Brewer's sparrow, and white-crowned sparrow.

MAMMALS: big brown bat, long-legged myotis, Townsend's big-eared bat, desert cottontail, black-tailed jackrabbit, Colorado chipmunk, golden-mantled ground squirrel, Abert's squirrel, Mexican woodrat, red fox, black bear, ringtail, long-tailed weasel, badger, striped skunk, elk, mule deer, and mountain sheep.

AMPHIBIANS / REPTILES: plains spadefoot, short-horned lizard, prairie lizard, eastern yellowbelly racer, bullsnake, and wandering garter snake.

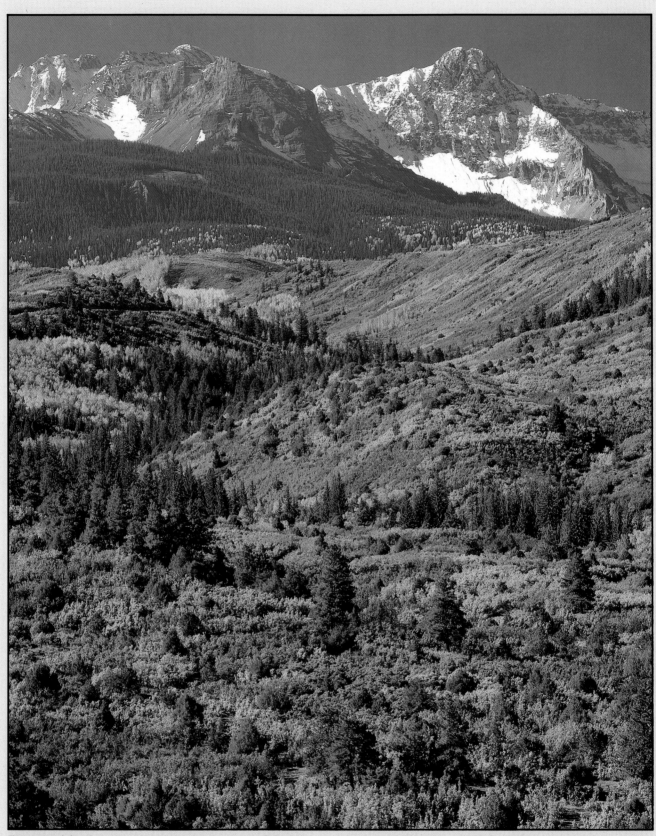

Foreground for the mountains, the montane zone in Colorado rises from about 6,000 feet to 9,500 feet. With a variety of vegetation, the montane zone produces substantial forage for large animals such as black bears, mule deer, and elk. In many areas of Colorado, quality montane habitat spells survival for big game herds. This photo shows montane habitat along East Dallas Creek in the San Juan Range, Uncompahgre National Forest. WILLARD CLAY

48

Sunlight and Shadows
The Montane Zone

I nterwoven with sunlight and shadow, the montane zone is an intricate pattern in the tapestry of life in the Colorado mountains. The flora of several ecosystems thread through the zone, which stretches from about 6,000 feet to around 9,500 feet. Ponderosa pine forests fringe the upper foothills and make up large patches of the montane to the east and south. On the shady north-facing slopes and over much of the western mountains, Douglas-firs dominate. In their shadows, where snowbanks last long into summer, moss thrives. Where fires have roared, lodgepole pine or patches of aspen grow. On dry soils in the lower elevations, cactus and yucca push down roots.

The two main vegetation types are ponderosa pine and Douglas-fir, which comprise two very different forests. Ponderosa pines grow in the eastern mountains along the Front Range and on dry, sunny slopes of the southern ranges, such as the San Juans. These forests are pleasant, park-like places. The trees are widely spaced, and the breezes hum in the long, elegant needles. "Of all the Pines," naturalist John Muir wrote, "this one gives forth the finest music to the winds." The forest floor is kept open by wildfires, and thin sunlight filters through the branches. There is little rain. Most of the 15 to 25 inches of annual precipitation comes as snow. The air smells faintly of vanilla because of a chemical in the sap of the trees.

A Douglas-fir forest is a much different place. Firs are found most often in the western mountains or on the cooler and moister north-facing slopes of the eastern valleys. Here, the trees are packed more closely together, allowing little room for the hum of winds. The trees' needles are short and stiff. Three-pronged bracts stick out of the cones like serpents' tongues. The branches interlock, keeping the forest floor in shadows

Colorado's mountains host a hardy year-round resident in the mountain chickadee, a small bird that sings its name, "chick-a-dee-dee-dee." With a resting heartbeat of 500 beats per minute and a core temperature of 104 degrees, chickadees are amazing bundles of energy. They must consume nearly their body weight in seeds and insects each day just to remain alive. To survive frigid winter nights, they reduce the flow of blood to their feet and fluff their feathers until they resemble a ball with a beak. JOHN & KAREN HOLLINGSWORTH

Billiant red head, bright yellow body, and black wings and tail identify the male western tanager, a resident of forests and riparian areas. Females are more muted in color, being dull greenish on their backs and yellowish below. In the spring and early summer, tanagers are often seen flashing through the air as they catch flying insects.
WENDY SHATTIL / BOB ROZINSKI

Near Washington Pass in Gunnison National Forest, mules-ears blossom in an aspen grove. Such groves are veritable flower gardens in Colorado. The variety of flowering plants, forbs, and shrubs make them major foraging areas for many animals, from elk to voles. Aspen groves also provide shade and cover.
WILLARD CLAY

that hold the snowbanks long into summer. Cold and dark, the understory of a fir forest is piled deep in the duff of needles. Sounds here seem muffled in the thick branches and the soft mounds of moss.

The aspen forests are yet another component of the montane. Aspen is a fast-growing, short-lived pioneer species that quickly settles areas disturbed by fire, logging, avalanches, road-building, mining, or insect infestation. In the sunlight of the forest floor after such a disturbance, a green sheen of aspen sprouts appears almost immediately, growing from an underground webbing of shoots called "suckers."

An aspen forest is more crowded than a ponderosa pine park but less packed than a Douglas-fir forest. It supports a more diverse understory than either,

including scores of wildflowers—blue columbines (the state flower), paintbrushes, geraniums, vetches, lupines, Mariposa lilies. The wide variety of plants in an aspen forest attracts a similarly wide variety of animals—swallows, black bears, elk, voles, mountain bluebirds.

The lodgepole is another pioneering species, a tree born of sparks. In a unique adaptation, the cones of the lodgepole burst open when heated to between 113 and 122 degrees Fahrenheit by the flames of a wildfire. Since the seedlings thrive in direct sunlight, they quickly take hold after a fire has passed.

With its ponderosa pine parks, Douglas-fir forests, patches of aspen, and stands of lodgepole pine, the montane zone holds a diverse collection of wildlife habitats. Mule deer are the most commonly seen large mammals. Herds of elk find winter range in the canyons and valley bottoms and summer range in the upper elevations.

The pine squirrel, or chickaree, is closely associated with the lodgepole pine forests of the montane, as are predator species such as the pine marten. The Abert's squirrel is common to the ponderosa pine woodlands. The claw marks of black bears sometimes stripe the trunks of aspen and pine trees. Porcupine move slowly among the branches. The tracks of bobcat and mountain lion may be seen in the soft mud.

The birdlife of the montane is varied and colorful, changing throughout the year. There are western bluebirds, pygmy nuthatches, and solitary vireos in the ponderosa; yellow-bellied sapsuckers, tree swallows, and house wrens in the aspen; dark-eyed juncos and hermit thrushes in the Douglas-fir; yellow-rumped warblers in the lodgepole. There are Townsend's solitaires and hummingbirds. Great horned owls fill the night with their hooting. A flash through the branches may be a goshawk or Cooper's hawk. Through the winter there are Steller's jays, ravens, mountain chickadees, and nuthatches. Even on the coldest days, one can hear hairy woodpeckers drumming on the snags.

Perhaps the only types of wildlife not well represented in the montane are reptiles and amphibians. Cold winters and snowfall keep most species at lower elevations. Still, the smooth green snake is found primarily in this life zone. There are chorus frogs, tiger salamanders, and boreal toads. Eastern fence lizards dart among the rocky areas in the northern mountains. In the warmer part of the montane, in the southern mountains, there are bullsnakes, many-lined skinks, short-horned lizards, and western rattlesnakes.

The montane zone has been extensively altered by human development. Logging and livestock grazing have had the greatest impacts. Douglas-fir and ponderosa pine forests are cut and used for everything from railroad ties to masts for sailing ships. Aspens have been logged for centuries; the Indians used them for lodge poles, modern industry for pulp wood. Fire—or more accurately, the fire suppression policy that dominated the early part of the century—has altered the distribution of lodgepole and aspen forests and changed the understories of ponderosa pine stands. The pleasantness of ponderosa stands and aspen groves has resulted in an increase in recreation. The development of summer homes during the past few decades has also affected the distribution of wildlife.

Still, much of the montane zone has been preserved as national park or wilderness. Rocky Mountain National Park has many fine examples of ponderosa pine stands, as do the San Juan Mountains to the south. Douglas-fir forests and their accompanying wildlife can be found in most of the western Colorado national forests and wilderness areas. Prime examples of aspen stands and lodgepole pine forests are scattered throughout the mountains.

The montane is a zone of sunlight and shadow, filled with birdsong and with silence as deep and soft as the moss in a Douglas-fir forest. Its complexity reflects the diversity of the Colorado mountains and the rainbow of life to be found here. ■

Yellow Warbler

Scientific name: Dendroica petechia
Range: Statewide
Habitat: Wooded areas, parks to 9,500 feet
Size: 4.5 to 5.5 inches long
Identifying traits: Yellow color, male's reddish-streaked breast, yellow tail spots

A flash of orange or yellow, a glimpse of olive green, red, black, or white. As if a rainbow has shattered and fallen into the trees, wood warblers fill Colorado with color. These are active birds, rarely still, chattering in the foliage, gleaning insects from branches or snapping them out of the air, bringing the sky alive with color and sound.

With its varied habitat and proximity to the migration routes of many birds, Colorado has recorded nearly every species of the North American wood warbler family. Some species are extremely rare, such as the prothonotary or the occasional golden-winged warbler. Others pass through regularly on spring and fall migrations, such as the Tennessee, the black-and-white, and the Townsend's warblers. Others nest in the state each summer, such as the yellowthroat and the Audubon's, Virginia's, Grace's, MacGillivray's, and Wilson's warblers.

The most conspicuous and widespread of the family is the yellow warbler, which has been recorded in almost every part of the state. Well-adapted to the human environment with its landscaping and open spaces, the yellow warbler is often found in city parks and golf courses. In the wild, the bird is most often seen along cottonwood-lined stream bottoms on the plains, along creeks running from the mountains, and in brushy areas in the canyons. The rusty red-streaked breast of the male makes this one of the easiest warblers to identify.

Yellow warblers arrive in Colorado in the spring from wintering grounds in South America. The males spend their days chasing females among tree branches or singing from highly visible perches. The birds' strong, tightly woven nests can be found high in cottonwood trees or just above the ground in thick brush. The female lays four or five eggs, which she incubates for 12 days while the male brings her food. As with most warblers, the diet is made up primarily of insects.

Yellow warblers have nested more successfully in Colorado since the curbing of extensive pesticide use. Changes in logging practices and reductions in livestock grazing have yielded more brushy habitat, increasing the bird's range.

But not all the news is good. Like other migratory warblers, yellow warblers are impacted by the continuing loss of habitat in South American rain forests. Closer to home, the nest of the yellow warbler is a favorite target for the parasitic cowbird, which will lay its own eggs there. Cowbird hatchlings are large and often will vie successfully with the warbler hatchlings for food. If cowbird eggs are discovered in the nest early enough, warblers often will build another layer of nest above them to keep the eggs from the warmth of incubation. Only about three percent of these abandoned cowbird eggs hatch, but they are enough to adversely affect the warbler population.

In a forest crowded with warblers, the various species use several strategies to avoid direct competition. In some parts of the range, species forage on different levels of the forest canopy. A classic study by ornithologist Robert MacArthur showed that several species of warblers can feed in the same trees by concentrating on various levels. Cape May warblers may feed on the top and outside branches, while bay-breasted warblers feed toward the middle and interior of a tree. Such strategies allow very similar birds to occupy slightly different places in the ecosystem.

In Colorado, the warblers are differentiated in another way: by nesting habitat. The yellowthroat nests most often in the cattail marshes, while the Grace's warbler prefers the mature ponderosa pines of southwestern Colorado, the orange-crowned warbler the aspens and upland willows, the MacGillivray's warbler the brushy areas along streams, the Audubon's warbler the conifer stands, the Virginia's warbler the ponderosa pines, the black-throated gray warbler the pinyon pines, and the yellow-breasted chat the riverbanks.

Mule Deer

Scientific name: Odocoileus hemionus
Range: Statewide
Habitat: Brushy areas near mountain parks, streams, and canyons
Size: Three to four feet at the shoulder, 150 to 250 pounds (bucks), 100 to 150 pounds (does)
Identifying traits: Large ears, small black-tipped tail

The meadows along Medano Creek in the Sangre de Cristo Mountains seem empty of all but the rustle of wind and a few notes of evening bird song. Then, as the shadows stretch toward evening, a single mule deer appears. Soon it is joined by others, mostly does and a few fawns already losing their spots as the summer grows into fall. Before darkness falls, a dozen deer browse quietly along the creek.

The mule deer is the most common large mammal in Colorado. It can be found anywhere from the wooded streambeds of the plains to above timberline in summer. It inhabits the foothills and the sagebrush and pinyon-juniper lands. Particularly dense populations can be found in the Piceance Basin, North Park, the Gunnison River Valley, the San Juan Mountains, and along the Front Range.

The mule deer has also adapted well to suburban life—sometimes too well. In cities along the Front Range and in mountainous areas, it moves down into backyards, causing damage to gardens, orchards, and ornamental shrubs. But it also gives suburban dwellers a close and often welcome glimpse of the beauty of wildlife.

The mule deer has not always proliferated in Colorado. Before European settlement, the animal's population on the American continent is estimated to have ranged

Sunlight and Shadows

More than half a million mule deer live in Colorado, the greatest population of any large animal in the state. Although most abundant in the mountains, mule deer also thrive on the eastern plains, in the southern canyons, and—to the occasional surprise of human residents—in metropolitan areas. This young doe shows the characteristic large ears of the species.
SHERM SPOELSTRA

between five and 10 million. Archaeologic evidence indicates that the mule deer was an abundant and important food source for early cultures. It was easier to bring down than the elk, slower than the pronghorn, and found in more accessible terrain than the bighorn sheep. Its hide was used for clothing and bedding. Its antlers and bones made good needles, awls, and scrapers. Petroglyphs of deer are found throughout the canyons of Colorado, and a mule deer headdress, ears intact, was found among the artifacts in Mantle Cave along the Yampa River.

Yet by 1911, Merritt Cary reported in the Biological Survey of Colorado that there were "...few mule deer in the Estes Park region in 1895," and "none in the foothills of Boulder and Larimer Counties in 1906."

With civilization in the 19th century came the need for meat. Market hunters, like those who contracted to bring more than three tons of game a week to Leadville, were hired to keep mining camps, butcher shops, and restaurants supplied. A single hunter's kill record for the week of August 11-18, 1878, listed 24 deer, 22 antelope, nine elk, five bighorn sheep, and one grizzly. Unrestricted hunting coupled with extensive loss of habitat and a few hard winters cut deeply into mule deer numbers.

With the passage of game laws in the 1930s, the deer began a comeback. Areas once disturbed by fire or timbering came back in succulent vegetation which, in the long run, benefited the deer population. Populations of many large predators, such as wolves and mountain lions, were reduced or exterminated. By 1960 there were as many as 60,000 deer in the Piceance Basin, twice as many as are found there today. There were too many deer.

The early 1970s saw another decline in the number of mule deer as the animal's habitat was overused. Today, with a wider knowledge of game management, tight controls on hunting, and protection of some critical winter range, the mule deer population in Colorado has stabilized at about 600,000 animals, one of the largest populations of any state.

Because it is so common, the mule deer has been studied more thoroughly than most species. The animal molts twice a year. Its summer pelage is reddish-brown, its winter coat a dull gray. Although its eyesight is good, the deer relies for defense mostly upon its large ears, which can pick up far-off sounds, and its quick and elusive gait.

The mule deer is a browser. Its diet consists mainly of shrubs, but it will also graze on succulent grasses and forbs in season. On poorer range, it will gnaw coniferous plants as high as it can reach, creating a "browse line." Because of its complex, multi-chambered stomach, the deer can consume great quantities of forage and can extract as much nutritional value as possible from available foods.

The mule deer's movement is governed both by time and season. Deer feed between dusk and dawn, spending the day bedded in thick cover. Some herds, particularly those in lower elevations, move little throughout the year; others undergo seasonal migrations.

As the snow line moves higher in spring, the bucks move into the high country to summer at or above the timberline. The does move later, often bearing young on fawning areas near the summer range. Twins are most common in does over two years old. The young are born in June and weigh six to 10 pounds. After nursing her fawns, the doe will hide them while she moves off to feed. Spotted coats and lack of scent help protect the fawns from predators such as coyotes, bobcats, and bears. In a few weeks, the young are steady enough to travel. They move with the does in small bands, spending the summers in high forests.

Summer and early fall are easy times for deer. There is almost no limit to the amount of summer range in Colorado; food is plentiful and predators few. But by October, the situation begins to change. Early snows drive the deer to lower elevations, and the season of the rut stirs the bucks.

The rut is a time of intense activity, literally a time of life and death for the deer. By mid-November the bucks are in prime condition. Their antlers, which were shed in February, have grown back and are now stripped of their velvet. The bucks stand ready for battle.

Unlike elk, mule deer do not gather harems. Instead, a buck will search widely for a receptive doe and then defend against intruders until mating occurs. Most often that defense takes the form of body postures. A dominant buck will flare his tail, snort, and lay back his ears to make his rack look larger. Glands on the buck's legs emit an odor as the animal approaches a rival in a stiff-legged gait. The buck may thrash bushes or trees with its antlers and even make bluffing charges. Most smaller bucks are convinced by this display to move on.

Actual full-scale battles are rare but awe-inspiring. The two usually closely matched animals approach each other and then engage their antlers, twisting and shoving violently. The tips of the antlers are like sharpened sticks, and the hides of bucks often display deep puncture wounds and slashes. Sometimes the outcome can be worse. In 1973 a pair of bucks, one a 17-point and the other a 14-point, were found dead at the base of Castle Peak near

Sunlight and Shadows

Eagle, their antlers locked, the ground around them torn in great chunks during what must have been an epic battle.

By mid-December the rut is over and an even bigger battle faces the mule deer: the survival of winter. The animal must find an area of little snow cover, about 14 inches or less. The area must provide both adequate cover from the cold and sufficient forage. The combination is increasingly difficult to come by.

Ski areas, highways, reservoirs, homes, and agricultural lands all have cut into available winter range for deer in Colorado, forcing the animals onto less than prime habitat and into even more danger. More than 3,000 deer a year, gathered onto winter ranges sliced by major highways, are killed by cars. In a normal winter, 10 to 20 percent of the state's mule deer—particularly the fawns, yearlings, and bucks weakened by the stress of the rut—will not live to see spring. In hard winters, as many as 75 percent of some herds may die.

The Colorado Division of Wildlife has initiated projects intended to ameliorate road-kill dangers and the losses caused by hard winters. Extensive use of eight-foot fencing along major highways has reduced accidents by as much as 75 percent. Deer underpasses such as those along Interstate 70 have kept mortality down.

And, in the harsh winter of 1983-84, the first successful program of supplemental feeding was undertaken. Biologists estimate that the program fed up to 20 percent of the state's mule deer, 70 percent of some herds. The result was a 50 percent increase in fawn survival in herds such as those in Middle Park. The program proved that, under the most extreme conditions, supplemental feeding can make a difference.

But on a warm summer evening along Medano Creek, in the shadow of the Sangre de Cristos, the perils of winter seem far away. Slowly the mule deer feed through the night, stopping now and then to listen or check the wind for the scent of predators. In the morning they will move off to cover in the hills—to rest, chew their cud, and wait again for the darkness of night.

Colorado Chipmunk

Scientific name: Tamias quadrivittatus
Range: Foothills to Utah border
Habitat: Rocky or brushy areas below 8,000 feet
Size: Eight to nine inches long including tail, three to five ounces
Identifying traits: Brown coloration, striped back, tail erect when running, relative size, lines through eyes

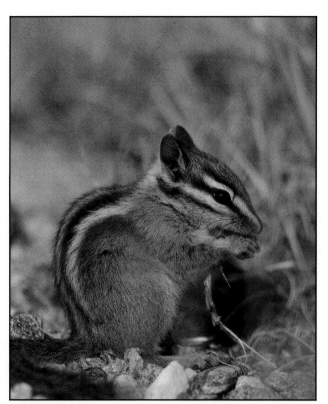

Colorado contains four species of chipmunks—the Colorado, Uinta, cliff, and the least which is shown here. Because the species look very similar, even experts have difficulty telling them apart in the field. Regardless of the species, all chipmunks provide wildlife watchers with common and enjoyable subjects. D. ROBERT FRANZ

They scurry across the picnic table or crawl out onto an overhanging branch to chatter before dashing off into the shadows. Chipmunks are seldom still for long. Their almost constant movement and the subtle differences among species makes identifying the Colorado chipmunk almost impossible.

Colorado is home to four species of chipmunk. The smallest is the least chipmunk, which can be as tiny as four inches long and weigh just over one ounce. The Colorado and the Uinta chipmunks are larger, about nine inches long and weighing about three ounces. The cliff chipmunk is only slightly larger still.

Location is one way of identifying a particular chipmunk species. The Colorado chipmunk is most often found in rocky or brushy areas below 8,000 feet in the western and southwestern mountains. The Uinta chipmunk is often seen in forest openings above 8,000 feet in the more northerly mountains. The cliff chipmunk has a very restricted range and is found only in a small area north of the Yampa River in Moffat County. The least chipmunk is widespread in central and western Colorado.

Yet the ranges of almost all of the species overlap, making location a less-than-foolproof means of identification.

All of Colorado's chipmunks are seed eaters, although they also will eat vegetation, insects, and even carrion when it is available. They are well-known scavengers in picnic areas. The animals are diurnal, most active during the day, and so are easily observed. In fact, they are so common and conspicuous that it is difficult to believe they spend much of their time below ground. Chipmunks dig a series of tunnels with an opening under a rock or brush at one end and a nest chamber at the other. In deep winter, they retreat to these dens to sleep, rousing occasionally to nibble at caches of food stored in their burrows. At lower elevations, they may move about outside their dens during warm spells, but in the mountains they normally stay below ground until spring.

Spring is mating season. Like most things in a chipmunk's life, mating seems to be done at full speed, with mad dashes through trees, over talus slopes, even across the feet of people sitting at picnic tables. Three to six young are usually born in the burrow—blind, naked, and helpless. They will stay in the den for the early part of summer before making short forays above ground. By the end of summer the young will be nearly full-grown.

Ironically, Colorado chipmunks, which are such a common sight in many wild places and picnic grounds, are relatively little-known to science. The difficulty in distinguishing among species, even for the expert, and the complications of studying winter behavior below ground have left great gaps in the knowledge of a creature that seems so much a part of the Colorado outdoors.

Broad-tailed Hummingbird

Scientific name: Selasphorus platycercus
Range: Plains to timberline, most common between 7,000 and
* 8,500 feet*
Habitat: Meadows, grasslands, mountain parks
Size: Four to five inches long
Identifying traits: Whistle or trilling of wings, red throat,
* iridescent coloration, small size, broad tail*

The high trilling of the broad-tailed hummingbird is as sure a sign of spring as the blossoming of wildflowers. Beating its wings as many as 50 times per second while hovering and up to 200 times per second while in courtship flight, the tiny bird can make the air over Colorado sing.

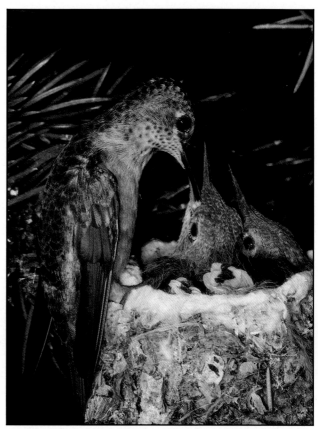

At a tiny nest woven with spider webs, a broad-tailed hum-mingbird feeds a pair of hungry young birds. When observing any nest, wildlife watchers should keep their viewing time to a minimum, remain at a distance by using telephoto lenses and binoculars, and never remove vegetation to get a better view.
WENDY SHATTIL / BOB ROZINSKI

Of the more than 300 members of the hummingbird family, seven have been recorded in Colorado. The most common Colorado hummingbirds are the broad-tailed and the black-chinned, the only two species to breed regularly in the state. The Rivoli's is a rare breeder here. Of the nonbreeders, the blue-throated and the Anna's have been observed only a few times. The calliope and the rufous hummingbirds are observed more commonly, the latter making its presence known with its aggressive behavior at feeding stations.

Hummingbirds live their lives at high speed. Their rapid wingbeats can propel some subspecies up to 60 miles an hour. Even on the inside, the hummingbird runs at a fast pace. Its body temperature ranges from 105 to 110 degrees Fahrenheit, and it can burn thousands of calories a day.

To keep its fires burning, the hummingbird often consumes several times its weight in nectar and high-protein insects during the day. On cold nights, it conserves energy by entering a mild state of torpor. Its body temperature drops as much as 10 degrees, and its metabolism slows by 90 percent so that it needs 30 times less oxygen.

The female broad-tailed hummingbird usually builds its tiny globe-like nest on the branch of a conifer, sheltered among the boughs. She may even weave spider webs into the lining. She lays a pair of eggs and incubates them for 14 to 17 days. From the moment they hatch, the female is kept busy feeding the young, which stay in the nest for 18 to 23 days after hatching. The male takes no part in rearing the family after mating.

By late August or early September, all of the Colorado hummingbirds have moved off to Central America or Mexico for the winter. The silence of the air where once it whistled with wings is as sure a sign of fall as the turning leaves of the aspens.

Mountain Bluebird

Scientific name: Sialia currucoides
Range: Mountains and western Colorado
Habitat: Mountain meadows and forest edges to 14,000 feet
Size: Six to eight inches long

There is a flash of blue over the meadow, as if a fleck of the summer sky has chipped away and drifted down among the grasses. It is one of Colorado's most beautiful birds, the mountain bluebird.

This sky-blue bird is primarily a summer resident of Colorado. Although a few winter in southern Colorado, the majority begin to arrive with the spring, sometimes too optimistically forecasting the weather and facing late winter storms. By the end of March, most of the mountain bluebird population has arrived.

The mountain bluebird is a "secondary cavity nester." It requires a cavity in which to nest, but its beak is not strong enough to gouge its own. The bird typically uses natural cavities or takes over the abandoned quarters of woodpeckers in the trees surrounding a meadow.

A number of factors have hurt the bluebird's reproductive success throughout its range. The timber industry has culled dead standing trees and ranchers have replaced wooden fence posts with metal bars. More than 85 other North American birds, including the English sparrow and the European starling, vie for cavities in which to nest.

With the lack of nesting sites, resourceful bluebirds do whatever they can. Pairs have been observed nesting in the burrow of chipmunks, on the floor of a road grader, and on the bumper of a motorhome. Perhaps the most unusual spot was recorded by Leander S. Keyser in his book *Birds of the Rockies.* He saw a pair constructing a nest "in the coupler of a freight car standing on a side track" and lamented that the nest "would soon be rolling hundreds of miles away, and all their loving toil would go for naught."

In some places, bird watchers have come to the rescue. In Cherokee Park, a consortium of groups including the Audubon Society, school children from Fort Collins, and the U.S. Fish and Wildlife Service, have constructed more than 100 bird boxes. A new type of birdhouse constructed of cement and vermiculite has been tried on the Arapahoe-Roosevelt National Forest.

Once a suitable nest is constructed or located, the less colorful female lays and incubates five to eight eggs. Once these hatch, the male assists with feeding the young and cleaning the nest.

In late summer, with the responsibilities of rearing young complete, the mountain bluebirds gather in family flocks and wheel across the Colorado mountains, feeding on insects frequently above timberline. As the sky begins to cloud up with the first snowstorms of November, most of the mountain bluebirds are gone. But a few remain behind, vivid reminders of the beauty of the summer sky.

Abert's Squirrel

Scientific name: Sciurus aberti
Range: Central and southwestern Colorado
Habitat: Mature ponderosa pine forests
Size: 20 to 25 inches long including tail, 1.5 to two pounds
Identifying traits: Tufted ears

No snow has fallen in the high country for days. The wind is still. In the open, drifts lay untracked and as white as clouds—everywhere, that is, except at the base of the tall ponderosa pines. There the snow is speckled black, littered with twigs, bark, and the scales of cones: sure signs of the Abert's squirrel.

The Abert's squirrel is one of the few Colorado animal species that is associated almost exclusively with a single plant community. The squirrel relies upon the ponderosa pine for almost all the essentials of its life. It eats the seed cones, the sweet inner bark of twigs, and the buds. It builds its nest in the high branches or in the "witches brooms,'' tangles of twigs grown in response to mistletoe infestation. It relies upon interlocking branches overhead for protection against airborne predators and upon its climbing ability to keep it safe from those on the ground. It will even have favorite feeding spots on protected branches and will eat there so often that the ground below becomes piled with debris.

The Abert's is a large squirrel, but its most distinguishing feature is the conspicuous tufts of hair on its ears. Up to two inches long, the tufts are more prominent in winter and give the squirrel a mischevious, elfish look. The squirrel's coat varies from light gray with a lighter underbelly to dark black with only a faintly lighter brown ring around the eyes. The color can vary within a population but more often varies among different regions. Almost all the Abert's squirrels found in the Black Forest of Elbert and El Paso counties are dark, while along the Front Range the ratio is about 65 percent dark and 35 percent light.

Mating, like almost everything the Abert's squirrel

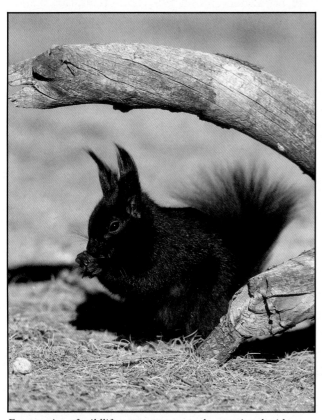

Few species of wildlife are more narrowly associated with a single plant species than the Abert's squirrel, a resident—almost exclusively—of ponderosa pine forests. In Colorado, as many as 65 percent of Abert's squirrels are black, such as the one shown here, rather than gray, but both colors may exist in the same population. The long ear tufts are typical of the species. SHERM SPOELSTRA

does, occurs in the trees. Males chatter noisily at one another and chase rivals through the branches. Litters of two to five young are born sometime between March and May in a nest lined with strips of pine bark. The young are born blind and hairless. Within two months they are fully furred and moving about in the area of the nest.

Since it does not hibernate, the Abert's squirrel continues to forage throughout the winter. Although it feeds on terminal buds and the cambium of young shoots, the squirrel looks to the cone crop for its survival. In a year of good cone production, the squirrel will eat fewer than 20 percent of the cones within its 20-acre home range. In a poor year, the number can be as high as 75 percent. The animal carries the cones to a favorite feeding spot and breaks them open to get the sweet pine seeds inside. The husks drop to the ground, littering the pure white snow, a sure sign of the Abert's squirrel.

Bullsnake

Scientific name: Pituophis melanoleucus
Range: Statewide below 8,500 feet
Habitat: Varied, riparian, forests, canyons, shrubby areas
Size: 36 to 110 inches long
Identifying traits: Triangular head, yellow with dark spots

It cuts across the trail suddenly, stopping us in our tracks. The canyons of the Yampa River are rattlesnake country, a place to step carefully. But this is not a rattler.

The bullsnake is often mistaken for a rattlesnake. When cornered or disturbed, it will sometimes hiss and coil, shaking its tail like the rattlesnake, even striking. Against some predators the ruse may be effective. Against humans, the snake often pays with its life. Yet the formidable-looking bullsnake is harmless, coiling around the arm of a fellow hiker while we stand in the trail admiring it, examining its yellow and black scales and the ridge of scales across its skull that gives it its common name.

Also known as gopher snakes, bullsnakes occupy a wide range of habitats, from sandy hills on the eastern plains to sunny ponderosa pine forests and rocky canyons in the west. Since rodents are the mainstay of the snake's diet, it can often be found around farms and suburban homes. Able to climb well, bullsnakes also will eat eggs and nesting birds. One snake was discovered 10 feet up a cottonwood tree along the Platte River; it had eaten five nestling flickers. Unlike the rattler, the bullsnake is a

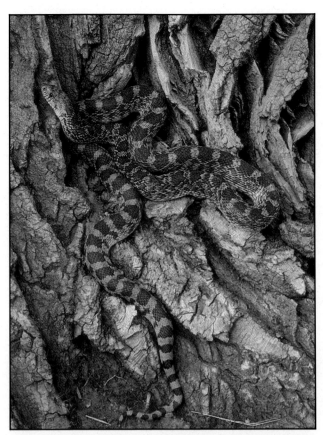

By mimicking the coloration and behavior of a rattlesnake—even to the point of shaking its rattle-less tail while making a rattle-like buzzing sound with its mouth—the bullsnake discourages predators. Unfortunately, the ruse also fools humans, who too often kill first and identify later. Despite its imitative appearance, the bullsnake poses no threat to humans. It preys effectively on gophers, mice, rats, and small snakes. SHERM SPOELSTRA

Black Bear

Scientific name: Ursus americanus
Range: Central and western Colorado
Habitat: Forested lands
Size: 40 to 80 inches long (male), 40 to 70 inches long (female); 220 to 350 pounds (male), 150 to 215 pounds (female)
Identifying traits: Black or brown color

constrictor, wrapping its coils around its prey and squeezing to death.

From October to April, the bullsnake hibernates in a den deep in the cracks of rocks or caves. Often it shares its den with other species, such as rattlesnakes, milk snakes, and garter snakes. In summer it hunts by day, except in the hottest weather. In the canyon country, it will move early and late in the day, lying still in the shade during the hottest hours.

Bullsnakes mate in April or May, after emerging from winter hibernation. The female lays a clutch of four to 20 leathery eggs in deep, warm soil and leaves them to incubate for as long as 11 weeks. The young resemble the adults, but despite their camouflage great numbers fall prey to hawks, coyotes, badgers, foxes, and other snakes.

After untangling it from our arms, we set the bullsnake back on the trail. With a soft swish in the dry grass, it moves off, quickly blends into its surroundings, and disappears.

Bear-paw petroglyphs, ancient bone spear tips, pictographs such as the famous bear on a cliff beside the Purgatoire River—the black bear has left its mark deep on the Colorado landscape. In bear country, the forest can be full of signs: claw marks on aspen trunks, rotting logs ripped apart, tracks in the mud. Still, few people ever get any closer to the animal itself than a good campfire tale.

Modern research has shed some light on the world of the black bear, but one question that remains difficult to answer with any scientific accuracy is the number of black bears in Colorado. Bears inhabit most of the forested ecosystems in the state; they especially are fond of areas abundant in nut- or berry-producing vegetation, such as Gambel oak, pinyon pines, and junipers. They also frequent aspen meadows with their variety of succulent grasses and forbs. These vegetation types occur in the greatest abundance west of the Continental Divide, as well as in the south-central ranges such as the Wet Mountains, the Sangre de Cristo, and the Cucharas.

Despite its reputation as a predator, the black bear consumes little freshly killed big game. It is lightning fast and extremely powerful, yet up to 95 percent of its diet is vegetation, including acorns, serviceberries, chokecherries, grasses, and forbs. Most of the animal matter in its diet is made up of ants and grubs. It also will eat porcupines, rabbits and hares, nesting birds, the young of elk and deer (especially during calving season), occasional livestock, and carrion when it is available.

The black bear is so dependent upon vegetation that in years when nuts and berries are scarce, mortality rates increase, and bears range farther in search of food. This often brings them into contact with humans. In 1976, a late spring frost in the Elk Range destroyed much of the sprouting vegetation, and black bears were spotted within the town limits of Aspen and Glenwood Springs. In lean years, the animals also have been seen wandering

Despite the name, black bears in Colorado are rarely black. As many as 75 percent are some shade of brown, such as the one shown here feeding on rose hips. Although black bears are fairly common in Colorado's mountains, the bear's nocturnal habits and generally shy behavior keep it out of sight much of the time. Still, the unexpected discovery of bear sign—tracks, diggings, and scat—suddenly makes any mountain seem a little more wild. DENNIS & MARIA HENRY

on the golf course at Steamboat Springs and raiding garbage cans in the affluent developments of Vail.

Fluctuations in food supply may be a reason for the bear's unique reproductive biology. Although mating takes place in late May or early June, the fertilized egg remains dormant in the female until she reaches peak condition for denning in late fall. If she has not gained enough weight to meet the additional energy requirements of birthing, the egg does not implant.

If implantation does occur, two or three cubs are born in the darkness of the winter den in January or February. They are naked, blind, and tiny, averaging just nine ounces. One of the first things to develop on the cubs are their claws, curved and sharp. Tree climbing is the

young bears' best defense, and by the time they emerge from the den in spring they are capable of climbing rapidly. The family group will stay together throughout the summer and fall, denning together the following winter.

For thousands of years, people have known that bears vanish with the first snows and reappear in spring. The Cree Indians relied upon the cycle as a means of telling time. The Shoshones considered the first clap of spring thunder to be a sign that the bear had emerged from its den. The Utes continue to celebrate spring with a bear dance.

Today the den is as much within the realm of science as of legend. Radio telemetry has revealed that the bear's winter behavior is even more complex and mysterious than the legend-makers ever imagined.

Each fall, the black bear goes into a feeding frenzy, consuming as much as 20,000 calories a day and gaining 30 percent of its body weight. As winter closes in, pregnant females move to prepared den sites in natural caves, thick brush, or dug-out hollows under logs and roots. Adult males and sub-adults den soon after.

Inside the den, the bear enters a state of hibernation different from that of many other wintering animals. Its heart rate drops to eight to 10 beats a minute and its metabolism can drop by half. But unlike other hibernators, the bear experiences little drop in body temperature. Also unlike other hibernators, the bear will not rouse to eat, drink, urinate, or defecate. It sleeps deeply, waiting out the winter.

As early as mid-April or as late as the third week of May, the bear comes out of its den. Emergence seems to have little to do with elevation, snow melt, or day length. It seems to be triggered most strongly by a little-understood biological clock. Bears often remain near their dens for the first few days, eating only small amounts of vegetation, particularly new shoots.

Science and myth seem to blend in the black bear. But modern technology has revealed much about this secretive creature that seems to contradict campfire wisdom. For instance, black bears do not mark their territory by clawing aspen trees. Home ranges can extend as far as 200 square miles for roving males, and they often overlap. Although solitary creatures by nature, black bears rarely battle over territory.

Black bears are not always black. In fact, in Colorado as many as 75 percent are some shade of brown. Only 25 percent are jet black, and as few as 15 percent have the familiar blaze of white on the chest that is so common to black bears in other states. Dramatic changes in a bear's color from one year to the next have also been recorded.

Every bear in every story is "a big bear," but research indicates that the shadow the bear casts around the campfire may be larger than life. Because of its thick hide, the black bear often appears larger than it is. In Colorado, males average about 260 pounds; an unusually large animal might weigh 350 pounds. Females are often not much bigger than large dogs, standing under three feet tall at the shoulder and sometimes weighing less than 150 pounds.

Still, even with the knowledge of science, the black bear ranges through the campfire tales and stares from canyon pictographs, a testament to the power of the animal on the landscape and the human mind.

Golden hair frames the face of a porcupine—and hides some 30,000 needle-sharp quills on its back and tail. Slow to move, often preoccupied with their own affairs, and highly tolerant of people who keep their distance, porcupines make wildlife-watching easy. They are found in forested areas throughout the state. SHERM SPOELSTRA

Porcupine

Scientific name: Erethizon dorsatum
Range: Statewide
Habitat: Ponderosa pine, aspen, and willow stands
Size: 25 to 30 inches long, 10 to 30 pounds
Identifying traits: Covering of quills

The track seems brushed, as if a broom has been swept back and forth across it. Large yellow scars, like open wounds, dot the trunks of the ponderosa pines. On the ground, scattered droppings look like wood shavings. These are the signs of the porcupine.

Next to the beaver, the porcupine is the largest rodent in Colorado. It is found in almost all forested areas of the state. Spending most of its time in the branches of aspens or ponderosa pines, it eats leaves, seeds, and buds during the summer. The porcupine will also feed on the ground, grazing grasses, forbs, and even cultivated crops such as alfalfa. In winter, it peels away the bark from tree trunks and branches to get at the sweet inner cambium, which contains large amounts of starch and sugar.

If abundant, porcupines can do extensive damage to a forest during a hard winter by chewing the bark from around the trees, cutting off the flow of nutrients from the roots. A forest culled by porcupines resembles a battlefied: strips of bark hang from the branches; large open patches like scabs mar the trunks. If not killed, a tree scarred by a porcupine is left vulnerable to beetle infestation or to mistletoe, a parasitic plant growth.

The porcupine is an agile climber, using its strong, curled claws for gripping and its tail for balance and leverage. On land it is slow and ungainly. This trait and its poor eyesight would make the porcupine an easy target for predators except for one thing—or more accurately, 30,000 things.

Starting at the forehead and growing thicker and longer toward the hump of the back, the quills of a porcupine can reach four inches long. A single animal has between 15,000 and 30,000 quills. When threatened, the animal hunches and displays them, a posture that earned it a scientific name that translates ''one whose back is arched in anger.'' Although a threatened porcupine will spin quickly, slapping with its tail, it cannot ''throw'' its quills as popular belief suggests. Yet each quill is needle-sharp and is barbed with tiny hooks that will pull it into the flesh of any animal or human unlucky enough to come within striking distance.

The quills are light-shafted and dark-tipped. Unless the animal is threatened, they remain hidden under long yellowish hair that many people mistake for the quills themselves. Indians in many parts of the porcupine's range dyed the quills and wove them into ceremonial clothing. They also used the quills as bristles in a kind of comb.

Coyotes and an occasional bobcat can overcome the porcupine's defense by slapping at it until it rolls over, exposing its unquilled belly and face. Mountain lions are perhaps the porcupine's most significant predator in the state, with individual lions becoming skilled at avoiding the quills. But against most predators, the quills are like a quiver of arrows, enough of a deterrent to ensure the porcupine a safe passage. Wolverines, foxes, and other predators have been found bearing the scars from a meeting with a porcupine.

In winters so cold that trees snap with frost, a pair of porcupines will sometimes share a den. But the porcupine is usually a solitary animal, moving alone from tree to tree in the dark hours of the night. It is active year-round. Because its incisors, like those of a beaver, continue to grow throughout its life, it continually gnaws—on branches, bark, even canoe paddles, rubber tires, and rake handles. The massive jaw muscles make up nearly half the weight of the head.

The mating of porcupines is one of the noisiest rituals in all of nature, a clamor of shrieks and screams that rings in the cold forests throughout late fall and early winter. The den used for sleeping and birthing is a simple affair, just a hollow spot in a log or a small natural cave. In spring, a gestation period of more than 200 days (one of the longest of any rodent), results in a single offspring.

The young porcupine is born with its eyes open and is equipped with a full set of soft quills that will harden within hours. It can walk within a day. It can climb within two days. In a week, it begins to eat green plants. Within a few weeks, it is weaned and sent out to face the world alone with only its quills to protect it.

Great Horned Owl

Scientific name: Bubo virginianus
Range: Throughout Colorado
Habitat: Cottonwoods, coniferous forests below 10,000 feet
Size: 19 to 25 inches long, females larger than males
Identifying traits: Long ear tufts, yellow eyes

In the cold winter woods, back in the thick timber, the great horned owl calls, a low sound shaped like the moon rising. It is March. The nights are still deep and long, but already the owls are incubating eggs. A pair calls to each other softly in the dark.

To the Romans, owls were evil spirits. To the Pima Indians, they were winged carriers that flew the souls of the dead to the spirit world. To hear the call of the great horned owl is to hear the echo of legends.

The great horned owl is the largest, most commonly seen, and most widespread of the 13 owl species that have been recorded in the state. It has been observed from the thick tangle of cottonwoods along the eastern rivers to the dark coniferous forests below 10,000 feet. Its nests, which can be used for many years, are found in juniper trees, cottonwoods, and pines. Often the owl

Colorado nights often echo with the deep, resonant hooting of great horned owls, the most widely distributed owls in the state. Besides hooting, they make a variety of sounds from squeaking to popping. In fact, many unidentified sounds of the night may be caused by owls. Great horned owls are readily identified by their large size and long ear tufts. RAY RICHARDSON

will use the abandoned nest of a hawk, magpie, or crow, or it will nest in a cavity or on the ground.

One of Colorado's earliest nesting birds, the great horned owl may begin mating in mid-February. The male presents the larger female with gifts of prey. The female lays one to five eggs and, to protect them from the cold, begins incubation immediately. The chicks, which hatch by mid-March, can vary greatly in size. Often a larger sibling will out-compete a smaller chick for food.

The great horned owl is a fierce, skilled hunter well-equipped for killing. As in all owls, the first primary feather on each wing is serrated rather than smooth, making the bird's flight as soundless as the wind. Its feathers are soft, its talons sharp, its grip sure and deadly. Its eyes have a high ratio of rods to cones to catch the faintest light and, although the eyes themselves are set in immovable sockets, the neck can swivel nearly 180 degrees, giving the owl a wide range of vision. The dished pattern of feathers on its face gathers sound waves, funneling them to the ears.

The great horned owl hunts mainly in the dark, preying on almost anything: rabbits, weasels, mink, squirrels, skunks, and birds as large as Canada geese. In places, rabbits seem to be its main prey, and its population swings follow closely the highs and lows of the rabbit cycles. It can and will prey on game birds and domestic fowl, earning it the enmity of sportsmen and farmers. Its efficient predation on the endangered peregrine falcon in some parts of the state has been a factor in the survival rate of peregrine broods.

The owl has enemies among the bird world as well. Crows and jays, if they discover an owl at its day perch, will mob the bird, diving and harassing it relentlessly. But the owl's territory is bordered by sunset and dawn. Its call can rise up through the trees like the full moon, echoing in the darkness and laying claim to the night.

Black-billed Magpie

Scientific name: Pica pica
Range: Throughout Colorado to 10,000 feet
Habitat: Foothills, forests, riparian, cities, rural areas
Size: 17 to 22 inches long including tail
Identifying traits: Long tail, black and white plumage

A flashy bird like the black-billed magpie is hard to miss. So it is not surprising that it was recorded early by explorers and naturalists in Colorado. And right from the start its reputation was in peril.

The first known report of the magpie was made by Zebulon Pike. On November 1, 1806, while camped along the Arkansas River, he and the men of his expedition heard a commotion among the saddle-weary horses they had staked out to graze. They turned to see magpies harassing the herd. The birds, according to Pike's journal, ''attracted by the scent of their sore backs, alighted on [the horses], and in defiance of their wincing and kicking, picked many places quite raw.''

This was not a very auspicious start for the magpie in the recorded natural history of Colorado. Since that time, many people have held the bird in contempt for its habit of raiding the nests of other birds, picking the sores of cattle, and attacking the eyes of injured or sick deer and elk. Even its name is less than complimentary, said to be short for ''maggot picker'' after its habit of eating maggots off of very rancid meat. Its call is harsh and raspy, like a file drawn across iron.

Despite its reputation among humans, the magpie thrives in Colorado from the plains to about 10,000 feet. It is an intelligent, adaptable bird whose stocky bill fits its varied diet of carrion, small rodents, eggs, and insects such as grasshoppers, caterpillars, and ticks. In fact, it eats more insects than any member of its family in the United States.

The magpie builds its nest as if it were here to stay. Nests are sturdy structures plastered with mud and reeds. They can be two feet in diameter, and many feature a side entrance. The insides are lined with fur, hair, or soft vegetation. With unusual architectural finesse, the magpie often adds a roof to its nest, a kind of half-domed structure usually built to block the prevailing winds.

Magpies form long-time pair bonds, using the same nest from year to year. As repairs are made, the nest may reach several feet in diameter. Nests are so sturdy that they indirectly contribute to the nesting success of

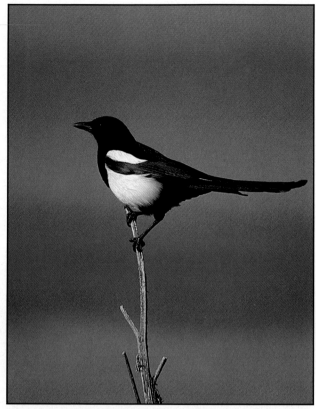

Big, flashy, boisterous, loud—all are traits of the magpie, one of the most commonly seen birds in Colorado. Its black and white coloration and long tail make it easy to identify. Equally at home in cities and in wilderness areas, the magpie thrives by being adaptable. Like its relatives the crows, it eats almost anything. SHERM SPOELSTRA

other species—great horned owls, long-eared owls, black-crowned night herons, and others—which will use old magpie nests as the foundation on which to construct their own. Kestrels, a cavity-nesting species, will use magpie nests if the roofs remain intact.

The magpie is a year-round resident. In the fall it gathers at roosts. Despite its tainted reputation, it is a favorite among many bird watchers who appreciate its elegant and colorful plumage. To describe a magpie to someone who had never seen one would stretch the power of words. Bailey and Niedrach, in their book *Birds of Colorado,* describe the adults as ''black, glossed with green, blue, purple and bronze.'' The underbelly and wingbars are white. In the direct sunshine, the bird's colors seem iridescent, its white feathers as bright as new snow. The plumage makes the bird look formal and straight-laced, as if it could not possibly be guilty of all the stories told against it.

Arguably the most beautiful snake in Colorado, the milk snake is sometimes wrongly and tragically confused with the deadly coral snake, a species not found in Colorado. The two species have similar colors. A constrictor, the milk snake kills its prey by squeezing. A taste for rodents frequently lures the milk snake to farms, ghost towns, and abandoned buildings, but it also thrives in wilder areas. W. PERRY CONWAY

Other Common Wildlife of the Montane Zone

BIRDS: red-tailed hawk, blue grouse, band-tailed pigeon, glammulated owl, northern flicker, western wood-pewee, tree swallow, gray jay, Steller's jay, red-breasted nuthatch, house wren, ruby-crowned kinglet, Townsend's solitaire, hermit thrush, orange-crowned warbler, yellow-rumped warbler, chipping sparrow, dark-eyed junco, red crossbill, pine siskin, and evening grosbeak.

MAMMALS: water shrew, long-eared myotis, Mexican woodrat, long-tailed vole, coyote, marten, long-tailed weasel, striped skunk, and elk.

AMPHIBIANS / REPTILES: northern sagebrush lizard, northern plateau lizard, red-lipped prairie lizard, and northern tree lizard.

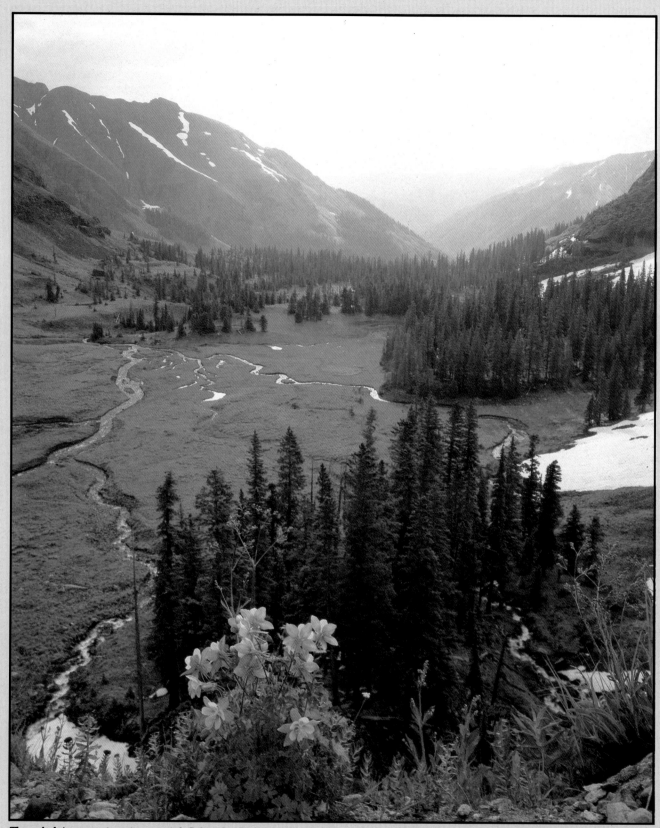

The subalpine zone is quintessential Colorado—high mountain meadows, spruce-fir forests, and, as shown in this view of Lower Ice Lake Basin in the San Juan Mountains, the blue columbine, Colorado's official state flower. A summer place to watch wildlife, the subalpine zone's cool weather, lush meadows, and sheltering forests attract deer and elk from lower elevations. Many birds such as warblers also summer here. LARRY ULRICH

A S t a g e   f o r   t h e   M o u n t a i n s

A Stage for the Mountains
The Subalpine Zone

I n our memories and in most photographs, the high peaks of Colorado are framed with a dark green band of unbroken forest. The trees are as sharp as the spires of the peaks. This is the subalpine zone, the stage for the mountains.

Stretching from about 9,000 feet to timberline at about 11,500 feet, the subalpine zone drapes the base of the summits. Conditions are harsh, summers are short, and the force of the high-country climate is reflected in everything that lives here.

Even on a still morning in the Colorado mountains, you can see the shape of the wind. On the flanks of many peaks, the "krummholz," wind-flattened mats of subalpine coniferous vegetation, ripples in green waves against the hillsides. Elsewhere "banner" trees, the branches stripped from the windward side of the trunk, flag a kind of war zone between life and climate.

The subalpine zone is cool; even in summer the winds can carry a chill. The growing season is only about two months long, even shorter at the higher elevations. The region gets vast amounts of snowfall and is covered as well in huge drifts blown off the alpine area. In the cool shadows, the snowbanks melt slowly, lasting far into the summer.

In Colorado, the subalpine zone is dominated by two tree species, the subalpine fir and the Engelmann spruce. Both species grow slowly and tolerate cold well. At the higher elevations, a spruce with a trunk just a few inches in diameter can be hundreds of years old. The trees are so well-suited to the cold, moist conditions at these elevations that there is little chance for successional plants such as aspen or lodgepole to gain a foothold.

Although less common than the spruce or fir, the bristlecone pine and the limber pine most poetically capture the wind's role in subalpine ecosystems. Squat,

Mountainous areas of Colorado often resound with the loud, chattering call of the chickaree, a year-round resident of coniferous forests. Also called a pine squirrel, the chickaree feeds on pine nuts, conifer seeds, mushrooms, berries, and insects. Large piles of pine cone scales often reveal its presence. These piles, called middens, form when generations of squirrels eat conifer cones in the same location, pulling off the scales to reach the seeds beneath. Some middens spread over several yards and may be knee deep.
DENNIS HENRY

twisted, and gnarled by the winds, these species are the jagged edge of life, taking hold in places few other species can survive. Their roots are like claws in the cracks of rocks as they face the wind straight on.

The bristlecone, in particular, is a patient species. It sheds its needles only once every 25 or 30 years, a tenth as often as most pines. Its bark is often scoured the color of rock by sand and ice particles blown by the wind. Its trunk twists like a broken bone in the force of the gales.

Yet, despite their harsh life, bristlecone pines dating back 1,500 to 2,000 years have been found in Colorado. They are the oldest living things in the state. A tree cut down in 1964 on the flanks of Wheeler Peak in Nevada dated back 4,844 years, at the time thought to be the oldest living thing on earth. Stands of bristlecone pine are visible at the Mount Goliath Natural Area near Mount Evans, in the Tarryalls on Bison Peak, and in other places across the high country. Limber pines are conspicuous around many high-elevation lakes in Rocky Mountain National Park.

Despite the harsh conditions of the subalpine zone, the area is vital to wildlife. To the species of the alpine area, the upper edges of the zone are like an oasis. Ptarmigan come down to find soft snow in which to burrow out beds for the night. Bighorn sheep sometimes seek shelter among the trees. Deer mice and least chipmunks feed on limber pine nuts. Mule deer and elk spend summer days feeding on the edge of the subalpine and alpine tundra, seeking the seclusion of the forests when disturbed or to escape the heat of the day.

On the strong winds of the subalpine zone fly many wings—blue grouse, golden-crowned kinglets, juncos, Townsend's solitaires, and woodpeckers. Many of the subalpine birds are seedeaters, including the pine grosbeak and Cassin's finch. Others, like the gray jay and Clark's nutcracker, eat some seeds but also take advantage of other food sources of the subalpine, such as insects and berries. Downy and hairy woodpeckers search tree trunks for grubs and insect larvae.

Because of the creatures drawn here by summer abundance, predatory birds are attracted to the subalpine forests. Golden eagles soar high above the alpine tundra and the subalpine zone. Goshawks

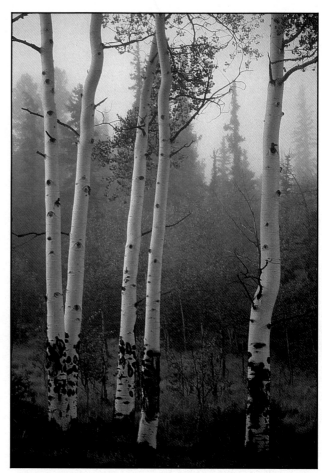

The black scars on the trunks of these aspen trees were caused by elk feeding on the bark. Aspen bark apparently meets a nutritional need of elk in the winter, and an entire grove may bear scars to the same height, forming a distinct browse line. Fresh scars appear greenish in color. Aspen leaves and sprouts are fed on by elk, deer, and moose.
WENDY SHATTIL / BOB ROZINSKI

speed silently through the branches. Scavengers such as ravens patrol on the cold, clear winds.

June afternoons ring with the musical notes of the hermit thrush, the cheery calls of the olive-sided flycatcher, and the thin warbles of the yellow-rumped warbler. In winter, the forest becomes quieter. Many birds migrate out of state or to lower areas. In the cold air of winter, the only sounds are the thin strains of the mountain chickadees as they seek insects among the conifer needles and in bark crevices, the rapping of hairy woodpeckers, and the faint rustle of feathers as ravens and jays cruise quietly overhead.

For most mammals, as well, the subalpine zone is a home only during the spring, summer, and fall.

Deer and elk, which often feed in alpine areas at night and bed down in subalpine forests during the day, move lower after the first snows. Marmots slip into hibernation; small mice and voles burrow beneath the snows. The longtail weasel changes colors for the season. The snow among the trees is almost trackless, marked occasionally by a snowshoe hare, an occasional bobcat, the scurry tracks of mice that soon disappear again.

The same cold and wind that sculpt the bristlecone pine and chase most birds and mammals out of the subalpine in winter also account for the small number of amphibian and reptile species here. More than 80 percent of Colorado's amphibian and reptile species do not venture above 8,000 feet, putting the subalpine ecosystem beyond their range. Only along the wetter riparian zones of the subalpine region can you find an occasional tiger salamander, chorus frog, wood frog, or western toad.

The force of the weather even manages to keep humans at bay. Slow-growing, gnarled trees on steep and rocky terrain attract little logging interest. Housing developments are more often set in the gentle montane. But ski areas and mining have taken a toll on parts of the subalpine, as have occasional fires, both manmade and wild. A recent increase in recreation has brought changes and disruption to certain areas of the forest.

The subalpine zone offers important breeding and feeding grounds for wildlife. Perhaps just as importantly, the pristine and unbroken mountain forests provide the solitude required by many wildlife species. We often think only in terms of food, water, and shelter when defining wildlife needs, yet many species also require a disturbance-free environment at least part of the year. Continual disturbances—cars passing on the highway that flush roadside birds or hikers unknowingly driving deer or elk from day beds—can drain the energy reserves of wildlife species.

Because of the lack of human development on the subalpine forest and man's penchant for high alpine scenery, large tracts of this zone have been preserved as national forests, national parks, and wilderness areas. The high country of Rocky Mountain National Park is composed largely of

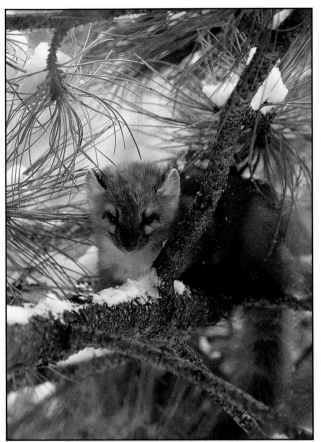

Equally at home in trees as on the ground, a pine marten rests comfortably in a pine tree. Pine martens live in dense coniferous forests above 8,000 feet, especially in areas containing old-growth forests. There they prey on mice, voles, snowshoe hares, and small birds, but their main prey is chickarees. Agile climbers and leapers, pine martens often chase chickarees through the treetops, a frantic and exciting sight for wildlife watchers. JUDD COONEY

subalpine forests. A drive over Cameron Pass in the Never Summer Mountains winds through prime examples of this habitat. Hiking trails in almost all of the state's designated wilderness areas lead through subalpine forests.

The subalpine zone is widespread in Colorado. Almost anywhere that high peaks cut into the sky, they are set on a stage of dark green trees—the subalpine forests. ■

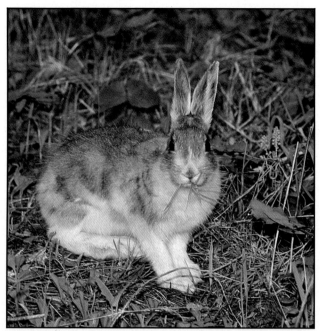

The color of the snowshoe hare reflects the changing season. White in the winter and brown in the summer, the snowshoe depends on its camouflage and quick bursts of speed to escape predators such as owls, coyotes, and bobcats. It is aptly named for its large rear feet that support it on snow.
WENDY SHATTIL / BOB ROZINSKI

Snowshoe Hare

Scientific name: Lepus americanus
Range: Mountainous areas from 8,000 to 11,500 feet
Habitat: Subalpine forests
Size: 16 to 18 inches long including tail, weighs about two pounds
Identifying traits: Large hind feet, coloration changes

The new snow tells an old story. The tracks of a snowshoe hare lead from a ''form,'' a day bed in thick brush beneath the branches of a spruce tree. The tracks move tentatively at first toward a clearing. Then they become more widely spaced. Suddenly there is a wild veering, great leaps of nearly 10 feet, and a dash for the brush.

The snowshoe hare is the target of many a predator. Perhaps the animal that made the tracks saw a hawk circling on the wind or the black shadow of an owl passing over the snow. Perhaps it caught the scent of a bobcat or coyote at the edge of the clearing.

The tracks of a snowshoe hare in fresh snow are unmistakable. The animal's back feet can be six inches long. They are thickly furred, giving them a webbed effect on soft snow and protecting them against the cold temperatures of the hare's habitat.

In Colorado, the snowshoe hare is most commonly found in the subalpine forests. It prefers areas of thick, protective undergrowth, where it will rest during the day and look for food under the cover of darkness. Its diet consists of grasses, sedges, and forbs in summer and the bark and buds of aspen, alder, birch, and willow in winter. Trees, especially saplings, are often left with browse marks at snow line.

In the face of heavy predation, the snowshoe hare can produce prodigious numbers of offspring. Females in Colorado produce between one and four litters annually, with each litter averaging three young. Unlike rabbits, the young of true hares are born fully furred and with their eyes open. Their growth rate is phenomenal. Birth weight doubles in just over a week. By the time the young are weaned, in about a month, they are almost 10 times their size at birth.

The hare that left its tracks in the new snow is likely in its full winter color phase—pure white except for black-tipped ears. By April, it will have completed a spring molt and become mottled brown with a lighter underbelly. The change of colors, which has earned it the name ''varying hare,'' is both to help in avoiding detection and to provide a better insulated fur for winter. The change apparently is triggered not by temperature or snowfall but by day length. An early blizzard or an early thaw can leave the hare very vulnerable.

Larger than the cottontail and smaller than the jackrabbit, the snowshoe hare is an important food source for such predators as the bobcat. In fact, populations of bobcats and hares depend significantly upon one another. For decades, ecologists thought that the presence of the predator kept the hare population in check. Today they believe that the balance may actually be kept by the hare. Fluctuations in the hare population set the limit on the number of bobcats. Fewer hares, fewer bobcats. More hares, more bobcats.

The dance steps in the snow indicate that this particular hare has triumphed over danger. The tracks continue from beneath a brush pile and wander downhill, where signs show the animal has stopped to gnaw at the bark of a sapling.

With its red neck sac partially inflated, a male blue grouse patrols its breeding territory in the Colorado mountains. Male blue grouse display for females in March and April. At this time they inflate their neck sacs to produce a low, booming rhythm that carries several hundred yards. To human listeners, the sound sometimes seems ventriloquial and difficult to pinpoint except at close range. In the fall, look for blue grouse in the mornings and evenings at the edges of meadows, where they feed on insects and seeds. PAT POWELL

Blue Grouse

Scientific name: Dendragapus obscurus
Range: Mountainous areas from 6,500 to 11,000 feet
Habitat: Coniferous forests, oak brush, deciduous forests
Size: 16 to 23 inches long, two to three pounds
Identifying traits: Orange or yellow comb above eyes and gray
  plumage (male), brown plumage and no comb (female)

In the tangled branches of the Douglas-fir, it stands perfectly still, patient, waiting for us to ski by. The motionless defense tactics of the blue grouse have earned it the nickname "fool hen." Its habit of standing still may account for the fact that it was the first bird ever accurately recorded in Colorado, observed in what is now Montrose County by the members of the Dominguez-Escalante

Expedition in August 1776. The dusky-blue coloration of the male and the mottled brown of the female make them blend in convincingly with their surroundings. More blue grouse may go unseen than not—a tribute to the wisdom of the tactic.

The blue grouse is the most numerous and widespread of the grouse family in Colorado. It makes an unusual reverse migration each year. In April, mature birds begin leaving the coniferous forests where they spent the winter feeding on needles and buds in the branches of Douglas-firs and spruce. They move down the mountains into aspen groves and more open country for their "booming" and breeding grounds.

The males are territorial during the breeding season, each one staking out a four-acre patch of open ground. The territory may overlap with that of several females but no other males. Within its site, the male blue grouse crawls atop logs or rocks and, with tail spread and wings dropped, inflates its throat sack to make a booming sound that can carry several hundred yards. The haunting, hollow sound is repeated five to seven times.

A loosely constructed nest is built on the ground. The female lays five to 10 buff-colored eggs and incubates them for just over three weeks. After mating, the male begins its journey to higher elevations, feeding on leaves, early berries, and grasses. The female and brood stay low, under cover near a stream or clearing. There they feed heavily on insects, which provide the young with the energy to spur their quick growth. Within two weeks, the young can fly, and in September they will begin the migration to higher elevations, feeding on acorns, snowberries, and seeds as they go.

If they survive, that is. Mortality is over 60 percent in the young. Predators such as the goshawk, coyote, and fox take their toll, as does inclement weather.

By midwinter, the blue grouse spends its time mostly in the trees, sometimes in small flocks, sometimes alone, searching for food and standing perfectly still whenever danger passes below.

Gray Jay

Scientific name: Perisoreus canadensis
Range: Mountains of Colorado from 8,500 feet to timberline
Habitat: Coniferous forests
Size: 10 to 13 inches long
Identifying traits: Gray and white plumage, no crest on head

On some of Colorado's busiest hiking and cross-country ski trails, you are likely to be met near the trailhead by a bold, gray and white bird: the gray jay.

While some Colorado birds will shy away at the sight of humans and even abandon nests if disturbed, the gray jay has realized that people can mean food. The bird will eat out of your hand, pick food off your plate, even try to pry open containers to get at the contents. It has been known to rob traps of bait without getting caught or to eat the carcasses of animals that did not get away. This boldness has earned it the nickname "camp robber."

The gray jay is a year-round resident of the coniferous forests. Besides seeds, it also eats small birds and mammals, carrion, and insects such as caterpillars and grasshoppers. To get through the winter, it stores large supplies of food, although these caches are often robbed by squirrels and other birds.

The gray jay's boldness where food is concerned seems

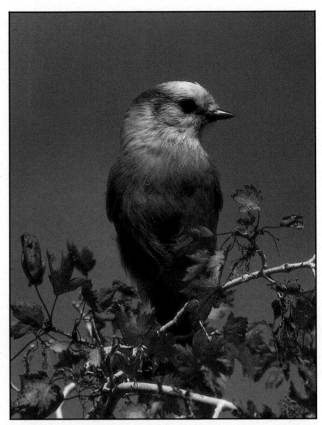

Backcountry travelers in Colorado nearly always see a gray jay, the boldest bird in the mountains. Curious and seemingly unafraid, gray jays often seek out human visitors, flying close to sit on a branch a few feet away. At campsites they frequently swoop down to look for scraps of food.
WENDY SHATTIL / BOB ROZINSKI

to be reflected in its attitude toward winter. It begins nesting while the snow is still deep in the forest, and it nests at elevations as high as 11,300 feet. It begins construction of its nest in late March, assuring extra warmth by lining it with rabbit fur, feathers, spider webs, and bark. The female lays from three to four eggs.

Colorado is home to five kinds of jay. The metallic blue Steller's jay is almost as bold as the gray jay when it comes to handouts. The pinyon jay, on the other hand, is flighty and spooks easily out of the branches of the pinyon pine whose nuts it depends upon for food. The blue jay, at the western extreme of its range, is found in urban areas of the plains and in thickets along waterways to the foothills. The scrub jay is associated with the oak stands of the low elevations.

But it is the gray jay that is most often seen by hikers and campers. It sits in the branches not far from your camp, waiting for you to turn your back for just a minute. Then a flash of gray and white feathers disappears into the trees with part of your lunch.

Goshawk

Scientific name: Accipiter gentilis
Range: Statewide in forested areas
Habitat: Forested areas, most common above 7,000 feet
Size: 20 to 28 inches long, 43- to 47-inch wingspan
Identifying traits: Large size, white eye streak, pearl-gray breast plumage

Before the last of the tiny, white feathers has even drifted to the ground, the goshawk is on its way back to its nest with the magpie it has snatched from the air above the clearing. The goshawk is the largest of the accipiters, which in Colorado also include the Cooper's hawk and the sharp-shinned hawk. It is a skillful and patient hunter, waiting hidden in the boughs near a clearing, watching for prey.

The goshawk's short, rounded wings make it an agile flier. Its long tail acts as a rudder for balance as it weaves through the branches after prey. Hunting from perches, the goshawk uses speed and surprise as its weapons. It can reach speeds of more than 70 miles an hour for short stretches, streaking out of the sky like feathered lightning.

The goshawk builds its nest in April or May. It often uses the same nest several years in a row, adding to it until it grows large and conspicuous high in the branches of an aspen, lodgepole, cottonwood, or ponderosa pine. Until the young are ready to fly, a mating pair defends the nest aggressively. Bears, coyotes, ravens, even humans that venture too near may be raked by the talons of the goshawk and, at the very least, barraged with loud screeching.

This noisy defense of its nest makes the goshawk easiest to spot during the nesting season. When food becomes scarce in the north, the number and range of goshawks in Colorado can increase dramatically. Pushed south out of their normal hunting territory by other birds, immature goshawks have been observed as far east as Bonny Reservoir. Even in normal years, they sometimes winter in the forests along the Arkansas or South Platte rivers, far out on the plains.

Except during these times, the goshawk is secretive and difficult to spot—so difficult, in fact, that it seems a much rarer bird than it really is. For hours the goshawk can remain motionless among the boughs of a hunting perch, moving only its eyes. As the largest of the accipiters, it preys on more mammals and large birds than the Cooper's or sharp-shinned hawks. It will take Abert's squirrels, ground squirrels, rabbits, snowshoe hares, and mice.

Among birds, its prey includes blue grouse, mourning doves, flickers, Steller's jays, robins—and an occasional unfortunate magpie.

Northern Flicker

Scientific name: Colaptes auratus
Range: Throughout Colorado
Habitat: Wooded streams, parks, coniferous and aspen forests
Size: 12 to 14 inches long
Identifying traits: Brown crown, red streak behind bill

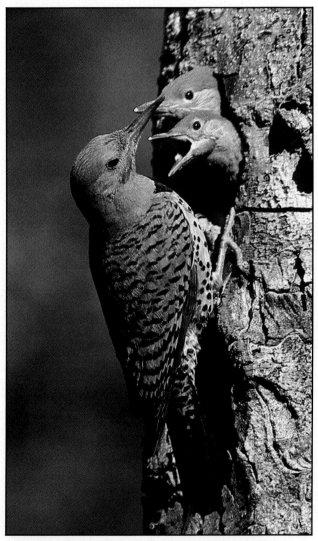

A northern flicker braves her brood of hungry nestlings. Formerly called red-shafted flickers, these birds can be identified in flight by the flashing of salmon-red color under their wings and tails. With their powerful beaks, flickers excavate nesting cavities in trees. These holes are later used by other birds such as bluebirds. BETTY SEACREST

73

A Fremont Indian headdress, estimated to be around 1,200 years old, is lined with ermine, strung with juniper seeds and bone, and adorned with more than 350 flicker feathers. The beak of a pileated woodpecker is found in an Indian grave site in Weld County. The birds of the Picidae family have a long history in Colorado.

The family here is represented by seven species and several subspecies of woodpeckers, three species of sapsuckers, and the flicker. Some are flashy birds: the flicker with its red, brown, and gray feathers and speckled breast; the yellow-bellied sapsucker; and the Lewis' woodpecker with its reddish face and underbelly. Others wear a more sedate pattern of black and white, such as the downy woodpecker. All have strong bills with which to gouge out cavities for nesting sites and to obtain food.

The birds of the Picidae family are mostly insect eaters. Studies have shown that the flicker consumes more ants than any other North American bird. At least three species—the three-toed, hairy, and downy woodpeckers —help to control outbreaks of the spruce beetle, a parasitic insect that ravages stands of Engelmann spruce. But members of the family also will eat seeds, nuts, and grains. The sapsucker uses its strong beak to drill a series of holes in live trees; these fill up with sap, which the bird drinks.

The northern flicker, like the others, nests in cavities in old trees, fence posts, or other suitable places. It either excavates its own cavity or forces other species out of ones they have already built. Flickers have been known to appropriate the nesting sites of woodpeckers, starlings, kestrels, and screech owls.

Nesting activity begins May in the lower elevations and as late as mid-June higher up. The female flicker usually lays five to eight white eggs but will lay more if the first brood is disturbed. In one experiment with yellow-shafted flickers, 71 eggs were removed from the nest in 73 days. Both sexes help with incubation, which takes 11 to 14 days, and with rearing the young.

One common trait shared by members of this bird family is the sound they make rapping on tree trunks. Sometimes they peck for food; other times, as with the flicker, the rapping is part of a mating song, with a pair doing a kind of duet on nearby trees. The hairy woodpecker drums in hundreds of bursts a day during mating. A light, almost tentative tapping may be a downy woodpecker. Like Morse code, the sounds of the tapping can tell the secrets of a forest.

Tiger Salamander

Scientific name: Ambystoma tigrinum
Range: Statewide to 12,000 feet
Habitat: Various habitats near standing water
Size: Three- to seven-inch-long body, up to 12 inches long including tail
Identifying traits: Long tail, four-toed feet, dark with yellow spots (eastern Colorado), light green with dark spots (western)

In a warm April rain, a tiger salamander ventures out of its winter burrow and moves to water to breed. The timing of the migration varies—those on the warm plains move first, those in the cold mountains later—but spring rains signal the trek of the salamanders.

The tiger salamander is the largest member of the mole salamander family and the only salamander found in Colorado. It inhabits a wide variety of habitats, including stock ponds on the eastern plains, glacial pools in the high country, beaver ponds, and small reservoirs. It also has been discovered in Colorado caves.

The tiger salamander is a secretive creature that moves in the shadows and most often at night. Its migration is dangerous. It may be killed by an automobile as it crosses a road. Its movement makes it more vulnerable to a host of predators, such as coyotes, raccoons, snakes, turtles, and hawks. Once in the water, it is preyed upon by ducks, gulls, bullfrogs, trout, bass, crayfish, and giant water bugs.

But the pull of the water is strong. The tiger salamander moves in the rain to its breeding grounds, where an average of 400 eggs from each female are fertilized by the male and strung along the stalks and leaves of submerged vegetation. Depending upon elevation and temperature, the eggs hatch in two to five weeks.

Adult salamanders hunt a variety of prey while at the breeding grounds. They have been known to take snails, caddis flies, mayflies, dragonflies, and other insects. The larvae, which can take from two months to two years to metamorphose into their adult form, feed on an even wider array of prey: water fleas, insect larvae, snails, amphipods, and the tadpoles of many frogs and toads.

In a strange process known as ''neoteny,'' some of the larvae never metamorphose. Instead they become what are known as axolotls, a word taken from an Aztec word meaning ''water dolls.'' These axolotls, although they look similar to larvae, are sexually mature, functional adults. Their breeding can result in either more axolotls or in normal metamorphosizing tiger salamanders.

Tiger salamanders are colorful residents of moist woods and wet areas. After rainstorms they may turn up away from water on lawns and porches. Despite their intimidating appearance, they do not bite. WENDY SHATTIL / BOB ROZINSKI

The coloration and life history of the tiger salamander vary greatly across its range and within the three subspecies found in Colorado. In the east, it is often dark with yellow spots. In the west, it can be light green with dark spots. At higher elevations, the adults move away from the breeding grounds as soon as mating is complete; on the plains, some adults remain near water all summer.

By the rainy nights of autumn, the young that have assumed the adult form are moving away from the ponds in another mass migration. Again they face hazards, but the pull is powerful as they move off toward the burrows in which they will spend the winter, waiting for the return of the warm spring rains.

Short-tailed Weasel

Scientific name: Mustela erminea
Range: Mountainous areas above 8,000 feet
Habitat: Coniferous forests, clearings, rocky areas

Size: Six to nine inches long including tail, one to four ounces
Identifying traits: Slender body, white in winter with black-tipped tail

To a mouse, chipmunk, or pika, the weasel is like a furred flash of lightning. It can come quickly out of nowhere and is just as deadly. The ferocity of the weasel is legendary. It is a tiny animal, Colorado's smallest carnivore, yet it will attack animals several times its size, and it will fight to the death. Naturalist Ernest Thompson Seton writes of an eagle shot out of the sky and discovered to have the remains of a weasel it had attacked firmly attached to its neck, the weasel holding tight even in death.

Colorado has two species of weasels. The short-tailed, also called the ermine, is found in the high country, while the larger long-tailed weasel can be found almost statewide. The two are very similiar in appearance and color—brown with a lighter underbelly in summer and white with just a tip of black on the tail in winter. The short-tailed weasel rarely gets longer than 10 inches or weighs more than six ounces, while the long-tailed weasel

75

can be twice as long and twice as heavy.

In habits, the two Colorado weasels are quite similar. Both are carnivores, feeding on rabbits, pikas, birds, mice, chipmunks, and ground squirrels. Although they can seem awkward in the open with their strange, spring-like gait, they are efficient predators, stalking the rocky slopes and even hunting beneath the snow in winter, killing with a swift bite to the neck. Often the carcasses of animals killed by weasels are discovered only partially eaten, giving the animal a bloodthirsty reputation for killing more than it can eat. Yet, more often, the weasel has only eaten its fill and crawled off to rest before returning.

The weasel is active all year, hunting mostly at night. Breeding takes place in midsummer, and the shorttail weasel bears four to eight young the next spring in a den located in a rocky area or under thick brush. The young are tiny, weighing hardly more than a tenth of an ounce, but they will be on their own in just six weeks and as large as their parents by the end of summer.

By then, the weasel will be turning a luxurious white, a color popular with furriers and royalty, a color giving it the appearance of lightning.

Elk

Scientific name: Cervus elaphus
Range: Eastern foothills to western border
Habitat: Forested areas, mountain meadows, foothills, canyons
Size: Four to five feet tall at shoulder, 400 to 900 pounds (bulls)
Identifying traits: Large size, dark color

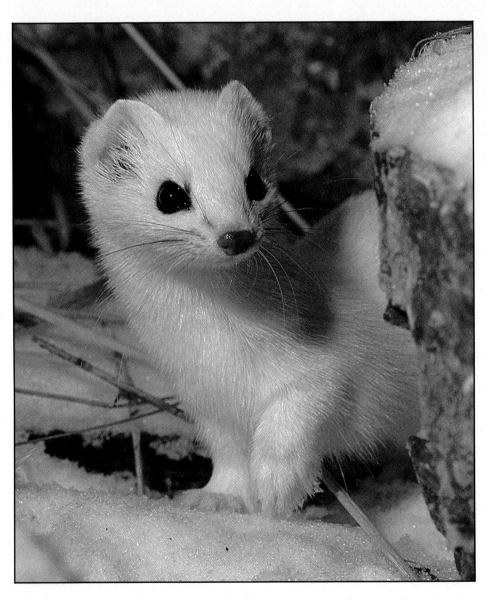

Short-tailed weasels are easy to see if a wildlife watcher spends much time around talus slopes where pikas live, and around rocky outcroppings and piles of downed timber where mice and other rodents live. Also called ermine, these weasels turn white in the winter and brown in the summer. A close relative, the long-tailed weasel is found throughout Colorado. JAN L. WASSINK

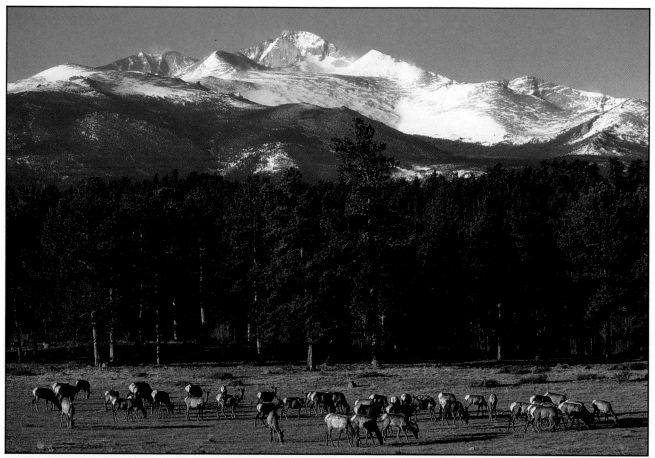

A herd of elk grazes below Longs Peak in Rocky Mountain National Park. Large herds of cows, calves, and young bulls spend the summer in subalpine habitat and are frequently seen. The best viewing occurs in high meadows in the early morning and late evening. Binoculars are useful to scan distant areas, while at closer distances hikers sometimes hear the low calls and squeals of cows and calves before seeing the animals. WENDY SHATTIL / BOB ROZINSKI

The first light of day has not yet touched the peaks of Rocky Mountain National Park. The October air is so still that fog is tangled in long strips in the trees surrounding the meadow at Horseshoe Park. For a time there is only silence. Then a long, sharp call cuts the air, unforgettable and indescribable. From the edge of the timber, a bull elk appears, silhouetted in the fog. The cold air smokes around its muzzle as it raises its head to bugle again.

Like the howling of a wolf or the midnight screech of a lynx, the bugling of elk has come to symbolize the power and beauty of the wilderness. The elk is one of the largest species of wildlife in the state, second only to the moose among the deer family. Some would say it is also the most majestic.

Mature bulls can stand five feet at the shoulder and weigh almost 1,000 pounds. The antlerless cows are usually one-fourth smaller. The elk's coat during the fall is a creamy brown on the back and sides, offset by a dark, rich brown mane and a distinctive off-white rump patch. In spring and summer, the coat is lighter.

The crowning glory of the bull elk is its antlers. By August these are full-fledged and covered with velvet, a blood-gorged skin covering that protects the antlers during growth. During August, the elk rubs the velvet off against tree trunks and branches. The rack of a mature bull can measure nearly five feet across and weigh as much as 30 pounds. In healthy animals, the rack is symmetrical, branching from a main beam and elegantly tined. Although elk shed their antlers every year, few castoffs are found in the woods. They are gnawed by rodents for their calcium and quickly disappear.

The elk once was among the most common hoofed mammals on the continent. Early cultures from across North America prized the ''wapiti'' for its hide (used as ceremonial robes, bedding, and shelter materials), its antlers (cut into needles and awls), and its meat. The

77

During the rutting season in September and October, mature bull elk are impressive monarchs of Colorado's mountains. Wildlife watchers at this time may hear the bugling call of bull elk and see small aspens and conifers that have been mangled by bulls thrashing their antlers. Sometimes bulls will engage in spectacular fights as they gather and defend their harems of cows. Bulls often expend so much energy during the rutting season that they enter the winter in poorer condition than the cows, a fact that accounts for higher winter mortality among bulls. TIM CHRISTIE

A Stage for the Mountains

base for the Plains Indians' feathered war bonnets was usually made of elk hide.

Of special importance to tribes such as the Arapaho, Ute, and Pawnee were the two over-sized canine teeth called "ivories." These teeth were used as ornamental jewelry on women's clothing. One robe still intact today contains 850 elk teeth. In more recent times, market hunting for the teeth cut deeply into the elk populations until game laws prohibited the practice.

As the United States was settled, the range of the elk shrank drastically. Today it is almost entirely a western species. Even in the West, populations once dipped dangerously low. As winter range and migration routes were cut off by development, as market hunting for meat and teeth began to take its toll, the number of elk began to drop.

By 1907, it was estimated that there were only 40,000 elk in the United States, most of them in the West. In 1910, biologists put the Colorado population at between 500 and 1,000 animals scattered in 10 herds, the largest found on the White River Plateau. From 1912 to 1928, a recovery program was undertaken in Colorado. Some 350 elk were shipped by train from Jackson, Wyoming, and released in several areas throughout the state.

Protection of habitat, strict hunting regulations, and wise management practices have helped the Colorado elk population to grow to more than 175,000 animals today—by most estimates, more than have been present since the dawn of the nineteenth century. Today there are healthy populations of elk in North and Middle parks, the Gunnison River Valley, the San Juan Mountains, the Rio Grande Valley, the Uncompahgre Plateau, Rocky Mountain National Park, and in several other areas from the eastern foothills to the western border.

In Colorado, the elk is a creature of the mountains, inhabiting almost all of the high, forested habitats in the state. It is a gregarious animal, moving in herds to favorite feeding grounds around dusk and to bedding areas during the day. Most of the herds undergo seasonal migrations, from the high alpine forests and meadows in summer to the low valleys in winter.

Other Common Wildlife of the Subalpine Zone

BIRDS: olive-sided flycatcher, red crossbill, Townsend's solitaire, hermit thrush, yellow-rumped warbler, dark-eyed junco, American robin, yellow-ringed warbler, western wood-pewee, tree swallow, violet-green swallow, Steller's jay, Clark's nutcracker, common raven, mountain chickadee, red-breasted nuthatch, ruby-crowned kinglet, pine siskin, and evening grosbeak.

MAMMALS: masked shrew, wandering shrew, Nuttall's cottontail, marmot, mule deer, mountain lion, hoary bat, least chipmunk, Colorado chipmunk, golden-mantled ground squirrel, bushytail woodrat, montane vole, porcupine, striped skunk, and bobcat.

AMPHIBIANS / REPTILES: boreal toad, boreal chorus frog, and wandering garter snake.

One of the most commonly seen mammals in Colorado's mountains, the golden-mantled ground squirrel is found in a variety of habitats. It often visits campgrounds and picnic areas to the delight of wildlife watchers. BOB HERNBRODE

79

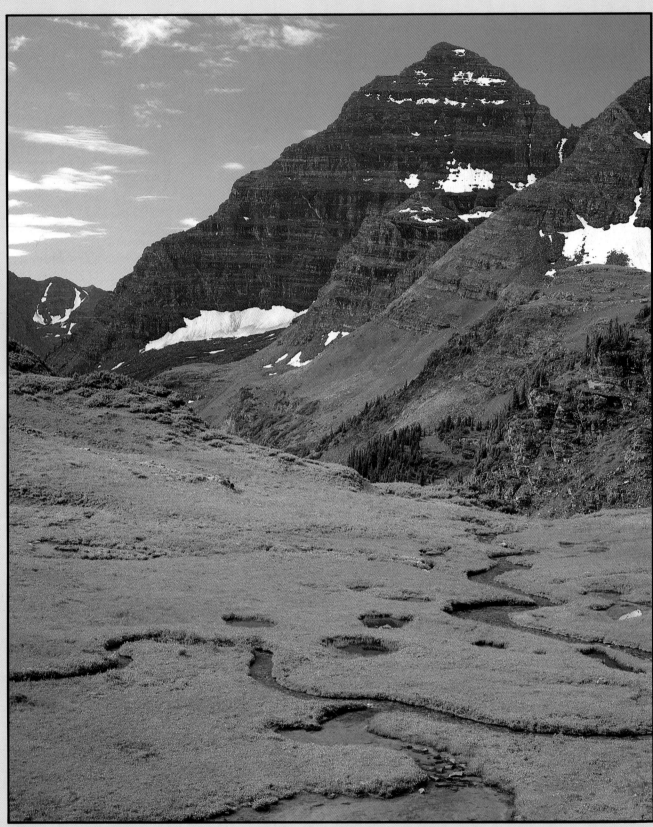

Far above timberline, North Maroon Peak soars 14,014 feet in the Maroon Bells-Snowmass Wilderness, located in the White River National Forest near Aspen. Colorado's highest mountains are crowned with the alpine zone, a land of tundra, rock, and snow. Severe weather dominates the alpine zone much of the year, but these areas provide important year-round habitat for hardy animals such as mountain goats and bighorn sheep, and summer habitat for deer, elk, and many other species. LARRY ULRICH

80

One Step to the Sky

One Step to the Sky
Alpine Tundra

Curious kid, a young mountain goat peers down from high ground in the alpine zone. Although mountain goats are well adapted to living in Colorado's high mountains, they are not native to the state. Instead, beginning in the 1940s, numerous mountain goats from other states were transplanted to Colorado. Wild herds now thrive in several areas. CHASE SWIFT

Here is where the sky comes to dance with the land—Colorado's high country. With 53 peaks over 14,000 feet and 830 peaks over 11,000 feet, Colorado is the crown of the country, the highest state in the nation. Just one step below the sky lies an ecosystem that is at once stunningly beautiful and unbelievably harsh: the alpine tundra.

Most ecosystems are difficult to define; they blend into one another, blurring their boundaries. Not the alpine tundra. It simply begins where the trees stop. Although this boundary is easy to see, the terminology sometimes gets tangled. The common term "timberline" denotes the end of continuous, unbroken stands of fully formed, upright trees—the end of the forest. Tree line is the point at which the growth of tree species, in any shape or form, becomes impossible.

Mats of "krummholz" (a German word for "crooked wood") lap up the hillsides like green waves, crawling before the force of the wind and cold. But where the krummholz ends, the alpine tundra begins.

The prime factor in the makeup of the alpine tundra ecosystem is the wind. Its moaning through passes and over summits is an endless background music. The open ridges above the Colorado tree line are some of the windiest places on earth. Wind gauges on Niwot Ridge in the Indian Peaks have recorded gusts of almost 150 miles an hour. At the summit of Longs Peak in Rocky Mountain National Park, wind gusts have been estimated at more than 200 miles an hour.

Ice and soil particles borne by these winds scour everything in their path. Exposed areas look as though they have been sandblasted; vegetation is ragged. Perhaps even more significant is the drying effect of the wind, which robs precious moisture from plants. To reduce the effects of the wind, most plant species grow low to the ground—

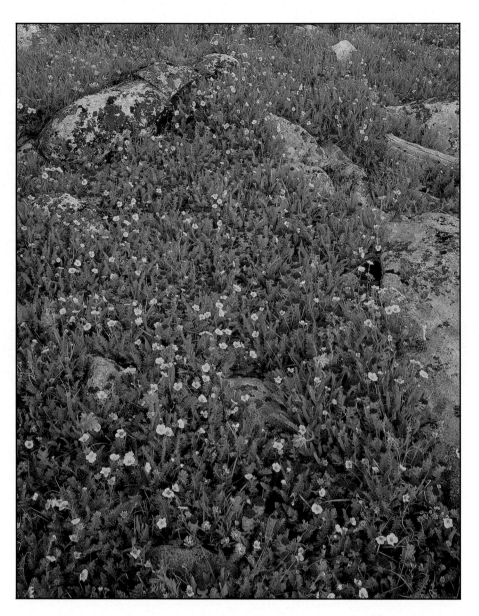

Yellow alpine avens and maroon kings crown brighten a patch of alpine tundra along Trail Ridge Road in Rocky Mountain National Park. Plants in the alpine zone must survive cold temperatures, strong winds, and short growing seasons. Yet despite these limiting factors, the alpine tundra supports the greatest diversity of wildflowers in Colorado. Their beauty adds enjoyment to any wildlife-watching trip. WILLARD CLAY

moss campion, sedge kobresia, arctic willow. To anchor themselves in the thin soils, many tundra plants have extensive systems of shallow roots.

The tundra receives more than 40 inches of precipitation a year, most of it in the form of snow. The wind determines its distribution. Most snow is blown right off the tundra and collects in the upper fringes of the subalpine zone. In protected areas, drifts of more than 10 feet high can form.

This snow pattern is vital to wildlife: If the snow is too deep, the bighorn sheep and mountain goat will be unable to paw through it to forage. If the snow cover is too thin, small rodents will be unable to tunnel under it to avoid the cold and predators.

If the snow is too crusty, the ptarmigan will not be able to burrow in for night cover.

Snow cover also plays a part in the distribution of plants. Those covered by insulating snow are protected from wind and cold. In spring, melting snow becomes a local water supply, nurturing blooms of Parry's clover, marsh marigolds, and king's crown, as well as a variety of lush grasses and sedges. Drier slopes support such species as alpine phlox and sandwort. The driest areas may provide habitat only for lichens and mosses.

Winter is the dominant season above tree line. It is a time of little movement, few tracks in the snow. The ptarmigan, the only bird found above tree line

The San Juan Mountains form the high roof of southwestern Colorado. As in other alpine areas, snow lingers on the San Juan peaks much of the year, but during the short, cool summers, alpine plants and animals rush to grow and reproduce. The types of plants found here are similar to the plants found in arctic areas of Alaska and Canada. DAN PEHA

all year, ranges through the willow brush. Ravens pass overhead. Pikas move among tunnels of rock and snow. Except for the wind, the land is almost silent. Except for the glare of the snow and the cold silver of the stars, it is all but colorless.

In contrast, the short summer is a crescendo of life. Snow buttercups push up around the edges of snowbanks by May. The greatest diversity of Colorado's more than 300 species of wildflowers can be found on the alpine tundra in summer: sky pilot, rose crown, saxifrage, old man of the mountain, avens, forget-me-not, spring beauty, shooting star—a constellation of flowers.

The tundra comes alive with wildlife during the brief summer as well. The water pipit moves up to nest in the rocky meadows. Herds of elk move onto the windy ridges to escape insects and find good forage. The rock fields ring with the calls of marmots and pikas; snow fields are pink with rosy finches picking for insects. White-crowned sparrows call from the willows; ravens call from the cliffs, their voices cracking like ice.

The abundance of summer brings mammals to the tundra that are more closely associated with other Colorado ecosystems: badger, coyote, marten, deer, elk, and porcupine have all been noted above tree line.

The few weeks of summer on the tundra are a celebration of life and its tenacity. And they are a boon to wildlife watchers. The lack of cover makes many creatures of the tundra among the most easily observed wildlife species in the state.

But summer is brief. By late August, the wind is cold and carries the threat of snow. The pikas have stashed their bushels of vegetation. The first feathers of the ptarmigan are turning white. One morning, the first snow blankets the high country and the land goes suddenly silent.

Until recently, man's tracks have been few in the high country of Colorado. Archaeologists have discovered game drives dating back hundreds of years, and evidence of hunting trails shows that humans have at least passed through the area since the glaciers receded. But the harshness of the climate has always pushed humans back to the lowlands each winter.

That has changed with the advent of high-altitude reservoirs, power lines, and mines. An increase in high-country recreation—from hiking and mountain climbing to off-road vehicles and motorhomes on the high pass roads—has brought the beauty of the alpine world to more of us, but it often threatens the very beauty that attracts us. The tundra is a fragile world. Scars made by off-road vehicles and by hikers cutting switchbacks can take decades to heal.

If we all show some respect for the landscape, the alpine tundra of Colorado can be shared by many. With roads such as Trail Ridge in Rocky Mountain National Park, the Mount Evans and Pikes Peak roads, Independence Pass, Loveland Pass, and others, the Colorado high country is some of the most accessible mountain scenery in the world. Many of the 27 components of the National Wilderness Preservation System in Colorado contain areas above tree line, as do many national forest lands and the Colorado State Forest in the northern part of the state.

During the brief summer months, the beauty of the land above the trees is like a gift—to be respected and savored. In winter, beneath the wind-blown snow, the tundra is a lesson in survival, in the tenacity of life, and in the simple beauties of snow shadows, wind song, and the star-shaped tracks of the ptarmigan. ■

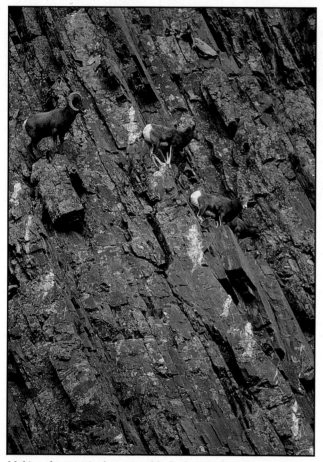

Making the seemingly impossible look easy, bighorn sheep traverse a cliff in Big Thompson Canyon south of Loveland. Bighorn use their legendary climbing ability to escape predators, so they are never far from steep terrain, whether on alpine summits or in rocky canyons at lower elevations. To help wildlife watchers find bighorns, the Colorado Division of Wildlife publishes a guide to 30 of the best sites in the state. LEE KLINE

Bighorn Sheep

Scientific name: Ovis canadensis
Range: Mountainous areas, particularly East Slope; some canyons
Habitat: Rocky terrain, including mountains and canyons, usually above 8,000 feet
Size: Three to four feet tall at shoulder, 350 pounds (male), 150 pounds (female)
Identifying traits: Grayish color, massive curling horns (male)

Sunset washes the Buffalo Peaks, a pair of 13,000 foot summits in the Mosquito Range overlooking the expanse of South Park. The light is soft on the mountainside, shining off the yellows, blues, and reds of wildflowers in full bloom and the orange and black of lichen on the rocks. The climb has been beautiful, but something is missing. We have come here looking for the bighorn.

Its signs are everywhere: tufts of brownish-gray fur clinging to the rocks, heart-shaped tracks in the dust.

One Step to the Sky

These rugged cliffs interspersed with green alpine meadows are perfect bighorn habitat—wild, high, and open. For two days, we have scanned the hillsides above timberline, looking closely for any movement among the crags.

Although the bighorn sheep is sometimes seen along roadsides, particularly in winter when snow drives it down to lower elevations, it is primarily a wilderness species. Its habitat includes some of the most remote and rugged country in the state. Bighorn sheep are found in the high mountains—on Pikes Peak and Mount Evans; atop the Sangre de Cristos, the San Juans, and the peaks of Rocky Mountain National Park—along steep river canyons such as the Arkansas, the Gunnison, the Poudre, the Taylor, and the Yampa, and on isolated buttes in places such as the Cebolla Creek Wildlife Area south of Gunnison.

The bighorn sheep is a magnificent animal. It is the largest mountain sheep in North America, with rams reaching 350 pounds or more. Against the rocks of the high country, it can be difficult to detect. Its coat is brown in spring, fading to a silvery-gray in winter. It has a prominent white rump patch year-round. Both sexes have horns, although those of the ewes are short, spiked, and not curled. It is the majestic curling horns of the ram that set it apart.

The bighorn's horns are true horns; they are not shed every year like the antlers of deer or elk. Annual growth rings form on the horns, helping biologists to determine the age of an animal. With good health and prime habitat, the ram's horns can reach enormous proportions, the skull and horns together weighing as much as 50 pounds.

In late November, the breeding season begins. The mating hierarchy of the bighorn is decided by a complex series of body gestures and interactions that take place throughout the year. Although more subtle, these interactions are as important as the dramatic horn-clashing battles of the breeding season.

When two contesting rams do square off, the battle begins with staring and body gestures as the animals attempt to avoid a fight. If neither animal backs down, the pair move toward each other, gaining speed and at the last moment rearing up on their hind legs to thrust their horns forward. The speed at impact has been estimated as high as 54 miles an hour. The sound of two rams battling is like cracking rock, and it can be heard in the still air as far as a mile away. During the height of the breeding season, the high country rings with the sound.

Battles between rams can go on for hours until one is injured or, rarely, killed. More often, the issue is decided in a single charge. Recognizing its inferior strength, one animal moves off, leaving the victor with the right to mate with the ewe.

But the battles take their toll on the victors as well. The effort of locating and defending ewes drains the energy of the rams at a time when food supplies are limited. During mating, the ram takes little time to feed, instead constantly checking the receptiveness of the ewes or defending a challenge. The stress can weaken the animal, making it more susceptible to disease, injury, or predation.

In May, the pregnant ewes move off to give birth to one, or rarely two, young weighing six to seven pounds. Within just three days, the young can clamber about the cliffs and move to join a herd of other ewes and young on nearby feeding grounds. The rams spend the summer separately on higher ground. The bighorn's diet consists mostly of grasses and sedges and a variety of plant material depending upon availability and season.

Because bighorns are so seldom seen, some people believe the animals range at random across the mountains. Actually, they will use the same feeding, bedding, and migration areas for years. An apparent aversion on the part of the animal to pioneer even nearby available habitat has hurt the bighorn; and the Colorado Division of Wildlife has relocated many animals with the hope of improving their distribution and ensuring the use of prime habitats.

The bighorn sheep once ranged much more extensively across North America—from northern Canada to the southern Rocky Mountains and from the Sierra to the Badlands. It is estimated that in the early 1800s there were nearly two million bighorn sheep on the continent. But today, less than two centuries later, there are only around 20,000. Colorado, which had an estimated 7,000 to 8,000 animals in 1897, saw its population dip drastically to something less than 1,000 in just a few decades. Now statewide counts place its number at about 6,000.

A number of factors have worked against the bighorn. Once, the herds in Colorado undertook long seasonal migrations out of the mountains to lower wintering grounds in the foothills, in river canyons, and on the plains. Encroachment by humans, the stringing of fences, and road-building have blocked many of the traditional migration routes, forcing the herds to winter on smaller, higher, and less favorable sites. Development of ski areas and the flooding of valleys for reservoirs have limited winter range. Decades of fire suppression have eliminated habitat by allowing thick forests to build up in areas once cleared by wildfire.

The effect of these and other factors has been to concentrate the herds into smaller and smaller ranges, stressing the animals and making them more vulnerable to the spread of diseases such as lungworm, a parasite picked up by consuming larvae along with forage. While the presence of lungworm parasites is often not, of itself, fatal to a mature bighorn, it can lead to pneumonia and a high mortality rate among the young when compounded with the stress of disturbance and less than favorable habitat. Grazing livestock have introduced other diseases for which the bighorn may have little or no immunity.

There have been dramatic deaths among the Colorado bighorn herds. The hard winter of 1952-53 saw 439 confirmed deaths in the Tarryall, Kenosha, and Pikes Peak herds, cutting the state's bighorn population by a fourth.

Other drastic declines in various herds during 1903, 1938, and 1946 have emphasized the dangerous combination of threats facing the animal.

Man has long tried to protect the bighorn. In 1872, even before Colorado became a state, the Territorial Assembly made it illegal to possess a bighorn out of season. A violation carried a $25 fine. Five years later, the hunting season for bighorn was closed, and it remained closed for 76 years, until 1953. In 1961, the bighorn sheep was designated the state mammal.

The creation of such places as Rocky Mountain National Park, where no hunting is allowed, and the preservation of prime habitats within designated wilderness areas have helped to stabilize bighorn populations in Colorado. An aggressive trapping and relocation program, which has

Although fairly common in the alpine zone, white-tailed ptarmigan may be difficult to see because of their exquisite camouflage— mottled brown and white in the summer, pure white in the winter. Look for ptarmigan in moist tundra areas, around rock outcroppings, and below snowfields. The Mount Evans Road, traveling to the summit of Mount Evans, and the Trail Ridge Road in Rocky Mountain National Park are two easily accessible areas to look for ptarmigan. GEORGE M. HAGER

One Step to the Sky

diversified the population and ensured the use of much historic range, has also aided in the recovery effort.

The bighorn sheep is the official symbol of the Colorado Division of Wildlife. To many, it is also the unofficial symbol of the Colorado high country. To see one in its natural habitat takes time, patience, hard work, and sometimes a little luck.

On this day on Buffalo Peaks, luck is with us. As we turn to take one last look before returning to camp, a flash of brown catches our eyes. A bighorn ram steps out onto a ledge, silhouetted against the sky. For an instant it is framed by the high clouds behind it, the last light of day caught in its fur. Then it moves slightly downslope. We sit and watch through binoculars until it is too dark to see and then move off towards camp, our quest fulfilled.

White-tailed Ptarmigan

Scientific name: Lagopus leucurus
Range: Throughout Colorado above 11,000 feet
Habitat: Alpine tundra, willow patches at timberline
Size: 12 inches long, one pound
Identifying traits: Seasonal plumage coloration, clucking call

By April, the snowdrifts on Cameron Pass in the Never Summer Range are slowly giving way to spring. Rocks and bare ground show through where the sun strikes, creating a patchwork of brown and white. By April, the ptarmigans on Cameron Pass wear a similar attire as their white winter plumage begins molting to summer brown.

The ptarmigan spends its life above or near timberline. By June, when the last of the year's snowdrifts are gone, its mottled spring plumage has turned brown and gray, matching perfectly the rocks of the mountainsides.

The ptarmigan can be difficult to spot—and not only because of its coloration. The ptarmigan feeds on willow buds, flowers, leaves, and insects, moving slowly across the tundra. In between feeding, it stands motionless for long periods of time. With its stubby wings, it can fly only short distances at a time, and cover is scarce above timberline. So avoiding detection is the bird's only defense.

The hen uses this same defense while sitting on her nest on the ground. Chicks hatch in mid-July and feed with the hen in areas of lush vegetation; the males stay on separate feeding grounds.

By fall, the ptarmigan has moved to a rocky area, feeding on mountain dryad and willow. The first snow

has dusted the high peaks, and the tapestry of white is slowly working its way down the hillsides. The ptarmigan's plumage begins its seasonal change, too. By October, it is as white as a snowdrift; only its black eyes and beak are visible.

The ptarmigan will spend the winter in the willows straddling timberline. Its feet, feathered for warmth, leave star-shaped tracks in the fresh snow. At night, it burrows into soft snowdrifts to escape the wind and cold.

Pika

Scientific name: Ochotona princeps
Range: Mountainous areas
Habitat: Talus slopes at or near timberline
Size: Eight inches long, seven ounces
Identifying traits: Sharp high-pitched whistle, rounded ears

Its sharp whistle pierces the high-country air. Its caches of vegetation sit like haystacks beneath overhanging rocks. The signs of the pika are easily detected. The pika itself is not.

Living in the maze of talus slopes and rock fields throughout the Colorado mountains above 8,500 feet, the pika is an elusive creature. With its gray fur and rounded body, it looks much like a rock itself. Yet, for people with a little patience, it can become one of the most

Tiny bundles of fur among large boulders, pikas appear and disappear almost like magic. More often heard than seen, the small animals emit a loud, sharp squeak when hikers—and other animals—venture near. To see pikas, find a rocky area where they live and sit quietly. Then watch carefully for any quick movements among the rocks. JEFF MARCH watchable species of wildlife in the Colorado high country. The pika is active during the day within a restricted territory. And its characteristic squeak and mounds of snipped vegetation give it away every time.

A relative of the rabbit and hare, the pika spends most of the short high-country summer gathering great bales of vegetation and storing them for winter. As much as four bushels of vegetation have been found in a single cache. When not foraging, it likes to find a safe perch near an escape route and keep an eye out for its predators: coyotes, weasels, martens, and hawks.

Unlike many other high-country mammals, the pika is active all year. Instead of hibernating during the winter, it moves about beneath the rocks and in tunnels dug through the snow. It lives off the stores of food it gathered throughout the summer.

The pika breeds in spring and often has two litters of from two to four young each. In Colorado, where summers are short, often only one litter will grow old enough to survive the winter. Pikas are born blind and hairless, but they reach adult size and establish their own territory by their first winter.

Hidden beneath the snow in winter, hidden among the rocks in summer, the pika can be a frustrating creature to observe. Still, its high-pitched call is familiar to any high-country hiker, a signal to sit quietly and watch for movement among the rocks.

Yellow-bellied Marmot

Scientific name: Marmota flaviventris
Range: Central and western Colorado
Habitat: Rock piles from 5,000 feet to above timberline
Size: 26 inches long, six to nine pounds

The routine is predictable: eat, sleep, and sunbathe. The marmot, a close relative of the groundhog, knows how to enjoy the short alpine summers.

Often seen stretched out on a favorite sunning rock, the marmot can be distinguished from the pika by its darker color and much larger size. It is the largest Colorado ground squirrel. Its name derives from the soft

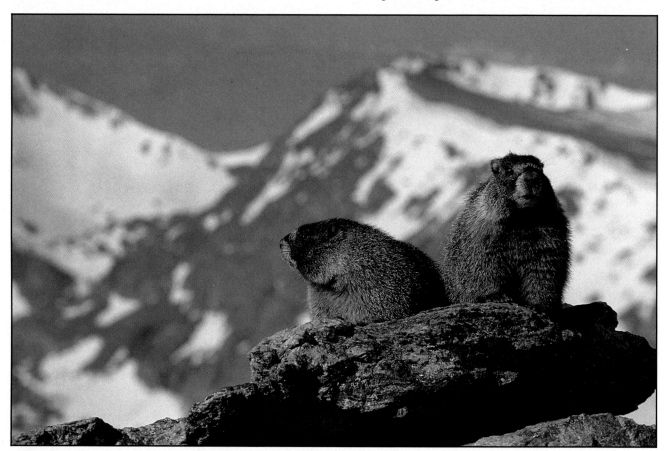

In typical marmot fashion, two yellow-bellied marmots sun themselves on a large rock. In addition to sunning, marmots are commonly seen feeding. They whistle when alarmed by predators or human passersby. Together with their roly-poly appearance, the loud, shrill blasts have earned marmots the unflattering nickname, ''whistle pigs.'' WENDY SHATTIL / BOB ROZINSKI

One Step to the Sky

yellow hair along its underside. Its distinctive whistle, which can be heard for almost a mile in the thin air at this altitude, has earned it the nickname "whistle pig." Besides its whistle, it also communicates with a scream and a tooth chatter.

The marmot lives in colonies. Although it can seem lazy and inactive, it uses the summer to raise a brood of four to six young. These are born blind, naked, and helpless, but they will be as large as adults by fall. The marmot eats prodigiously, storing up to 60 percent of its body weight as fat for the coming winter. A single warning cry given at the sight of a coyote, fox, badger, human, or even a shadow passing overhead will send it scurrying for cover.

Unlike the pika, the marmot is a hibernator, content to sleep away the long winters of the tundra in the same burrow it uses for birthing. At the first sign of snow and the first gust of cold wind, usually in September, the marmot retreats underground to its den. In May, it returns to its favorite rock to soak up the warm sun again.

Mountain Goat

Scientific name: Oreamnos americanus
Range: Along the Rocky Mountains
Habitat: Rocky outcroppings, cliffs, and tundra
Size: Three feet tall at shoulder, five feet long, 300 pounds (males), 80-150 pounds (females)

They look like cloud tatters snagged by the sharp summits. Mountain goats drift across the highest, most remote places in Colorado. Their world is made up of dizzying heights, cold wind, blue sky, white snow, and gray rock. They live out their lives, for the most part, beyond the reach of human eyes, just one step below the sky.

The mountain goat is not a true goat at all. It is most closely related to the chamois of the Alps and the antelope of Africa. It has no close relative on this continent.

Although the mountain goat's coat may look like a piece of drifting cloud, its hooves are designed to keep it on solid ground. A concave rubbery pad rimmed by a hard shell, each hoof gives the mountain goat sure-footed traction. Powerful hind legs and a precise sense of balance make its climbing prowess legendary. Mountain goats have been seen on near-vertical cliff faces, calmly grazing the sparse vegetation. When an animal reaches an impassable place, it can pull itself to a higher ledge using its forelegs. The young, called "kids," can climb with agility just hours after birth.

Because of its ability to inhabit a land of ice and sky, the mountain goat has few enemies. Isolation is its defense. A mountain lion may stalk it in the snow-free months. A golden eagle may swoop down on an unsuspecting kid in the spring. But it is the same steep country that protects the mountain goat that presents it with its greatest danger. In winter, avalanche chutes are often the only way across cliff faces, and entire herds have been found buried in the run-out of snow slides. Even for all their dancer-like grace on the cliffs, mountain goats have been known to slip and fall when a sudden ice storm coats the cliffs. Many animals carry the scars of such accidents: broken limbs or missing horns.

Although it seems at home among the summits of Colorado, the mountain goat is not a native species. It is abundant in the mountains to the north of the state, but the low dip of South Pass in Wyoming, with its lack of water, high temperature and low terrain, has effectively barred natural migrations farther south.

Between 1948 and 1971, some 51 animals obtained from other states were released in such places as Mount Evans, Collegiate Peaks, Mount Shavano, and the Gore Range. The most famous herd inhabits Mount Evans, where it is often seen along the roadside near the summit, grazing on grasses and willow shoots.

Mountain goats molt in great tatters during the warm months, giving them a shaggy, unkempt appearance. In summer, tufts of hair shed from winter coats are strung like cottonballs on rocks and branches. The Indians of the Northwest, where the goats are native animals, called them "white buffalo" for their shaggy coats, and they collected the shed fur to be woven into warm blankets for the winter.

In May and June, the females move off alone to steep, isolated cliffs to give birth. Each nanny bears one, or very rarely two, kids weighing six pounds. Within hours the kids can stand. Within a few days they can climb, and they follow their nannies back to common feeding grounds, usually on sunnier south-facing slopes. There they will spend most of the summer on the alpine tundra, feeding on grasses and shrubs.

Winter is a time of testing. In the high country, temperatures drop far below zero, and winds can whip up to a hundred miles an hour. The mountain goat faces the season head on, not bothering to move to lower

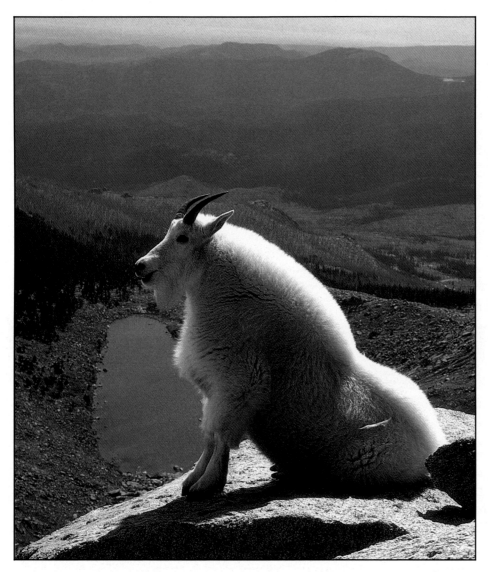

ground. Seeking out windblown areas where browse is exposed, it paws through the snow for food. Although its coat is good protection against wind and cold, the mountain goat has little natural protection against rain and sleet. In the harsh conditions of the tundra winter, some of the young, old, and injured animals will perish from exposure.

Few people see the Colorado mountain goat in winter. It is lost in the wind and snow and storm clouds. But it is up there on the peaks, staring straight into winter and waiting patiently for the return of spring.

Other Common Wildlife of the Alpine Tundra

BIRDS: blue grouse, horned lark, Clark's nutcracker, water pipit, white-crowned sparrow, and rosy finch.

MAMMALS: masked shrew, wandering shrew, snowshoe hare, least chipmunk, montane vole, porcupine, coyote, red fox, marten, long-tailed weasel, and striped skunk.

AMPHIBIANS / REPTILES: none common.

One Step to the Sky

Horned larks are commonly seen in alpine areas during the summer, but they also inhabit open, grassy areas at lower elevations throughout the state. They are small, active, ground-dwelling birds that walk rather than hop. The distinctive black "horns" (actually feathers) on their heads are not always noticeable from a distance. SHERM SPOELSTRA

91

Alpine Tundra

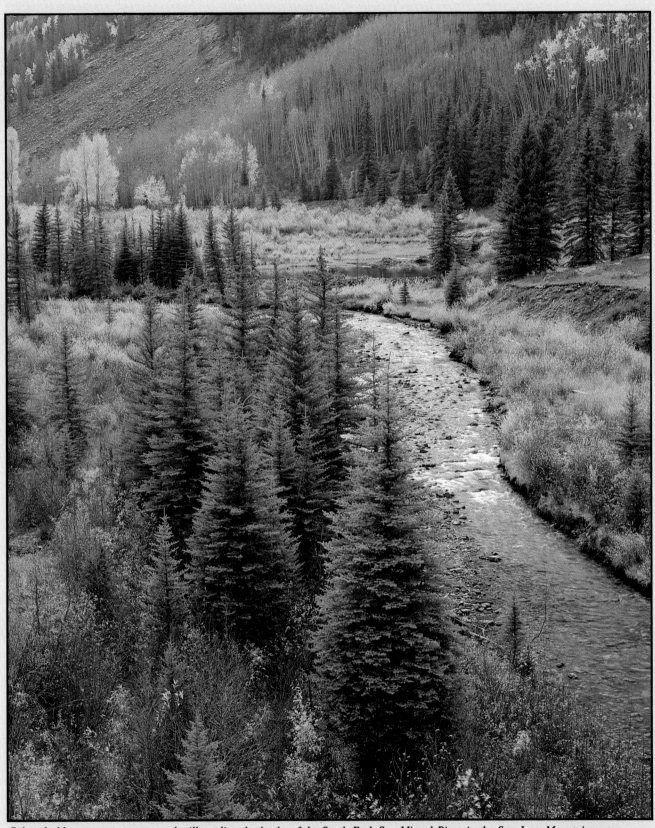

Colorado blue spruce, aspens, and willows line the banks of the South Fork San Miguel River in the San Juan Mountains near Telluride. Water-associated plant communities along rivers, streams, lakes, ponds, and other wet areas form riparian habitat, one of the most important wildlife habitats anywhere. Some 75 percent of all vertebrates depend on riparian areas for at least a portion of their life requirements. LARRY ULRICH

The Waters of Life

The Waters of Life
Riparian Habitats

Tiny amphibians, striped chorus frogs rarely exceed 1.5 inches in length, yet their mating calls, especially when thousands of frogs gather in huge colonies, fill spring nights with sound. The call is distinctive, if not exactly melodious. It is often described as the sound made by running a fingernail along the teeth of a comb. JEFF MARCH

Colorado is a land shaped by water. Long ago, glacial ice carved the face of the state, slicing mountains, cutting canyons, and gouging wide valleys. Today, the waters of rivers, creeks, lakes, ponds, and wetlands give shape to the land around them, creating what are called riparian habitats, our most diverse and life-filled areas.

With an average annual precipitation of just under 16 inches, Colorado is considered a semi-arid state. But that number is misleading. In the mountains, immense quantities of snow fall each winter. Cumbres Pass in the San Juans is one of the snowiest places on the continent, buried under an annual average of 370 inches. Out on the dry flats of the San Luis Valley, less than seven inches of precipitation falls each year.

Snow is a frozen fountain, melting in the spring and watering the landscape. Snowmelt flows into almost 100 named rivers. It gathers in wetlands and marshes. It forms shallow ponds on the plains.

Riparian habitats occur from less than 4,000 feet on the plains to over 14,000 feet in the mountains. They differ greatly in the plant and animal communities they harbor. But wherever they are found, riparian habitats display a greater diversity of life than non-riparian habitats of equal size. The reason is water.

On the eastern plains away from water, there are mostly grasses and sagebrush. Where the long, meandering rivers flow—including the South Platte and the Arkansas—there are trees such as cottonwood, willow, box elder, and hackberry, and shrubs such as wild plum, Russian olive, hawthorn, and wax currant. The lakes and ponds that pockmark the plains are ringed with cattails, snowberries, bulrushes and cord-grass.

On the dry flats at higher elevations, there are thick, silent stands of lodgepole pine with little but dark shadows as understory. Wherever the ground is watered by streams or wetlands, there are trees such as aspen and Colorado blue spruce; shrubs such as river birch, alder, and honeysuckle; plants such as subalpine rush and Canadian reed grass; and constellations of wildflowers, such as queen's crown, shooting star, columbine, and monkeyflower. Most of the more than 300 wildflower species in the state are associated with riparian habitats.

The wildlife species here are also diverse. Some species are like reflections on the water, never found far from it. Along the high-country streams, the call of the dipper is common. Quiet water is often rippled by the V-shaped waves of swimming beaver. On the lowland ponds are muskrats, kingfishers, plains

With golden feathers streaming behind fiery red eyes, the eared grebe makes a wild-looking mother as she approaches her nest. The fringed toes reinforce its unusual appearance, but they also help make the grebe a superior diver and swimmer. Grebes lay their eggs on a floating nest, which is anchored to reeds. These birds may be observed at several locations in the San Luis Valley, including Russell Lakes, San Luis Lake, and Monte Vista and Alamosa national wildlife refuges. SHERM SPOELSTRA

leopard frogs, and snapping turtles. If the water were gone, they would be gone, too.

Other species less directly dependent upon the water are drawn by the forests at the water's edge. Mule deer extend their range out of the mountains along the rivers, east onto the plains and west through the canyons. White-tailed deer, blue jays, oppossums, and red-headed woodpeckers follow the vegetation cover provided by rivers into the state from the woodlands of the east. Deer mice, raccoons, eastern cottontails, and skunks take advantage of the cover and live in greater concentrations in riparian habitats than in most other areas. Many bird species—chickadees, nuthatches, several species of warblers—move to the riparian forests in winter.

To still other species, the water acts as a stopover during long migrations. The Pacific Flyway includes the western side of the Continental Divide, and the edge of the Central Flyway takes in the high mountain parks as well as the plains. Along these routes, millions of birds move through the state each spring and fall—ducks, geese, cranes, terns, mergansers, and others. Huge congregations can be seen at the Monte Vista and Alamosa national wildlife refuges in the San Luis Valley, in North Park, and along the rivers and reservoirs on both sides of the Divide.

This congregation of life draws predators. Cliff swallows skim low over the water collecting insects. Flycatchers work the forest edge. Rodents are hunted by red-tailed hawks by day, great horned owls by night. There are coyotes, red foxes, raccoons, and snakes.

At Barr Lake State Park northeast of Denver, more than 300 of the state's 439 bird species have been noted. Although cottonwood thickets cover only about two percent of the state, more than half of the state's birds have, at one time or another, been observed in this habitat type.

Perhaps the creatures most closely tied to the riparian habitats of Colorado are the reptiles and amphibians. While some, such as the rattlesnake, are often found in even the driest areas, others define their ranges by the availability of water. Riparian habitats below 6,000 feet on both sides of the Divide show the greatest diversity of species: chorus frogs, painted turtles, tiger salamanders, water snakes, to

T h e   W a t e r s   o f   L i f e

Carrying a piece of vegetation in its mouth, a muskrat hightails it across a Colorado pond. The distinctive, vertically flattened tail is usually held in the water and serves as a rudder for this efficient swimmer, which is found mostly in marshes, ponds, and slow-moving rivers on the eastern plains. While it often shares a pond with beavers, the muskrat is much smaller, weighing about two to four pounds. Muskrats may be observed throughout the year, although many winter days are spent inside their dens feeding on stored vegetation. SCOTT NEILSON

name a few. The number of species of reptiles and amphibians declines at higher elevations; 70 percent of the amphibians and 80 percent of the reptiles in Colorado are not found above 8,000 feet. The species that are found at high elevations are found along waterways. Tiger salamanders, wood frogs, western toads, and chorus frogs are found in mountain riparian habitats.

Water is so important to life that even the flood pools, puddles, and intermittent streams teem with living things. Spadefoot toads, plains leopard frogs, red-spotted toads, and others have been known to breed in temporary pools, ponds, and puddles.

As much as water has changed the face of Colorado, humans have changed the face of riparian habitats in the state. From the start, water was a central part of human history in Colorado. Rivers were pathways for early explorers. Mountain men trapped beaver in every creek. Prospectors panned for gold, altering streambeds and causing erosion. Settlers built farms along rivers, diverting water for irrigation, draining marshes, and allowing stock to destroy riverside vegetation. Industry began to

release pollutants into the streams and lakes.

The greatest changes have come in the wake of our need to quench the thirst of our large cities. There are 1,900 reservoirs in Colorado, with a combined capacity of 8.85 million acre feet—enough to hold about half of the state's annual precipitation. There are 16 ditches and eight tunnels through which more than one million acre-feet of water is pumped or gravity-fed out of its native drainage and into another. About 630,000 acre-feet of that is pumped off the West Slope and diverted through or under the Continental Divide onto the East Slope, where 80 percent of the state's population lives. Groundwater has been pumped hundreds of times faster than its rate of replenishment, lowering the water tables.

The effects on riparian habitats have been enormous. Areas above dams are flooded by reservoirs. Below dams, flow pattern, water temperature, and silt load are drastically altered. Where water is diverted, stream flows are reduced. Where rivers are augmented, stream flows increase. Each has a different effect upon wildlife.

95

Some species of waterfowl have probably benefited from the creation of reservoirs, stock ponds, and irrigation ditches. The white pelican was not known to breed in the state until a nesting population was discovered on an island in Riverside Reservoir. However, high-country reservoirs have often destroyed winter range for bighorn sheep or cut off migration routes for deer and elk. The clear, cold water released from dams has helped to produce and sustain quality trout fisheries throughout the state, but it has all but eliminated warm-water species such as squawfish, bonytail chub, and razorback sucker.

Water is a dynamic element. Where it flows, it can create habitat for some species of wildlife and destroy it for others. Wise management of our riparian habitats is critical to the survival of an entire spectrum of wildlife species—birds, reptiles, amphibians, and mammals. Colorado truly is, as poet Thomas Hornsby Ferril described it, a state where "life is written in water."

Belted Kingfisher

Scientific name: Ceryle alcyon
Range: Throughout Colorado below timberline
Habitat: Along streams, rivers, lakes, and ponds
Size: 11 to 15 inches long

The kingfisher flys along a few feet over the stream like a splash of cold blue water; its rattling call cuts the air. The crown of blue feathers on both sexes and a distinctive wingbeat make this bird easy to identify, even from a distance. The female also wears a rust-colored "belt."

The kingfisher is most often found along waterways throughout the state, from below timberline to the plains. Unlike most bird species, it is most abundant in Colorado during the winter, when migrant kingfishers from northern states come south to the Colorado plains in search of open water, augmenting the resident populations.

The kingfisher is most often seen patroling its territory, a stretch of water up to a mile long. It can be heard calling raucously from a hunting perch. Its eyes are glazed with a kind of oil that reduces glare off the water, allowing it to see below the surface.

When the bird spots prey, it hovers for a moment as if taking aim and then dives beneath the surface of the water to capture small fish in its beak. Only a small percentage of its dives are successful, but when it does take prey, it flies to a nearby perch, kills the fish with blows from its powerful beak, and swallows it whole. It coughs up bones and other indigestable materials in pellets later, and successful hunting perches can be littered with debris.

For years the kingfisher has had a bad reputation among fishermen who see its hunting skill as a threat to populations of sport fish. But the kingfisher most often takes sunfish, carp, and suckers, thinning out species that compete with game fish for habitat and allowing the game fish to grow bigger and more abundant. The bird also eats crayfish, dragonflies, nymphs, small rodents, even berries.

The hunting skill of the male comes in handy during

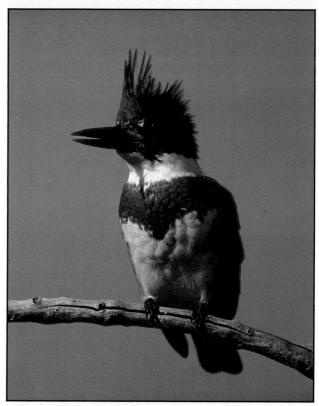

Bluish color, broad breastband, and ragged, bushy crest identify the belted kingfisher, a common sight along rivers, ponds, and lakes throughout Colorado, including waterways in urban areas. Kingfishers are sometimes seen hovering above the water with rapidly beating wings before plunging down to capture small fish, their favorite food. Fishermen and wildlife watchers often observe kingfishers flying above a stream or hear their loud, rattling calls. WENDY SHATTIL / BOB ROZINSKI courtship. The male often presents a catch to a prospective female before nesting begins. The nest consists of a tunnel up to 15 feet long dug into the side of a streambank. The site can often be recognized by the two-toed tracks leading into the tunnel. The female lays six to eight eggs, which because of their underground location are vulnerable to predation by snakes and raccoons.

Both parents share in incubation and hunting. By the time the young are two months old, they are testing their wings at the lip of the tunnel. Their flights are clumsy at first. Hunting skills, like flying skills, must be practiced. An adult bird will sometimes teach a chick to feed by dropping its catch back into the water and allowing the chick to finish the kill.

By the time the birds are adults, they are skilled hunters and superb fliers. Kingfishers have been known to outmanuever goshawks in the open air. Others have escaped danger by diving under water until the danger has passed and then heading for cover, just a flash of blue in the green of the forest.

The little bird even has a place in legend. According to Greek mythology, Alcyone, the daughter of the wind god Aeolus, jumped into the sea in a fit of grief over the drowning of her husband Ceyx on his way to consult the oracle of Apollo. Apollo then turned both the husband and wife into kingfishers and forbade Aelous to let the wind blow for two weeks while they mated. Sailors from many parts of the world know the legend and say that as long as the kingfisher is nesting the weather will be calm.

Beaver

Scientific name: Castor canadensis
Range: Central to western Colorado, eastern plains along waterways
Habitat: Streams, rivers, and creeks
Size: 39 inches long including tail, 30 to 60 pounds
Identifying traits: Large, flattened tail

Few animals had as much impact on Colorado history as the beaver, a furbearer that lured trappers to the Rockies in the early 1800s. These trappers, or mountain men, paved the way for settlers that came later. Today, wildlife watchers may see beaver from central to western Colorado, and along waterways on the eastern plains. Largely nocturnal, beavers are best seen by sitting quietly near an active beaver pond from sunset to dark. DENNIS HENRY

The names are the stuff of legend—Kit Carson, "Old Gabe" Bridger, "Broken Hand" Fitzpatrick, Bill Williams. As guides in the late 1800s, these men and others like them opened the way for settlement of the West. They knew the country like the scrollwork on the stocks of their rifles, and they learned it from the beaver.

A gentleman's top hat made of felt pressed with the hairs of beaver pelts was in vogue during the early years of the 1800s in the fashionable cities of the world. When the beaver became extinct in England and was all but trapped out in much of the eastern United States, a kind of gold rush for beaver began in the Rocky Mountains. The pelts were almost as good as gold, bringing $8 a pound on the open market.

Taking beaver from the streams of Colorado was nothing new. Several Indian tribes that hunted here had many uses for the animals: ground teeth were used as medicine for lung inflammation, tanned hides were used as leggings and cut into strips to make thongs, furred skins provided bedding and clothing, the meat was eaten. But the Indians hardly touched the beaver population compared to the trappers. By 1830, more than 200,000 pelts a year were being shipped to London. Hundreds of thousands more were used by U.S. clothing manufacturers. The beaver was vanishing from the West.

The beaver was saved only by a swing of fashion. In 1832, a new process was discovered for creating silk hats, and the bottom dropped out of the beaver market. George Frederick Ruxton, who explored Colorado in 1839, wrote that the "beaver has so depreciated in value within the last few years that trapping has been almost abandoned— the price paid for the skin having fallen from six and eight dollars per pound to one dollar, which hardly pays the expenses of traps. . .and is certainly no adequate remuneration for the incredible hardships, toil, and danger."

The beaver began a comeback, this time indirectly helped by the hand of man. Programs to control the populations of predators such as wolves, bears, and mountain lions decreased predation on beavers and may have inadvertently aided in the comeback. In an early conservation move, the 1887 Colorado Legislature placed the beaver on a list of protected animals.

Today the beaver is common in Colorado on creeks and rivers from 4,000 feet to timberline. Its habitat requirements are specific. If a stretch of river or creek meets those requirements and the density of beaver in the area is low, the animal does not build a dam. It simply digs a den into the riverbank. Where the habitat is not as suitable, the beaver takes matters into its own hands.

Dams can be over six feet high and hundreds of feet long. They are built of sticks, mud, and debris across slow-moving streams. The dam serves several purposes. It provides protection for the lodge, which is built surrounded by water. It assures that the water will be deep enough that winter ice will not reach all the way to the stream bottom. And it gives the beaver access to its food supply.

The beaver is well-suited to life in its pond. Its hind feet are webbed, and membranes close over its eyes and nostrils when submerged. It has a thick, waterproof coat. Oversized lungs allow it to remain underwater for as long as 15 minutes when threatened, although most dives average only four to five minutes long.

In Colorado's high country, a colony of beavers needs about eight to 10 acres of aspen forest to survive. The animals eat leaves, buds, sedges, and forbs in summer, as well as the bark of aspens, willows, and alders. The large incisors of the beaver grow throughout its life. With its sharp teeth and strong jaw muscles, the animal can snip through saplings an inch thick or patiently gnaw through the trunks of trees much larger. Campfire stories extol the beaver's ability to predict what direction a tree will fall while it is cutting through its trunk. But the number of beavers found crushed beneath the trunks of fallen trees seems to suggest otherwise.

Since the beaver does not hibernate, it must collect large caches of twigs and branches to eat during the winter. Drag marks and trails are often a good sign of beaver. Awkward on land, the beaver builds channels as far as 100 yards back into the forest and uses these to float its food supply back to the main pond.

Winter is spent in a lodge made of stick and branches. The outside of the lodge is often slapped with mud that, when dried, makes it almost impenetrable to predators. The entrance of the lodge is underwater. Inside, a typical lodge consists of separate areas for sleeping and eating. All through the winter, the beaver retrieves sticks from its underwater cache. Once the bark is eaten off, the animal may use the sticks in the spring to patch its dam.

Beavers mate for life, which can be as long as 20 years. Breeding takes place in late January or February. In the spring, three to six young are born furred and with their eyes open. They are capable of swimming within four days, but they often stay in the lodge for their first month. The young will usually stay with their parents for two years before striking off in search of suitable habitat of their own.

Before the turn of the century, it seemed that the beaver's only legacy to Colorado would be the open meadows that grow up over abandoned ponds. Beaver habitat is still threatened by high-altitude diversions, pollution, and development. But thanks to the shifting whims of fashion and conservation techniques, the beaver's legacy is now found in the V-shaped ripples it leaves on the water and in the sound of its tail as it slaps out a warning to dive.

Striped Chorus Frog

Scientific name: Pseudacris triseriata
Range: Throughout Colorado below 12,000 feet except in the southeast and extreme west
Habitat: Ponds, marshes, reservoirs, meadows
Size: Up to 1.5 inches long
Identifying traits: Dark stripe through the eye, three dark stripes down back

To school children on a spring field trip, the chorus frog is often nothing more than a tiny plop in the water as they walk around a pond or marsh. Mostly silent except for its mating call—which has been compared to the sound made by running fingers over the teeth of a comb—this small frog can be found in many water-related habitats across the state.

The chorus frog emerges in spring from a secluded den. From March to September, it is most active during the day, hunting the water's edge for flies, spiders, and ants. While mating, its call can sound throughout the night.

In the warm puddles created by spring rains, in ponds and pools and bogs, the chorus frog lays its eggs, as many as 500 at a time, on underwater leaves and stems. Very few of the young survive. As many as 99 percent fall victim to cold water, disturbance of the eggs, or one of many predators. Those that do survive metamorphose to the adult stage in two months. Even then they are preyed upon by jays and robins, fish and snakes.

Still, enough chorus frogs survive to fill the spring nights in Colorado with their distinctive call. Sometimes they gather in huge colonies numbering in the tens of thousands, making the spring air shimmer with sound.

Canada Goose

Scientific name: Branta canadensis
Range: Statewide
Habitat: Wetlands, rivers, reservoirs
Size: 22 to 43 inches long
Identifying traits: Black, white, and gray coloration; honking voice

It is sunset. The first storm clouds of an early winter snow lie low and heavy along the horizon. Over the South Platte River, the air is filled with a faint honking and the rustle of wings. Canada geese in two loosely-held V-shaped flocks are passing overhead, knitting a thread of black color into the gray clouds.

Although scientists do not fully understand why geese fly in V formations, the sight of a flock piercing the autumn sky is one of the most memorable in nature. It conveys a restlessness that speaks of adventure, of new places, of moving on. Like the migration of the caribou or the spawning runs of the salmon, the passing of the geese is part of the essence of autumn.

Canada geese are loyal mates, pairing for life and returning each year to a successful nesting site. Although the mortality rate among the birds is high, some geese live as long as 23 years. Pairs have been recorded nesting in almost exactly the same spot for two decades.

Both the male and female will aggressively defend the nest, which is usually set in the reeds near the water's edge. The four to seven eggs hatch in a month, and within a day or two the young follow the female to open water, where they will be safer from predators. During the day, they may move off to open fields to peck for grain, bulbs, and grass, or they may stay in open water, feeding on crustaceans, insects, and plant shoots. They mature quickly, doubling in weight almost every week for the first month. They quickly become strong fliers in preparation for the flights of autumn.

The presence of open water and short grasses and the lack of predators in such places as golf courses, city parks, and cemeteries has attracted great numbers of Canada geese to urban and suburban landscapes. They are often the largest and most conspicuous birds many city-dwellers see. With their young waddling behind them as they cross roads, or during the mid-July molt, which leaves adults flightless, geese have been known to cause traffic jams on city streets. Their droppings can stain the paint of cars. Flocks of several thousand have wintered on Denver-area golf courses. Large numbers

99

Canada geese take flight from the South Platte River in eastern Colorado. Large birds, Canada geese may weigh 10 pounds or more and have a wingspan exceeding five feet. As a result of successful transplanting programs by the Colorado Division of Wildlife, thousands of geese are year-round residents in many parts of Colorado. In addition, tens of thousands of migratory geese pass through the state in the spring and fall. The calling, or honking, of flocks of migrating geese on cold autumn nights is an ancient sign of approaching winter. RAY RICHARDSON

can be seen at places such as Washington Park and the grounds of City Park in Denver and in the city parks and agricultural fields of Fort Collins.

The first confirmed encounter with Canada geese in Colorado comes from the journals, and the dinner table, of the Pike Expedition. On February 26, 1807, a pair of Spanish Army officers dined on goose with Pike on the banks of the Conejos River. The goose remains a popular game bird with hunters today.

The Canada goose will always be seen as a symbol of the changing seasons. Heard over the roar of traffic from the window of a high-rise office building or seen on a cloudy day over the South Platte River, a flock of Canada geese passing overhead raises our eyes to the sky.

Red-winged Blackbird

Scientific name: Agelaius phoeniceus
Range: Throughout Colorado to about 9,000 feet
Habitat: Marshes, wetlands, open fields
Size: Eight to nine inches long
Identifying traits: Black with red shoulder patches

On a cold, gray day in late September, a stand of creekside cottonwoods is peppered with birds. The branches are weighted as though with a dark fruit by grackles, cowbirds, Brewer's blackbirds, starlings, and red-winged blackbirds. A flock is gathering to migrate. In a burst of wings that ruffles the air, the birds are gone.

The branches of the trees are left swaying as if in a breeze.

The red-winged blackbird is one of the most common breeding birds in Colorado. With its crimson shoulder patches, bordered with yellow and worn against a plumage of sleek black, the male is easily distinguished from the other blackbirds in the state—the yellow-headed, Brewer's, and rusty—as well as from the grackles, starlings, and cowbirds.

The red patches are more than just decoration. They also serve as a kind of flag. When a bird stakes out its territory, an event that can begin as early as January, it will sing from a traditional song perch, its wing bands prominently arched. In courtship, the male will spread its tail, drop its wings to display the red, tip slightly forward, and sing. Studies have shown that the red can also be used as a sign of aggression. A bird knowingly invading the territory of another breeding pair will shield the red patches on its wings submissively, while battling males will flash their wings wildly.

After wintering as far south as Costa Rica, red-winged blackbirds arrive in Colorado so early that the males often are seen singing upon perches while snow and ice still lock the marsh. The birds are polygamous; several females mate with a single male. The female weaves a nest within a defendable range. Although red-winged and yellow-headed blackbirds nest within the same general area, they prefer different specific locations. The latter will build in the cattails over deep water, while the red-winged variety chooses to nest over shallow water.

The drab female lays three or four blue-green eggs that are streaked with purple. She incubates these for 12 days and then assumes total responsibility for feeding the young. The male stays nearby, singing and keeping watch. The adults and young feed on insects, spiders, grass seed, and some fruits.

The birds raise two or even three broods in a season. Once the final brood is reared, the birds gather in flocks that can reach enormous proportions. One flock near Lamar was estimated to contain almost a quarter of a million birds. The Crown Hill cemetery is the site of

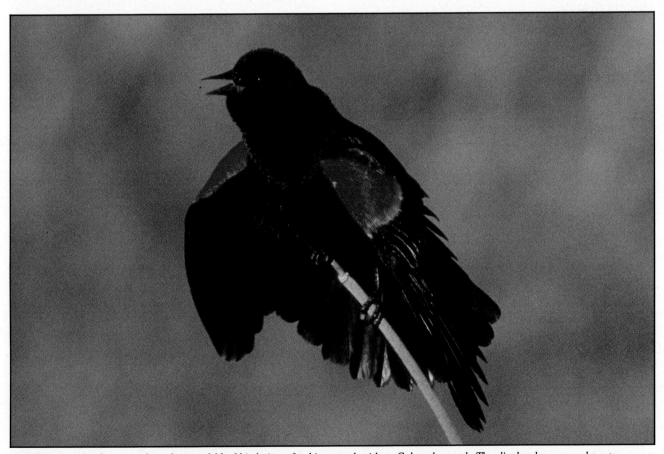

In full mating display, a male red-winged blackbird sings for his mate beside a Colorado pond. The display has several parts— flared tail, spread wings to show the bright red wing patches, and loud, clear song. During March and April, displaying males perch atop bullrushes and cattails around ponds, marshes, and lakes throughout the state. Such areas also provide excellent opportunities to watch warblers and ducks in mating displays. WENDY SHATTIL / BOB ROZINSKI another popular roost. The weight of the flocks bends the branches of the trees, their sound fills the air, so that when the birds finally leave, the sky behind them seems empty and quiet.

White-tailed Deer

Scientific name: Odocoileus virginianus
Range: Eastern Colorado, scattered groups in mountains and northwest Colorado
Habitat: Deciduous forests along rivers
Size: 125 to 200 pounds (male), 90 to 170 pounds (female), three to four feet tall at shoulder
Identifying traits: White flaglike tail, shorter ears than mule deer, tines of antlers rise from main beam, smaller than mule deer

The heart-shaped tracks of a deer are imprinted in the light frost atop the muddy bank of the South Platte River. It is impossible to tell from the tracks alone whether their maker was a white-tailed or mule deer. But a rustle in the brush and a flash of white reveal the animal's identity—a white-tailed deer.

The conspicuous white tail is the main distinguishing feature of the white-tailed deer. It is also smaller and has shorter, less conspicuous ears than the mule deer. Its antlers are tined from a main branch rather than forked. Its coat is usually redder and less gray in the winter. It is more distinctly marked with a chin patch, eye rings, and more contrasting underparts. And the white-tailed deer is more likely found in the bottomlands than the mule deer, apparently being better adapted to riparian habitat and farmlands.

Moving in thick, brushy habitat most often along waterways, the white-tailed deer in Colorado has always been difficult to spot and even more difficult to count. Early records indicate it ventured along the South Platte River as far west as Fort Collins and Golden and up the Cache la Poudre River. Along the Arkansas River, it has been reported in the Wet Mountain Valley, near Cotapaxi and Montezuma. Sightings have also been made along the Rio Grande to Del Norte.

Colorado is the western edge of the white-tailed deer's range. It has never been as abundant here as the mule deer, and its numbers suffered early from changes in riparian habitat and from the guns of meat hunters. A 1947 report by the Colorado Division of Wildlife cites no resident white-tailed deer population in the state.

In the 1960s, a few whitetails were reintroduced into the state. But by this time, human impacts upon habitat had benefited the animal and a natural expansion into Colorado took place from the east. The coming of agriculture provided a more stable food source. Changes in the riparian zones provided necessary cover. Successional habitat that follows fires, timbering, or land clearing tend to favor species such as the white-tailed deer.

Today the whitetail is found most commonly along the South Platte, the Arkansas, and the Republican rivers. There are also small local populations along the White River in northwestern Colorado, the Laramie River in north-central Colorado, in the mountains surrounding Kremmling, along the Yampa River, and in the foothills west of Fort Collins.

Whitetails breed in the fall. By October, the antlers of the bucks are in prime condition, and noisy battles occur over mates. Unlike mule deer, whitetails breed as fawns, and usually they have twins by their second year. While the doe feeds nearby, the spotted fawn lies still in the grass; its stillness, spotted coat, and lack of scent are its only defenses against such predators as the coyote.

Large bucks are usually solitary animals, while does and their young often graze in small herds. Deer have favorite feeding grounds for grass, forbs, and the leaves of woody plants. They supplement their diet with cultivated crops, such as alfalfa and corn, feeding mostly at dusk and dawn. Much of the day is spent in thick cover. In the worst winter weather, deer of both sexes will often gather in places with enough food and cover so that they do not have to plow through deep snow. Bucks lose their antlers in February and begin growing them back immediately.

Moose

Scientific name: Alces alces shirasi
Range: Northcentral Colorado
Habitat: Streambeds, meadows to timberline, mixed forests
Size: Five to six feet tall at shoulder, 1,100 pounds (males); four to five feet at shoulder, 700 pounds (females)
Identifying traits: Size, large muzzle, palmated antlers (male)

For many years, one of the only sure places to see a moose in Colorado was the Routt County Courthouse in Steamboat Springs. There, a mount of a young bull

102

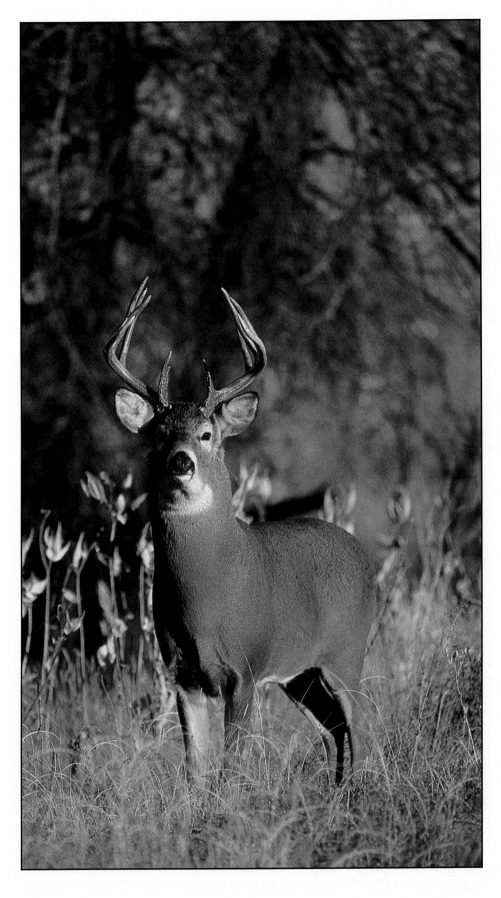

Seldom far from dense cover, a whitetail buck pauses near the edge of a cottonwood forest near Denver. A 1947 report by the Colorado Division of Wildlife concluded there were no resident populations of white-tailed deer in the state. Today, whitetails are almost as abundant as mule deer from the eastern border to the foothills, the result of a natural population expansion from the east. Although mule deer and white-tailed deer may be encountered on the open plains, whitetails prefer riparian areas, especially cottonwood river bottoms.
WENDY SHATTIL / BOB ROZINSKI

A cow moose and calf exchange information by nose. Prior to 1978, moose were not resident in Colorado. But in 1978 and 1979 the Colorado Division of Wildlife transplanted several moose into North Park near Willow Creek Pass. A later transplant was made in the Laramie River drainage. Both were successful, and moose can now be observed in North Park, Middle Park near Granby, on the west side of Rocky Mountain National Park, and along the Laramie River. R. E. BARBER

hung on the wall with a plaque reading "Killed 4 November 1941 on Storm Mountain." There was an occasional track found in the mud along the streams of North Park. A passage in the journal of the 1871 Wheeler Survey talks of discovering the remains of a moose in South Park. Sometime in the early 1860s, one was shot in Estes Park. But, for the most part, the moose roamed Colorado only in campfire tales. Despite a hundred-year record of occurrence in Colorado, living proof was hard to come by.

The moose has long been established in southern Wyoming. Occasionally a yearling bull or young cow would wander into North Park, a broad, high valley on the Colorado-Wyoming border, or into the northcentral mountains. But the wanderers had little chance of survival, despite the willow thickets and stands of spruce, fir, and pine to serve as habitat. Most were taken by poachers before a viable population could take hold.

Then on March 14, 1978, the story changed. Using private donations, the Colorado Division of Wildlife began transplanting into the state a dozen moose trapped near the Bear River in Utah. The animals were tranquilized and transported by helicopter to waiting cattle trucks. There they were tested for brucellosis and leptospirosis, diseases that could infect livestock and native Colorado wildlife species. Finally, they were trucked 350 miles to the headwaters of the Illinois River, near the western boundary of Rocky Mountain National Park.

In 1979, 12 more moose were brought in from Wyoming. In 1987, another dozen were released along the Laramie River near the Rawah Wilderness Area. Colorado had its moose.

Released into prime habitat with no major predators and no competition from existing moose populations, the animals have thrived. Today there are an estimated 180 to 250 moose in Colorado. The largest concentrations are

The Waters of Life

found in and around North Park, in the Never Summer Mountains, and in the Laramie River valley. A smaller group can be found in the Kawuneeche Valley in Rocky Mountain National Park, along the Colorado River. Moose sightings have occurred as far away as South Park, almost 100 air miles away from the release site.

The moose introduction program has been so successful that the Division of Wildlife has decided to increase the population from its original target of 100 animals to 300 and to introduce the animal into other parts of the state.

The moose is the largest member of the deer family. Even though the subspecies in Colorado is smaller than the Alaskan moose, bulls are formidable animals, standing six feet tall at the shoulder and weighing up to 1,200 pounds. Cows weigh around 700 pounds.

Moose are solitary animals except during the mating season. They are most likely seen where there is water—along streams or ponds or in marshes. Aquatic plants, willows, and grasses are their main summer foods. Moose sometimes spend summer days in the krummholz near timberline in an effort to avoid pesky insects.

In September, the rut begins. Bulls thrash the trunks of trees, stripping the velvet from their antlers. The echoes of their bellowing calls shake the frosty air. Clashes between rutting bulls are epic battles that occasionally end in injury or even death. The bones of great bulls that starved to death after their antlers became locked in battle have been discovered in other parts of the moose's range.

Bulls do not gather harems like elk but will defend one cow until mating and then move off in search of other receptive females. Single calves, sometimes twins, are born in late May or early June weighing about 30 pounds. A cow moose is extremely protective of her young and when threatened becomes one of the most dangerous animals in North America. With sharp hooves and snapping teeth, she will fend off any perceived danger—coyotes, mountain lions, black bears, wolverines, or humans.

Dark brown against the winter white, snow gathering on its back, the moose stays put during winter rather than moving to lower elevations. Its thick coat protects it from cold and snow. Unlike deer and elk, which can tolerate only a few feet of snow, the moose can move about in as much as five feet of snow. The availability of browse sets the boundaries of its winter range.

Willow is the chief food of the moose in winter. Thickets that hold large numbers of moose can look like piles of matchsticks, littered with broken branches and tree trunks. The branches of other trees will be gnawed as high as the animals can reach, creating a "browse line" and giving the forest a strangely pruned look.

Its preference for thick willow stands and deep forest makes the moose a difficult animal to see. Still, the tracks along the riverbank are real, the bellowing voice in the autumn aspen is no longer just a hopeful echo. Once just a campfire story, the moose now roams the thickets and forests of northern Colorado.

Great Blue Heron

Scientific name: Ardea herodias
Range: Statewide
Habitat: Riparian areas below 8,000 feet
Size: Stands 42 to 52 inches tall, six-foot wingspan
Identifying traits: Long neck, trailing legs in flight

The great blue heron steps slowly along the edge of the marsh without rippling the water, its long neck bent like a bow, its yellow eyes intent. It is a patient and disciplined hunter. For long moments, it stands completely still, looking like a reed set at the edge of the pond. An unwary frog surfaces. The sharp beak of the heron flashes downward. The few ripples left on the surface of the water slowly disappear.

The great blue heron is the largest and most widely distributed heron in North America. In 1872, when it was first described in Colorado, the heron was a common sight, its image reflected in rivers, ponds, streams, and marshes from the plains to the canyon country on the western slope.

The great blue heron is a water bird rarely found far from a marsh, pond, river, or slow-moving creek. Its long legs allow it to hunt in shallow water for small fish, aquatic insects, frogs, reptiles, amphibians, snakes, small birds, and crustaceans such as crayfish. It sometimes hunts plowed fields away from water, searching for insects or rodents. Occasionally, aquatic plants become the mainstay of its diet.

Some herons winter on patches of open water in the state, while others migrate, returning in February, often to the same grove of cottonwood trees year after year. The bird prefers to nest in groups, and congregations of more than 100 nests have been recorded.

The female lays three to seven eggs in April or May, just as the first leaves begin to appear on the branches to provide cover for the nests. Although adult birds have few natural predators, mortality among the chicks is high,

105

up to 70 percent. Harassment by humans, even unintentional, can cause the adults to flush from their nests, leaving the eggs and the young vulnerable to heat, cold, or predation from hawks, owls, and ravens. If disturbed often, herons will simply abandon their nests.

The traditional use of old-growth cottonwoods for nesting sites has caused some problems for the heron. The best sites are often also prime development locations, since they are near waterways. As a result, many nesting sites have been lost to highways, reservoirs, and residential construction.

But others have survived, even thrived. Two of the state's largest nesting sites—Chatfield Reservoir and Boulder Creek—are near metropolitan areas. A large heronry straddles Interstate 70 near Debeque. Others have sprung up in cottonwoods lining manmade lakes such as Barr Lake near Brighton and Empire Reservoir west of Fort Morgan. In 1986, a new heronry containing eight nests was discovered in an unusual place: a ponderosa pine forest.

Perhaps the best-known great blue heron nesting site is Chatfield Reservoir, a manmade lake on the South Platte River. Records indicate that it has been used since around 1900. In 1972, just nine nests were counted. Recently, as many as 175 nests have been in use.

Of all Colorado birds in flight, none is more distinctive than the heron—the long, slow wingbeats, the neck bent into the shape of an S, the long legs dangling behind like a rudder. Following slowly the bends of a river, the heron seems at once awkward and graceful. The powder-blue feathers of its upper back and wings, the colors along its breast and neck like the gray of storm clouds, and its sun-yellow eyes make the heron seem like a chip of the summer sky.

In silhouette against the setting sun or reflected in a still prairie pond, the sight of a great blue heron is unmistakable and beautiful.

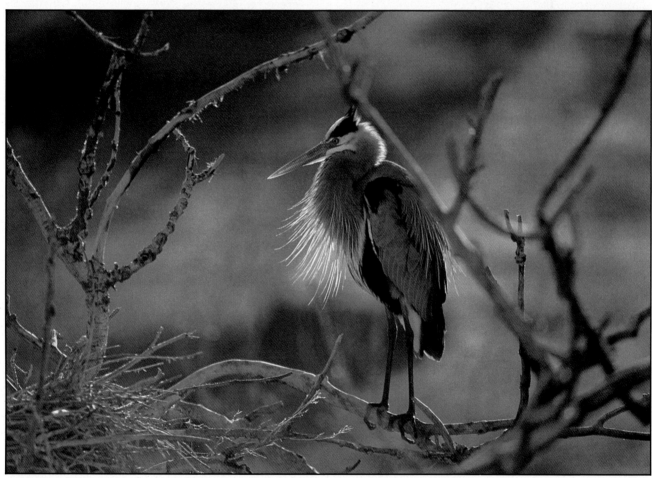

Great blue herons are large, stately birds usually seen standing alone in shallow water along ponds, lakes, and rivers. They nest in communal roosts in large trees, and these colonies range from a few nests to several hundred. The largest wading bird in Colorado, great blue herons search shorelines for crayfish, frogs, and small fish. W. PERRY CONWAY

The Waters of Life

Sandhill Crane

Scientific name: Grus canadensis
Range: Northwestern Colorado, flyways on East and West
  slopes
Habitat: Marshes, wetlands
Size: 40 to 48 inches long, 10 to 12 pounds, six-foot wingspan
Identifying traits: Large size, long legs, bare red patch on
  head, neck extended in flight

Theirs is a dance without music, grace without equal in the bird world. On their traditional dancing grounds, the sandhill cranes bob and weave, bowing, unfurling their wings, and then springing into the air only to settle softly to the ground again.

Colorado has seen the mating dances of two subspecies of sandhill cranes. The lesser sandhill is a migrant. Both spring and fall, lesser sandhill cranes pass in flocks that sometimes can grow very large. A 1957 observer reported that "skein after skein passed for hours late into the evening." Large numbers often stop at Prewitt Reservoir, and along the lower Arkansas and North Platte rivers. Others can be seen over Delta and the Grand Valley on the western slope. But the glance is fleeting. The breeding grounds of the lesser sandhill crane are in Canada and Alaska.

Although 17,000 to 18,000 greater sandhill cranes migrate through Colorado in the spring and fall, the mating dance of the greater sandhill crane is becoming rare in the state. Once it nested throughout much of the state, even above 9,500 feet. But today breeding is restricted principally to two areas in northwestern Colorado: a stretch of islands on the Yampa River and a few wet meadows and beaver ponds in portions of Routt and Jackson counties. As a result, Colorado's nesting population of greater sandhill cranes has been placed on Colorado's endangered species list.

The huge birds leave their southern wintering areas and gather on dancing grounds in Colorado. There the pairs, which mate for life, dance in the growing spring sunlight until the snow has melted off the breeding grounds at higher altitudes. The female usually lays two eggs, and both sexes share in the month-long incubation. Survival of both chicks is rare.

Sandhill cranes need solitude to nest successfully. Disturbances can cause them to abandon a site. In undisturbed habitat, sandhill cranes have been successfully used as foster parents in an ongoing program to revitalize the population of whooping cranes, an endangered species.

During exploration and early settlement of the state, many sandhill cranes were shot for food. Like many bird species, particularly the heron and the egret, the sandhill also suffered losses during the late 1800s, when elaborately feathered hats were in fashion for women.

But the real beauty of the sandhill crane is not to be found in a few feathers on a woman's hat. It is in the graceful spring dance, in the duets sung at dusk and dawn, in the echo of a flock overhead, calling to each other in the dark.

Mallard

Scientific name: Anas platyrhynchos
Range: Statewide
Habitat: Wetlands, rivers, lakes
Size: 21 to 27 inches, two to three pounds
Identifying traits: Brilliant green head and neck (male), blue
  wing patch (female)

On the maps it has no name; it is just a pothole lake on the plains of Kiowa County. On an autumn morning, its waters are laden with waterfowl—geese, coots, pintails, buffleheads, and so many mallards the lake seems to ripple with a metallic green. The mallard drake is one of the most common and easily identified wildlife species in Colorado.

The ponds and reservoirs of eastern Colorado are a kind of crossroads for waterfowl. Between the northern breeding grounds and the southern wintering grounds, these small bodies of water are a resting place for huge flocks of migrating birds. Colorado has recorded 28 species of duck, some of them seasonal migrants, others regular nesters.

The mallard is by far the most numerous and widespread nesting duck in the state. It breeds everywhere from the plains to high-country headwaters. Major breeding areas include North Park, the San Luis Valley, South Park, and the watersheds of the South Platte, Arkansas, Gunnison, and Cache la Poudre rivers. These and other areas in the state produce more than 100,000 young each year. Although many of the nesting mallards move south in cold weather, other flocks move in from the north. An estimated 250,000 mallards winter here.

Mallards begin laying eggs in April. If a brood is destroyed early in the season, a second batch may be laid. The female lays between seven and 10 eggs, one each

107

day, and pads them with down plucked from her breast. The drake leaves the area soon after the eggs are laid, gathering with other males while the hens incubate their nests for about 26 days. Soon after the eggs hatch, the hens lead the young to open waters. Although the chicks can swim early, it will be another eight weeks before they can fly. The water serves as both a feeding ground and protection from predators.

The mallard needs the protection. It is faced with many threats. Snakes, coyotes, badgers, raccoons, magpies, crows, and foxes are among the creatures that will eat eggs and prey on both chicks and adults. Humans have both helped and hurt the mallard. Almost three-quarters of the game birds taken in the state are mallards. Almost three million ducks nationwide are poisoned each year by ingesting lead shot used by hunters. When agricultural lands are plowed too close to the perimeter of ponds, the cover necessary for successful nesting is destroyed. The U.S. Fish and Wild-

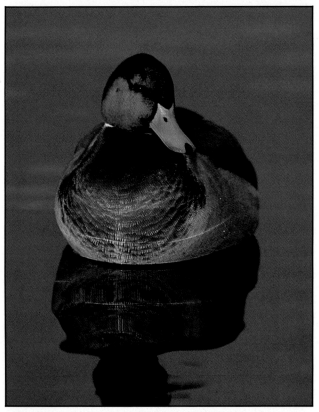

A bright green head and rusty breast distinguish a male mallard in breeding plumage. Mallards are the most common ducks in Colorado, both as resident and migratory species. They often inhabit city ponds in addition to prairie potholes, slow rivers, and shallow lakes and reservoirs. Large concentrations of mallards and other waterfowl may be seen at any of Colorado's eastern reservoirs during the fall migration, usually the first three weeks of October. CHASE SWIFT

life Service estimates that, due to draining and filling, the United States has lost 54 percent of its original wetlands.

On the other hand, major conservation efforts have been aimed at protecting the mallard and other waterfowl in Colorado. More than 25,000 acres in the San Luis Valley, representing one of the southernmost major duck breeding grounds in the United States, have been set aside as the Monte Vista and Alamosa national wildlife refuges. While many wetland areas have been lost, irrigation of croplands has inadvertently created new habitats.

Congress recently passed a law that, as of the 1991-92 hunting season, will ban the use of lead shot nationwide. And, in one of the largest undertakings in wildlife history, the United States and Canada have recently agreed to implement a $1.5 billion, 15-year North American Waterfowl Management Plan. Its goal is to increase the number of birds flying south in the fall to 100 million. That number will include geese, coots, mergansers, and a collection of duck species.

As on an autumn morning on a prairie pond, a large number will flash the bright green head and neck feathers of the mallard drake.

American Dipper

Scientific name: Cinclus mexicanus
Range: Mountainous areas
Habitat: Clear, fast-moving streams from foothills to timberline
Size: Six to eight inches long, two ounces
Identifying traits: Slate-blue color, bobbing motion

Its song is as clear and fluid as a mountain stream. This small, dull-gray bird with its short upturned tail, conspicuous whitish eyelids, and stubby wings is, as naturalist John Muir described it, "the humming-bird of blooming waters." Appropriately, the dipper, or water ouzel, is heard most often in Colorado along clear streams—from within the shadows of the mountains at the edge of the plains to timberline.

The dipper is an aquatic bird, the only member of the Passerine order that has evolved to feed underwater. Standing at the edge of a flowing stream, bobbing up and down in the dipping motion from which it takes its common name, it will suddenly plunge and disappear into the current.

The Waters of Life

Using a shelf of ice as a diving board, a dipper plunges into the South Platte River. These small gray birds actually dive underwater and walk on the stream bottom to feed on aquatic insects. But they are most often seen flying just above a rushing stream or standing on a streamside rock, where they bob, or dip, almost constantly. WENDY SHATTIL / BOB ROZINSKI

The dipper seems more at home underwater than in the air. Its short wings allow it to "fly" below the surface, holding to the bottom, working against the current. Its unwebbed feet clutch at river stones to provide balance. A membrane closes over its nostrils to keep out water. The bird can stay under for as long as 45 seconds, searching for aquatic insects, fish eggs, even small crustaceans.

The dipper's thick plumage and an enlarged gland at the base of its tail that secretes a waterproofing oil for its feathers seem to make it impervious to cold. Even when ice lines the banks and every rock is domed with snow, the dipper can be found diving for food.

From the very beginning, the dipper's life is closely tied to the water. The nest is woven of moist moss and set just at the edge of spraying whitewater, on a rock ledge behind a small waterfall, or under a bridge. The female lays three to six tiny white eggs. From the moment the chicks hatch, they are surrounded by the sound of falling water, a sound echoed in the song of this streamside bird.

Other Common Wildlife of Riparian Habitats

BIRDS: western wood-pewee, killdeer, least sandpiper, Wilson's phalarope, ring-billed gull, mourning dove, house wren, Virginia's warbler, American dipper, European starling, yellow warbler, yellow-rumped warbler, lark sparrow, Lincoln's sparrow, and yellow-headed blackbird.

MAMMALS: water shrew, eastern cottontail, rock squirrel, fox squirrel, raccoon, spotted skunk, and river otter.

AMPHIBIANS / REPTILES: tiger salamander, Woodhouse's toad, plains leopard frog, western painted turtle, orangehead spiny lizard, wandering garter snake, and western plains garter snake.

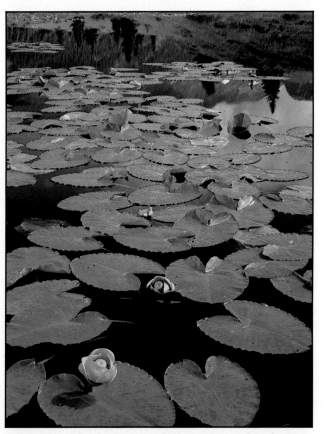

Yellow water lilies blossom in a high country pond in the San Juan Mountains. Although the pond and its adjacent vegetation constitute a riparian area, it is surrounded by the subalpine habitat reflected on its surface. Riparian areas actually occur in all major habitat zones and frequently form the most productive wildlife areas within those zones. LARRY ULRICH

109

Oblivious to the Denver skyscrapers rising beyond it, a coyote searches for prey at the Rocky Mountain Arsenal. Coyotes and other wild animals often inhabit urban areas, much to the surprise of human residents. But like wild areas, urban areas offer food and shelter, two basic requirements for wild animals anywhere. As a result, animals in urban areas provide excellent wildlife-watching opportunities close to home. SHERM SPOELSTRA

110

The Hand of Man
Human-influenced Habitats

A European starling waits out a Colorado snowstorm. The first flock of starlings appeared in Colorado in 1937. Since then, they have colonized the entire state and seem equally at home in the mountains and the cities. In the fall and winter, starlings and blackbirds gather in huge flocks, sometimes numbering in the hundreds of thousands. DENNIS HENRY

A bus roars by. Footsteps clatter on the pavement. A siren wails in the distance. Machinery hums. The heart of downtown Denver is not a place usually associated with wildlife. It is a landscape of steel and glass and concrete, a place totally dominated by man—almost.

Although a big city at heart, Denver is wild around the edges. On top of the skyscrapers along 17th Street, killdeer build their nests. Geese fly in V-formations over Washington Park. Fox squirrels chatter on the Capitol lawn. Short-eared owls sit silently in the cool, dark warehouses at Union Station. Coyotes hunt along Cherry Creek. Peregrine falcons streak across the slits of blue sky visible between buildings.

In the 200 years since Zebulon Pike came to what is now Colorado, humans have come to dominate the landscape. Immense tracts of prairie have been plowed under and converted to cropland. Cattle have replaced herds of elk, deer, and bison in the valleys. Sparkling cities have grown up against the foothills. Dams have flooded the valleys upstream and drained them dry downstream. Much of Colorado wears a human face.

But with its national parks, national forests, and wildlife preserves, Colorado is fortunate to have tracts of untouched landscape remaining. In pure numbers, the percentage of the state's acreage that has been lost to wildlife would seem small compared to other places. Yet wildlife habitat is more than numbers. It is space, food, water, solitude, and denning and breeding areas. If human development has not taken it all, it has taken some of the best.

Humans need many of the same things as wildlife: ease of travel, a good climate, flowing water, cover. So humans have chosen to live and develop many places that are also vital wildlife areas. Our roads follow rivers along

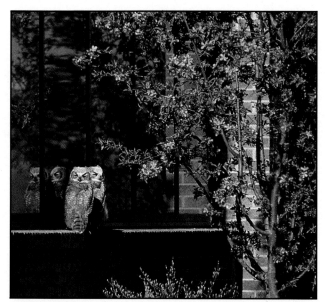

A matched pair of young great horned owls decorate a window ledge in Littleton. City dwellers may be surprised to find owls sitting on their windows, foxes prowling their backyards, and peregrine falcons flying overhead, but Colorado's urban areas support a variety of wildlife. WENDY SHATTIL / BOB ROZINSKI

Many residents of the Denver metropolitan area would think something was wrong with the world if they didn't see Canada geese (left) every day, so common are these birds in Denver and its suburbs. Flocks of several thousand winter on Denver-area golf courses, and large numbers inhabit Washington and City parks. Geese also live in Fort Collins' city parks and golf courses. GEORGE M. HAGER

which wildlife migrates. Our towns are set in valleys that serve as winter range. Our vacation homes and ski areas are built in prime calving, nesting, and denning spots. For many wildlife species, the result of human encroachment upon their habitat has been simple and predictable: the animals vanished. But for others, the outcome may be surprising.

Whether in the wild or in the heart of downtown Denver, wildlife still requires the basics of life: food, water, and shelter. Although the creation of cities may destroy the ability of some species to survive, it actually may meet the needs of others. Some species are tolerant of human development and adaptable to human presence. Small parks, roadsides, even backyard bird feeders, have helped to create conditions suitable to a wide array of species.

Birds are among the most adaptable creatures.

They are small, often inconspicuous, and usually do not require huge tracts of land on which to live. To a starling, the nook of a storefront sign is as suitable a cavity for nesting as the trunk of a tree. To a killdeer, the gravel on a rooftop makes as good a nesting site as the gravel of a riverbank. The lawns of golf courses and cemeteries make excellent feeding grounds for geese. A parking lot full of cars, each with a windshield full of crushed insects, makes a feast for a flock of house sparrows.

Home bird feeders have had a dramatic effect upon birds, changing their migration patterns and expanding their ranges. Some of the more reclusive birds that refuse to be lured to feeders can be found at the edges of Denver. Great blue herons nest at Chatfield Reservoir. Black-crowned night herons are commonly seen along the South Platte Greenway. Of more than 440 bird species noted in Colorado, almost 300 have been recorded in and

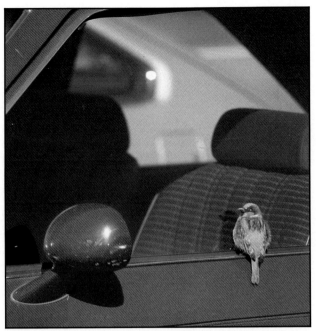

The first house sparrows in Colorado were observed in Pueblo in 1895. They were described as having "a very dingy appearance" as if they had been riding the rails. Perhaps that explains why this sparrow seems to be checking its appearance in the side mirror of a car in Littleton. Often ignored because it is so common, the high-pitched chirping of house sparrows is as much a part of city life as the rumble of traffic. SUSAN JENKINS

ornamental shrubs. Forays into town expose the animals to new dangers: unleashed dogs, fences, plate-glass windows. More than 3,000 deer a year are struck by automobiles across the state.

Although not a true urban species, the mountain lion has established a small but stable population in the foothills along the Front Range, preying on the deer. When the deer move lower toward the city, mountain lions are sometimes spotted within the limits of such cities as Boulder and Fort Collins. Another predator, the coyote, preys on smaller mammals at the edges of cities, in such places as the Fort Logan National Cemetery near Denver.

The smaller, less conspicuous mammals are more common in the city. Eastern fox squirrels are fed by picnickers in city parks. Cottontails move quietly among the shrubs around suburban areas. Beaver are found along the South Platte River and Cherry Creek. Where their towns have not been bulldozed or flooded, blacktail prairie dogs still burrow in vacant lots. As darkness falls over the city, nocturnal creatures such as freetail bats, raccoons, and striped skunks move among the streets.

The creation of ponds in parks and the protection of fringe areas along waterways have helped sustain populations of amphibians and reptiles within the city. The densities of some species, such as garter snakes and lined snakes, may actually be higher in the city than in the wild. There have been almost 30 species of amphibians and reptiles noted within the Denver metropolitan area: painted turtles, leopard frogs, eastern fence lizards, chorus frogs, tiger salamanders, and milk snakes among them.

Cities are not built with wildlife in mind. Yet urban settings offer adaptable animals several major advantages. A lack of large predators can mean lower mortality rates. Bird feeders, garbage cans, and gardens often provide more stable and concentrated food supplies. The nooks and crannies around buildings and bridges can provide good sites for nests and dens.

As cities grow, urban wildlife becomes an increasingly valuable resource. For some people, the deer along the roads, the birds on the telephone wires, and the frogs heard at sundown may be the only Colorado wildlife they experience. In 1979, the Colorado Division of Wildlife initiated an urban

around the capital city, including the five peregrine falcons released by the Colorado Division of Wildlife atop the Civic Center Plaza in 1988.

Large mammals have had a harder time in the city. They are more conspicuous than birds, and cover is scarce. They require more space. Still, some have come to thrive at the edges of our cities. Mule deer and white-tailed deer are the largest urban mammals. Preserved river corridors, such as the South Platte Greenway, have provided habitat for them. They also are at home on the grounds of the Air Force Academy in Colorado Springs, along the edges of the Rocky Mountain Arsenal near Denver, and at the National Center for Atmospheric Research in Boulder.

Such large animals can, at times, present problems in a city setting. Deer must regularly be chased off the runways at Stapleton and Jefferson County airports to prevent collisons. In winter and spring, deer move down into the backyards of Boulder, causing damage to gardens and wildlife program to enhance this important resource. The program encourages creation of backyard habitat; management of city wildlife areas such as Crown Hill in Jefferson County, Barr Lake outside Brighton, and the Littleton Floodplain Park; and education of the public about wildlife viewing opportunities.

The hand of man has deeply touched some parts of the Colorado landscape. Nonetheless, some creatures have adapted, even thrived, in the wake of development. The sight of a raccoon prowling the edge of a pond or the flutter of wings as starlings come to roost can make even the heart of the city seem suddenly wild. ■

Black-crowned Night Heron

Scientific name: Nycticorax nycticorax
Range: Mostly Eastern Colorado to foothills
Habitat: Riparian, reservoirs
Size: 23 to 28 inches long
Identifying traits: Shorter bill and neck, black back and crown

For several minutes, the black-crowned night heron holds as still as stone. On a boulder in midstream, it stands watching the waters of the South Platte flow by. The traffic noise from Interstate 25 is audible over the sound of the river. Unlike the great blue heron, which often stalks its prey, the night heron relies upon patience, waiting for what the river will bring it.

The night heron, as its name suggests, is most active at dusk, dawn, and in the dark. It hunts the waterways of eastern Colorado for snakes, fish, and small reptiles. With the protection of parks such as the Platte River Greenway, it is a more common sight.

A few night herons winter in Colorado. Migrants arrive on the plains or in the San Luis Valley in late March. They nest in colonies, often with other herons, their large nests set in midsized cottonwoods and box elders.

In early May, the female lays three to six light blue eggs. These are incubated by both sexes for 25 days until they hatch. The young are covered with a light brown fuzz that seems scruffy next to the stylish plumage of the adults with their black crowns and dark gray backs and wings.

The night heron is a less common sight than the great

Black-crowned night herons are stocky birds with black and white plumage and piercing red eyes. In flight, they almost seem to be headless, so inconspicuous is their neck and head. As their name implies, they are most active at dawn, dusk, and dark. W. PERRY CONWAY

blue. In flight, it does not seem as elegant. When it is spotted, it is most often hunched motionless upon a rock, waiting. Its beak flashes downward, taking something from the water almost too quickly to be seen, and it flies off around a bend.

Desert Cottontail

Scientific name: Sylvilagus auduboni
Range: Statewide below 7,000 feet
Habitat: Foothills and plains with abundant cover
Size: 12 to 15 inches long, one to three pounds
Identifying traits: Large ears, white tail

In the low light of dawn or dusk, a hillside or patch

114

The Hand of Man

of prairie can seem filled with them. The desert cottontail is the most numerous rabbit in Colorado, a status achieved as a result of its prodigious biotic potential.

In favorable weather conditions, the cottontail's breeding season can stretch from February to August. Females have been known to breed again just one hour after giving birth. With a gestation period of less than a month, the cottontail can produce five to seven litters of five young each during a single breeding season.

The nest is a simple hollow in the ground lined with fur or vegetation. The young rabbits are born blind and without fur. Their eyes open in a week, and their coats grow in by the time they first leave the nest, at the age of about two weeks.

Summers are spent feeding on such plants as blue grama grass, scarlet globemallow, western wheatgrass, and fringed sandwort. The cottontail travels over a system of trails, and in areas of high density the trails can become deeply worn into the soil. Active mostly at night, the cottontail spends its days in ''forms,'' small depressions scraped out beneath the cover of brush or overhanging branches.

The cottontail has been documented in a wide range of habitats, from rocky canyons to open plains and foothills up to 7,000 feet. It prefers areas of dense brush, in which it can hide from predators. Although it is often seen in residential areas, it is also abundant in wild habitats, such as the undeveloped lands along the South Platte River.

The desert cottontail does not change color in winter like the snowshoe hare. Through the winter, it forages on twigs and inner bark, often scarring the trunks of saplings and sometimes killing trees by eating bark in circles around them. It does not hibernate, but it may seek cover and remain inactive during periods of particularly harsh weather. It has even been known to take over the burrows of other animals.

With such a high reproductive rate, the cottontail could overrun the state. But an exceedingly high mortality rate brought about by winter and predators helps keep the population in check. It is estimated that as few as 15 percent of the young make it through their first year. Those seen grazing in the soft light of dusk or dawn are the survivors, escaping the cold, the hawks, the coyotes and foxes, slipping away from the owls, at least for the moment.

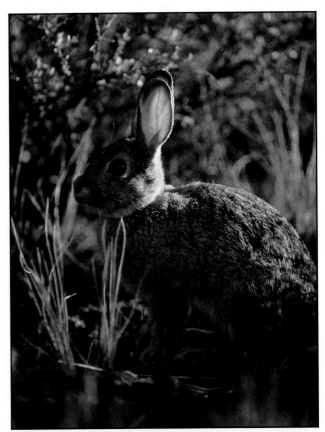

Ever alert, a desert cottontail listens and looks for predators such as owls, hawks, coyotes, and foxes. Its prodigious rate of reproduction helps compensate for heavy predation and high winter mortality. Enough desert cottontails survive to make the species the most abundant rabbit in Colorado and the most common rabbit observed in backyards and city parks.
TERRY WYGANT

Raccoon

Scientific name: Procyon lotor
Range: Throughout Colorado below 8,000 feet
Habitat: Cottonwood thickets, wetland forests, farmlands
Size: 20 to 45 inches long including tail, six to 30 pounds
Identifying traits: Black facial mask, ringed tail

For a species that is mostly nocturnal, the raccoon is one of the best-known creatures in North America. The distinctive ''mask'' around its eyes, its playful nature, and its track, which looks like a tiny human hand, make it unmistakable and memorable, even if it is not always popular.

The rattle of garbage cans at night, a sudden panic in the chicken coop, stalks of corn ravaged in the garden, these have become as common a sign of raccoons as their tracks in the riverside mud. The raccoon is intelligent and adaptable. It is one species that has likely expanded its range since the coming of modern civilization.

In Colorado, the raccoon is found mostly along the streams and near the agricultural lands of the eastern plains. On the Western Slope, the raccoon is less abundant and most often found along rivers such as the Colorado, the Yampa, and the San Juan. Although it is rare in the mountains, at least one animal has been recorded at over 11,500 feet in Rocky Mountain National Park, another sign of how readily adaptable this species can be.

A part of that adaptability comes from its varied diet. Raccoons will consume just about anything—birds' eggs, small mammals, snakes, frogs, berries, crayfish, melons, domestic corn, garbage. They will rest during the day

Tucked in the crook of a cottonwood tree, a bright-eyed raccoon seems ready to fulfill its reputation as a nighttime raider of suburban garbage cans. Although raccoons survive very well in wild areas, they readily exploit urban habitat, often denning in fireplace flues, eating dog food, and leaving distinctive, five-toed tracks in plundered gardens.
W. PERRY CONWAY

in any kind of cover they can find, from abandoned magpie nests to barn lofts. They often follow the same foraging routes at night.

The stories of raccoons washing their food before eating are true, more or less. The Latin name of the raccoon—*lotor*—translates to "the washer," and if water is nearby the raccoon will often rinse its food. But much of what it consumes is found far from water and is eaten as is.

Mating occurs in February or March. Birthing takes place most often in tree cavities, but it also has been recorded in rock caves, hollow logs, and even birds' nests. Around human developments, raccoon dens have been found in attics and chimneys.

After a gestation period of 63 days, the young are born just as spring is making a bountiful food supply available. At birth, the young are blind and deaf, and they weigh just two ounces. They are covered with a fine, yellowish fur, and the markings of the facial mask are visible as pigmentation in the skin. Within two months, the young grow to over two pounds and begin taking short foraging trips in the company of the female, who raises the young by herself. By fall, they are weaned and on their own.

Once the young reach full size in the second year, they have few predators. Raccoon coats were once popular, as was the "Daniel Boone" raccoon hat. But trapping has not cut significantly into the population. Coyotes will take a few, but raccoons are not easy prey for any species. They are good swimmers, agile climbers, and fierce fighters if cornered. With so few predators to worry about, raccoons can live for more than five years, rattling garbage cans, raiding gardens, stealing into chicken coops, and then vanishing back into the night.

Striped Skunk

Scientific name: Mephitis mephitis
Range: Statewide below timberline
Habitat: Varied, farmlands, open parks, riparian
Size: 25 to 30 inches long including tail, five to 10 pounds
Identifying trait: Black and white coloration, musky odor

With its white-on-black pelage and musky odor, the skunk is one of the most common and easily identifiable wildlife species in Colorado. Whether you see it waddling along a creekbed or just catch its scent from afar, there is no mistaking the skunk.

The most obvious identifying trait is the scent, a defensive device with few equals in the animal world.

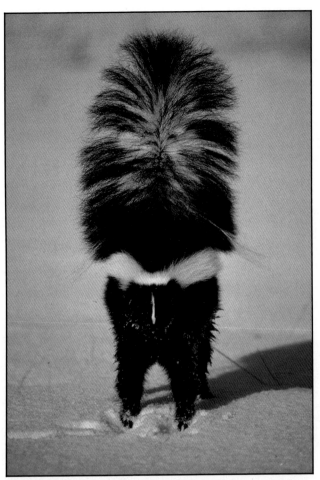

Some wildlife, such as this striped skunk, is better watched from afar. In fact, skunks don't seem to mind being observed when humans maintain a reasonable distance, and their behavior makes fascinating wildlife-watching. Still, skunks are smelled more often than they are seen, their olfactory calling card usually distributed at night when the animals are most active. WENDY SHATTIL / BOB ROZINSKI

The skunk can squirt musk stored in a pair of glands below its tail as far as 10 feet with amazing accuracy. Besides its indescribable smell, the fluid stings the eyes and temporarily blinds the victim.

Some predators learn their lesson with just a single dose. But the skunk still has a few dangerous enemies. Foxes, coyotes, and great horned owls can learn to take it without being sprayed. But the skunk is not a mainstay in the diet of any predator. Its greatest threats are disease and automobiles.

Even without much fear of predation, the skunk is mostly a night creature, foraging for everything from crayfish and birds' eggs to grasses and grasshoppers. The insects and mice the skunk consumes are almost enough to endear it to some homeowners who find skunks denned under their outbuildings or porches. Almost.

There are four species of skunks in Colorado, ranging almost statewide below timberline: the striped skunk (the most common), the eastern and western spotted skunks, and the hognose skunk.

The spotted skunk, as its name implies, has white markings in a mottled pattern across its back. It is smaller than the striped skunk; the male rarely exceeds two pounds or 18 inches in length. Because it is an agile climber, the spotted skunk is often called a "civet cat." It uses its climbing ability to prey upon birds and their eggs.

The fourth Colorado skunk is rare. Found mostly in the southeastern part of the state, the hognose skunk is at the northern extent of its range in Colorado. It can be identified by its flattened snout, its small ears, and the broad patch of white that covers most of its back.

Skunk tracks in the snow are a rare find. Although the males often stay active all winter, the females and young retreat to dens to sleep through the worst weather. The old dens of coyote or badgers are often appropriated, although the skunk has little problem digging its own into the south-facing slope of a hillside. The skunk's den is lined with twigs, grasses, and leaves.

Although each skunk species in Colorado breeds at a different time, the young of all are usually born in May or June. Anywhere from two to 10 young are born in a single annual brood, and they stay with their mother for up to a year.

With its effective defense, its varied diet, and its nocturnal habits, the skunk has managed to exploit many habitats in the state and has often done well in human-influenced areas. Residents near city parks or undeveloped waterways may be surprised at the number of skunks living nearby, venturing out at night, undetected except for the sharp, stinging scent that sometimes blows in on the night breeze.

Red Fox

Scientific name: Vulpes vulpes
Range: Statewide except extreme southeast
Habitat: Brushlands, forests, wetlands, farmlands
Size: Eight to 12 pounds, 38 to 50 inches long including tail,
*   14 to 16 inches tall at shoulder*
Identifying traits: Reddish color, white-tipped tail

The scene could have come out of Aesop's Fables. In eastern Colorado, a fox established a den right in the middle of a sheep pasture. Because the rancher was

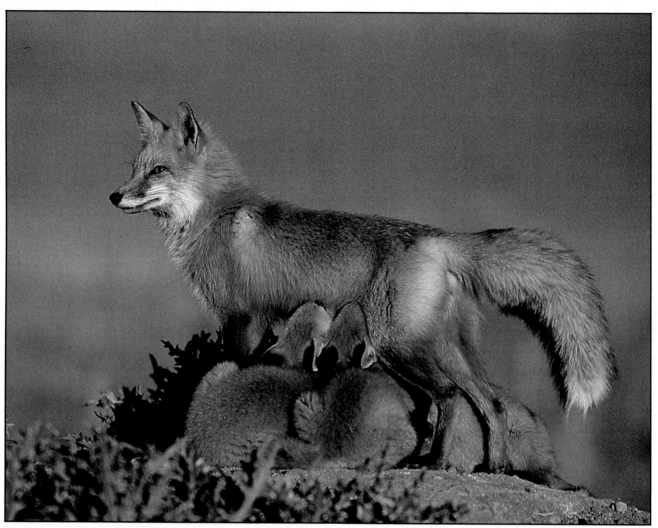

A red fox mother provides a stand-up meal to her hungry pups. Red foxes live in city areas quite well, although most human residents are unaware of their presence. Feeding mostly on small rodents, foxes utilize open areas such as cemeteries, parks, and golf courses. Of course, red foxes also inhabit agricultural and undeveloped areas throughout most of the state. GEORGE M. HAGER

concerned about possible predation, a wildlife manager stood watch for more than a month. The fox hunted mice, never bothering the ewes or lambs.

A highly adaptable species, the red fox is capable of many surprises. It is the most widely distributed of the four fox species in Colorado; it has been reported from above timberline to the eastern plains and western canyons. Within its range, it does not wander far. It covers the same well-worn hunting trails every night in search of food—grouse, quail, ducks, rabbits, muskrats, gophers, mice, and voles. It does not seem to be a picky eater and also consumes grass, berries, earthworms, corn, grasshoppers, and forbs. But mice are its primary prey. An adult fox can take up to 100 mice a week.

Despite its name, the red fox is not always red. It can be any one of three other colors—silver, black, or marked with a dark cross across its back—and all four colors can be found within one litter. No matter the color, the red fox can always be identified by its white-tipped tail, which does not appear in other Colorado foxes.

The red fox is a solitary animal except when mating and rearing its young. The fox takes a single mate as early as February, and the pair remain together until the young are on their own in the fall. A den is established, often in the burrow of another animal, such as a marmot, or in a rock crevice, culvert, or hollow beneath an old building. After a two-month gestation period, four or five (sometimes as many as 10) kits are born blind and lightly furred.

By their fifth week, the young begin to poke their noses out of the den and take short foraging trips with the adults, both of which hunt to feed the family. Dens are often littered with bones, feathers, and sticks that the young use as toys while the adults are off hunting. Once the kits leave the den, they are very playful; spring is a good time for fox-watching because of the frolicking.

The fox population in Colorado suffered from predator-control programs aimed at coyotes and wolves; foxes were attracted to the tainted meat used in the traps. Foxes also are preyed upon by eagles, coyotes, and bobcats. Those that do survive spend the winters alone, hunting by night and then curling up in whatever cover is available during the day, wrapping their bushy, white-tipped tails around their bodies for warmth.

Cliff Swallow

Scientific name: Hirundo pyrrhonota
Range: Plains to foothills
Habitat: Cliffs, buildings, bridges, waterways
Size: Five to six inches long
Identifying traits: White forehead, square tail, buffy rump patch

Pass in a canoe beneath a bridge on the South Platte River in suburban Denver and the air may suddenly be filled with swallows, flashes of orange and brown and white. While most birds nest singly and some in small rookeries, the cliff swallow nests in huge colonies that have been known to contain more than 3,000 pairs. They are the most dense gatherings of breeding vertebrates on the continent.

Once, the cliff swallow nested mainly on cliffs and the

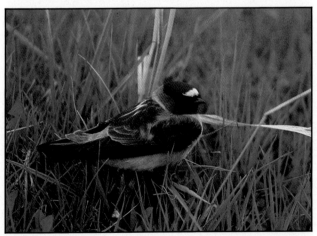

Like few other animals, cliff swallows take advantage of human settlement. To them, a bridge over a stream or river substitutes very nicely for a cliff, and Colorado bridges support thousands of cliff swallow nests. The insect-eating birds also nest on buildings near water. Cliff swallows are one of six swallow species in Colorado. SHERM SPOELSTRA

steep embankments of rivers, as its name implies. Since the coming of humans, it has taken in great numbers to culverts, bridges, and other overhanging structures. This colonial habitat has both advantages and disadvantages for the species. Against predators, there is safety in numbers, both because there are many eyes watching for danger and because in a dense colony a predator cannot destroy all the eggs or young in a single attack. Also, cliff swallows have been known to share information about food supplies. An unsuccessful forager, seeing a bird return to the nest with food, will often follow that bird back to the food source.

But closeness also has a price. A vast array of parasites pass through cliff swallow colonies. Studies have shown that as the number of birds in the colony increases, so does the prevalence of parasites. Increases in parasites have been shown to cause both a decrease in chick size and an increase in chick mortality. Big colonies also run the risk of being wiped out by a single incident, such as a flood, storm, or human disturbance.

The cliff swallow can be distinguished from other swallows in Colorado by its squared tail. Like all swallows, it is a summer resident, often arriving later than its relatives. Legends have arisen about the punctuality of the bird, such as that regarding the swallows of Capistrano. But the cliff swallow's return to its summer home actually depends upon weather conditions.

Egg-laying begins in June on the plains, later in the mountain parks. The female lays four to five eggs, sometimes in the nest of a different pair. Cowbirds sometimes lay their eggs in the swallows' nests, and house sparrows have been known to take over the completed structures. Within a month of hatching, the young can fly, and the birds gather in great flocks, slicing back and forth over the water to feed upon insects.

By late September, the cliff swallows have moved south to wintering grounds in South America. The endless rows of mud-daubed nests are as empty as a ghost town. Because of the parasite build-up, nests are rarely reused. The swallows will often alternate sites for successive breeding seasons. The once thriving nest site is left to crumble slowly in the late autumn rains.

European Starling

Scientific name: Sturnus vulgaris
Range: Throughout Colorado
Habitat: Farmlands, urban areas, parks, riparian
Size: Seven to nine inches long
Identifying traits: Shorter tail, noisy flocks, bill yellow in summer and black in winter

It was a small article in *The Denver Post*, on February 16, 1937. Few people took notice. It didn't seem like big news at the time. The first confirmed flock of starlings had been observed in Colorado, near Sterling. It was, however, another chapter of the amazing bird that has conquered a continent.

Not a native species, the starling was introduced into the U.S. in New York City in 1890-91. A hundred birds, and the seeds of a major controversy, were released.

From that small beginning, the North American population of starlings has reached an estimated 200 million, one-third of the world's starlings. It is now found from Alaska to Mexico and on both shores. In fall and winter it congregates with other birds in huge roosts. A mixed roost of blackbirds and starlings near Lamar, Colorado, was estimated to contain more than a million birds. Other roosts of over 100,000 have been recorded near Ione and Fort Lupton.

The starling is an aggressive breeder, outcompeting species such as mountain bluebirds, flickers, and small woodpeckers for nesting sites. Both parents aid in nest building, incubation, and rearing of the young. Reproductive success is high, accounting for the prodigious population growth in the last century.

This competition with other native species has turned many birders against starlings, and in places a kind of war has been waged against the birds. In the early part of the century, roosts were sprayed with water at night in hopes of freezing the birds. Explosive devices were put up to scare flocks off public property. Stuffed owls were set in trees to keep the birds at bay. Nothing worked for long or had any lasting effect on starlings.

Despite its less admirable traits, the starling has its finer qualities. Its intelligence is evident not only from its adaptability to human environments but from its ability to mimic other birds. Although their calls are raspy, starlings can mimic the songs of 56 U.S. species, according to one authority. In Denver what seem like the calls of killdeer, nighthawks, or yellow warblers often turn out to be starlings. They have even been known to echo the sounds of dogs and cats and a few words of human speech.

A starling's diet consists mostly of insects, beetles, caterpillars, grasshoppers, and even garbage off the city streets. For city-dwelling bird watchers, it is one of the most accessible species. And, in its own way, it can be considered beautiful. Its summer plumage seems metallic with tinges of purple and green on a black background. Its wings are woven with straw-colored specks.

Because it is so common, few people take notice of starlings on city streets. But had someone known that the birds reported in 1937 were to be the first of what is estimated to be over one million starlings in Colorado today, perhaps more notice would have been taken.

Other Common Wildlife of Urban Areas

BIRDS: Canada goose, American kestrel, rock dove, mourning dove, broad-tailed hummingbird, northern flicker, western wood-pewee, western kingbird, eastern kingbird, blue jay, black-billed magpie, American crow, black-capped chickadee, American robin, Bohemian waxwing, yellow warbler, house finch, pine siskin, lesser goldfinch, evening grosbeak, and house sparrow.

MAMMALS: big brown bat, black-tailed prairie dog, fox squirrel, Norway rat, house mouse, eastern yellowbelly racer, bullsnake, coyote, and beaver.

AMPHIBIANS / REPTILES: tiger salamander.

A male barn owl brings a white-footed mouse to feed his mate on the nest. The barn owl's relationship with people is indicated by its name. Where barns or belfries are not available, the bird nests in caves, hollow trees, and cavities in cliffs. Barn owls are scattered throughout Colorado. GEORGE M. HAGER

Wildlife in Colorado has survived better than wildlife in many other states, but some species have declined and even disappeared. More than 20 species are listed by the state as threatened or endangered. Recovery programs are helping some species, but the future for others remains uncertain. In this photo, an alpine lake in San Isabel National Forest near Colorado City reflects the fading light of day, a symbolic image of the fading tracks of these rare animals. WILLARD CLAY

122

Fading Tracks

Fading Tracks
Threatened & Endangered Species

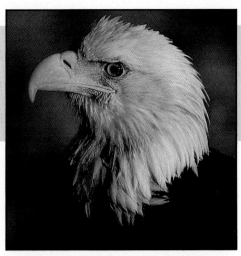

Bald eagles are still listed as endangered in Colorado and throughout the United States, but the nation's symbol is making a comeback, thanks to protective laws and the banning of the pesticide DDT. In Colorado, the number of eagles wintering in the state has increased in recent years.   J. B. HAYES

Something is missing from Colorado. The mountains still pierce the sky. The plains still stretch to meet the sunrise. The aspen leaves still turn gold in autumn. Yet, something is missing.

Gone is the opportunity to watch herds of bison spread like dark waves across the plains. Gone is the chance to see a grizzly trotting along a ridgeline in the San Juans or to hear the sound, as sharp as stars, of timber wolves howling. We are in danger of losing the flashy dance of the plains sharp-tailed grouse. We may never again see the ripples made by a bonytail chub on the mud-colored waters of the Yampa River. We may no longer hear the chorus of the wood frog on a spring night.

There are 23 species on Colorado's Threatened and Endangered Species List—six mammals, 10 birds, one amphibian, and six species of fish. Thirteen of the 23 are also on the federal list of threatened and endangered species.

The Secretary of the Interior decides what species will be included on the federal list, while the state list is overseen by the Colorado Wildlife Commission. A species is classified as ''threatened'' when its population has declined, its habitat is in danger of being reduced, and it is on the verge of becoming ''endangered.'' A species is ''endangered'' when its population has declined drastically and it is in immediate danger of becoming extinct.

Species are added to or dropped from the lists as their status changes. In 1985, several species were dropped from the lists, including the white pelican and five fish: the Colorado River cutthroat trout, the Rio Grande cutthroat trout, the plains orangethroat darter, the Johnny darter, and the Arkansas River speckled chub.

Perhaps more than any other species, grizzly bears are not compatible with civilization. The bears once roamed Colorado from the mountains to the plains, but their numbers dwindled as the land was settled. Grizzlies were shot, poisoned, trapped, and simply overrun as wilderness vanished under farms, ranches, and cities. For many years, grizzly bears were thought to be gone from Colorado. Then in 1979 a female grizzly was killed when it attacked a bowhunter in the San Juan Mountains. A subsequent, two-year search in the area failed to find another grizzly. But reports of grizzlies persist, especially in the San Juans. Do grizzlies still exist in Colorado? A definite answer remains as elusive as the great bear. TOM & PAT LEESON

There are two other state classifications that reflect species needing additional attention. Species of "special concern" are those species recently taken off the state's threatened and endangered list or those species that may need to be added to the list. Species of "undetermined status" are species about which too little is known to accurately determine their status in the state. The Colorado Division of Wildlife has established a priority system to study animals in these classifications.

Of all our environmental concerns, extinction is the most critical. We can stop acid rain. We can devise ways to rid the environment of toxic chemicals. We can recycle scarce resources. But no technology exists to recreate a wild species. The extinction of a species quakes with finality. Once a species is deemed extinct, it will require, as

scientist William Beebe has written, "another heaven and another earth . . . before such a one can be again."

Fluctuations in wildlife numbers, even in the number of species on earth, are a natural occurrence. Nature's balance is not a straight, unwavering line. It is dynamic. Extinction is a natural part of that balance.

As many as 90 percent of the species that have existed on earth are now believed to be extinct. Some were victims of long-term climatic changes; some lost the competition for limited resources to other species. A species, like an individual, may have a natural lifespan on earth. When conditions become unsuitable, it dies out.

As a natural principle, extinction is, by itself, not alarming. It is the rate of extinction and the human influence on that rate that is troubling. An estimated seven species disappeared during the 17th century. In the next 100 years, 11 species became extinct. By the 19th century, the rate had increased to 27. In 1974, the extinction rate hit 100 species each year, and it has continued to grow. One species may now be lost to the world with each passing day. In the lesser known regions of earth, species may actually be going extinct before they are documented by science. Before we know they exist, they are gone.

The main cause of extinction has been the alteration of habitat caused by human development. As much as 60 percent of the nation's wetlands, areas vital to a wide array of wildlife, have been drained, plowed under, or paved over. The world's rain forests, the most diverse and least understood ecosystems in the world, are being destroyed at the rate of 17 million acres a year.

Even in Colorado, some 40,000 acres of habitat, an area the size of Aurora, is altered every year by road-building, urban sprawl, agriculture, logging, ski-area development, the construction of reservoirs, and other development. That translates to more than four acres lost every hour of every day. With the population of Colorado expected to double not long after the turn of the century, that rate will likely increase.

In an effort to combat this, the Colorado Division of Wildlife was one of the first state wildlife agencies in the nation to begin a nongame program. Initiated in 1972, the program focuses on the management of more than 750 nongame species in Colorado. Through this program, more than 500 peregrine falcons have been reintroduced to the state. More than 100 river otters have been released. Some 100,000 fry of greenback trout have been stocked. Efforts have been made to purchase or lease habitat critical to wildlife or to work with landowners to ensure proper management.

Much of the funding for these efforts has come from a check-off on state income tax returns. Begun in 1977, the check-off program was the first of its kind, providing taxpayers with the opportunity to help wildlife programs through donations made directly through their tax forms. Already, the state program has raised more than $6.5 million.

Today, radio telemetry is used to follow the movements of elusive creatures. Satellites are used to map vegetation types and habitat loss. Solar-powered stream gauges warn of drastic changes in water flow or quality. Still, even with all our technology, there is much we do not know about the status of wildlife. No one can say with scientific certainty whether grizzly bears survive in the state. Our knowledge of wolverines and lynx is too scant to document the extent of the decline in the population and range of either creature. No one, not even the experts, can say if the Arkansas River speckled chub will ever again be found.

More research, continued public support, and individual involvement are needed to more fully document the status of wildlife in our state and to come to understand the consequences of our own actions upon the natural world. And, too, we need to foster a deeper respect for wildlife and its place on the landscape. Wildlife is more than just something to hunt, photograph, or check off on a list.

In the face of such gaps in our knowledge, the extinction of any species, no matter how seemingly obscure, has the potential to sever ties in the complex web of life, ties that we do not yet fully understand and ties which, eventually, may prove vital to man's own survival on the planet. ■

Although rare, both the greater prairie chicken, shown here, and the lesser prairie chicken provide excellent viewing opportunities on their mating grounds in March and April. The Colorado Division of Wildlife and The Nature Conservancy lead tours to watch greater prairie chickens on private land near Wray, Colorado; while the lesser prairie chicken may be seen at a developed viewing location in Comanche National Grassland near Campo in southeastern Colorado. Dancing usually takes place at dawn, so viewers should arrive before daybreak. DENNIS & MARIA HENRY

125

White pelicans preen before their reflection. The "centerboard" on top of the beaks of the three pelicans in the middle appears only during the breeding season. Although these large white birds with black wing tips may be seen at many reservoirs on Colorado's eastern plains, they nest only at Riverside Reservoir near Masters. Saving the nesting islands there has been a success story for Colorado's endangered wildlife program. JOHN & KAREN HOLLINGSWORTH

White Pelican

Scientific name: Pelecanus erythrorhynchos
Range: Northeastern Colorado
Habitat: Waterways, marshes
Size: Up to five feet long, up to 20 pounds, eight- to nine-foot wingspan
Identifying traits: Black-tipped wings, yellow bill, white plumage, neck folded in flight

On a routine aerial survey in May 1962, two Division of Wildlife biologists came across a sight in Riverside Reservoir that was anything but routine: nesting white pelicans. Although pelicans had been known to summer in the state since 1873, no pelican nests had ever been observed here. But the excitement of the discovery was soon tempered by a grim realization. The only island ever known to hold nesting white pelicans in Colorado was rapidly eroding away.

Set far out on the plains, treeless, barren, often lost in swirls of sand, Pelican Island in Riverside Reservoir is unimpressive. Yet, although it rarely attracts humans, the island is a summer haven for the white pelican.

Pelicans have very specific nesting requirements. The best sites are on islands in freshwater lakes with little brush to impede takeoffs and landings. There must be few predators, solitude, and a supply of rough fish such as carp and suckers within flying distance. But there seem to be other factors that even biologists cannot discern. Although there are other islands in other reservoirs nearby, none supports nesting pelicans. An attempt to coax them to a manmade island in Latham Reservoir was unsuccessful.

Unfortunately for the birds, wind and wave action destroyed the original Pelican Island. They moved to another island on the south side of the reservoir. That one also was threatened by erosion until a major reconstruction effort was undertaken. Despite the work, the stability of Pelican Island continues to be in question.

Even with whole islands disappearing out from under

them, the pelican population has thrived. From the original 250 nesting pairs in 1962, the population has grown to 600 to 700 pairs today. Including non-breeding birds, there is a total of 2,500 pelicans summering in the state. In 1985, the pelican was removed from the Colorado list of threatened and endangered species.

The white pelican is built to fish. Unlike the brown pelican, it does not dive headlong into the water. Instead it swims rapidly along, scooping up fish in its large, pouched bill. Flocks of pelicans have been known to work together, encircling a school of fish in a kind of water-borne roundup.

The young are born blind and featherless but quickly get a covering of white down. They grow to three or four pounds in just a few weeks. When they leave the nest, the young band together in large groups known as ''pods.''

By fall, the birds have migrated to wintering sites in Mexico. Each spring they return to a dubious future. With the construction of numerous reservoirs, the breeding population is higher today than ever. Yet islands, each one of them dutifully dubbed ''Pelican Island,'' continue to disappear out from under them. Without the island in Riverside Reservoir, the birds may not breed here. But without continued human assistance, the latest Pelican Island may soon vanish beneath the water—along with the hopes of keeping a breeding population of white pelicans in Colorado.

Lynx

Scientific name: Felis lynx
Range: Mountainous areas
Habitat: Coniferous forests
Size: Average of 18 pounds, up to 40 pounds
Identifying traits: Tufted ears, dark-tipped tail
Status: Endangered in Colorado

In February 1980, researchers discovered a set of tracks crossing West Chicago Creek in Clear Creek County. The catlike tracks cut between two thick stands of spruce and did not sink deeply, even in the snow. They were the first documented evidence of lynx in Colorado since 1974. Only a few scattered signs have been seen since.

Colorado represents the southern extent of lynx country. An animal trapped near Cumbres Pass in 1919 is the southernmost lynx ever documented in North America. Lynx have never been abundant in the state, nor very thoroughly studied. Since lynx and bobcat are so similar,

visual sightings are at best inconclusive. Still, the observation records date back to 1870.

The lynx is similar to the bobcat in appearance, but it is larger and its tail has an unbroken dark tip. Tufts of stiff, dark hair rise prominently from the tips of its ears. It hunts mostly at night within a home range of six to eight square miles, taking snowshoe hares, mice, grouse, and, sometimes, deer or elk. When larger prey is taken, the lynx hides any meat not initially consumed and returns to it later. Lynx prefer thick stands of spruce-fir forest on cold, northern slopes.

The lynx breeds in February, and the female bears a litter of about four in May. Survival rates in the young are closely tied to the abundance of snowshoe hares.

The lynx is a secretive creature, and much of the existing knowledge about it is tentative. With so little evidence, scientists cannot even pinpoint with authority the extent or causes of the decline of lynx in the state. Pushed by development and human encroachment, lynx seem to have moved to higher elevations. Rarely, if ever, is sign of a lynx found today below 9,000 feet. In the early part of the century, observations were made as low as 6,000 feet.

The dearth of information about the lynx is why a single set of tracks can be so important. Each scrap of evidence is a step toward documenting a simple fact: lynx do still

Oversized paws act like snowshoes for the lynx, a secretive cat of spruce-fir forests on cold, northern slopes. More commonly found in Canada and Alaska, lynx rarely appear as far south as Colorado, but they have been sighted near the Vail ski area and in a few other remote, high-country locations. CLAUDE STEELMAN

127

The sun set quickly on the vast bison herds that once blackened Colorado's plains. Although bison no longer roam wild in Colorado, several semi-domestic herds still exist. Two excellent places to see bison are Genesee Park near Denver and the Rawhide Power Plant north of Fort Collins. SHERM SPOELSTRA

exist in Colorado. Perhaps with this knowledge, we will have the time to come to know this elusive creature, to make sure its tracks will always be found somewhere in the fresh Colorado snow.

Bison

Scientific name: Bison bison
Historic range: Throughout Colorado, extinct in the wilds today
Habitat: Plains, mountain parks
Size: Five to six feet tall at shoulder, up to 2,200 pounds (male); females a third smaller
Identifying traits: Large size, shaggy mane

At first glance, the long, rolling expanse of South Park has the look of bison country. You feel that at any moment you could top a small rise and discover a herd big enough to shake the earth with its stampede. To the south lies Cochetopa Pass, named "Buffalo Gate" by the Utes for the deeply rutted trails made by the herds crossing from the plains. Both Pike and Fremont came upon huge herds here. Pike claimed that on the banks of the nearby Arkansas River there were enough animals "if used without waste, to feed all the savages in the

United States territory for one century." But then it hits: less than two centuries later, the bison are gone.

Once an estimated 60 million bison of two subspecies—plains and mountain—ranged the continent. The sight of immense herds of this, the largest terrestrial mammal native to North America, was impressive. James Wilkinson, a scout for the 1806 Pike Expedition, returned from a day's ride near Cimarron claiming, "I do solemnly assert that, if I saw one, I saw more than 9,000 buffaloes during the day's march."

In those days, both subspecies lived in Colorado. The plains bison turned the horizons of the eastern plains dark with their passing. The slightly smaller mountain bison could be found in the high parks and mountain meadows. There are even stories of Arapaho Indians hunting bison atop Thatch-top Mountain in what is now Rocky Mountain National Park. In 1983, hikers discovered a pair of bison skulls in a melting icefield near the headwaters of the Big Thompson River, confirming the historic range of the mountain bison.

Almost as soon as early explorers began marveling at the size of the bison herds, the shooting started. Bison were shot for food by Indians, trappers, prospectors, and explorers. Pike's party shot 56 while in Colorado, taking 19 shots to bring down one animal and verifying a remark of George Frederick Ruxton that "No animal requires so much killing as a buffalo." Market hunters

Fading Tracks

were commissioned to supply meat to workers laying the tracks of the transcontinental railroad. One of them, "Buffalo Bill" Cody, killed 4,200 animals in just eight months.

Bison were also shot for their hides. A huge tannery built in Greeley processed more than 10,000 hides a year. In 1882, the Northern Pacific Railroad hauled more than 200,000 hides from all over the West. Bison were killed from trains for sport. People could buy special tickets to shoot the animals from the safety of the railroad cars. Bison were shot so that their bones could be used as fertilizer. A pile of bones taken from an estimated 90,000 animals was once hauled by rail out of Springfield, Colorado.

But the demise of the bison can be attributed mostly to the U.S. Army. Annihilating the bison was seen as a way to wage war on the Indians who depended upon the species for survival. Only 80 years after the Louisiana Purchase, more than 50 million bison had been exterminated.

In 1872, the territorial governor passed laws attempting to protect many of Colorado's wildlife species. The laws did little good in the case of the bison. The last wild buffalo in northwestern Colorado was killed in 1884 near Juniper Springs on the Yampa River. Four years later, the last animal of the eastern plains herd was killed near Springfield.

By 1893, only five herds of mountain bison were known to exist anywhere in America. One, in Yellowstone National Park, was protected by a law passed by Congress in 1894. The other four herds were in Colorado—a few animals in Middle Park, just over 20 in the Kenosha Range, a dozen surrounding Hahn's Peak in the Park Range, and a few in the area of Dolores. These were left unprotected, setting the stage for a dubious distinction for the state of Colorado.

In 1897, a small herd of two bulls, a cow, and a calf were cornered in the Lost Park area of South Park and shot. The last unprotected herd of wild bison in America lay dying on the hard ground. With it, a sad chapter in North American wildlife history came to an end on Colorado soil.

From a few animals protected on game farms and reserves, the bison population in America has grown to about 30,000 animals today. Domestic herds can be seen at game farms throughout Colorado, but the wild herds are gone. The wind across South Park echoes as if through a hollow, sun-bleached bone.

Bald eagles can be seen at several locations in Colorado. In the spring, nesting eagles can be observed from a boardwalk at Barr Lake near Brighton. In the winter, as many as 500 bald eagles migrate to Colorado, and many of these birds may be seen along the South Platte and Arkansas rivers, Barr Lake, the Rocky Mountain Arsenal, many reservoirs along the Front Range, the San Luis Valley, and along the Colorado River from Rifle to the Utah border. SHERM SPOELSTRA

Bald Eagle

Scientific name: Haliaeetus leucocephalus
Range: Scattered winter visitor along waterways and in San Luis Valley
Habitat: Open waterways, reservoirs, riparian zones
Size: Six- to eight-foot wingspan, up to 12 pounds, 31 to 37 inches long
Identifying traits: White-feathered head and tail, large size
Status: Endangered in Colorado and nationally

Snowflakes falling as big as feathers over Horsethief Canyon make it difficult to see the bald eagle on the branch of a cottonwood beside the Colorado River. Our canoes float silently on the water, our paddles drawn up. In winter, these canyons west of Grand Junction are almost deserted. But, drawn by the open waters, the bald eagles gather here. Our canoes drift closer.

The bald eagle is a majestic bird, whether perching stoically on a cottonwood snag or soaring in wide circles in the sky. It is a symbol of power and mystery that has been recognized for thousands of years. The Hopis fired its symbol onto pottery. Ancient cultures scratched its likeness onto silent canyon walls. The Utes coveted its feathers for ceremonial clothing.

The bird was chosen to symbolize a fledgling United States in 1782, although the decision was not a unanimous one. "For my part," Ben Franklin said in a letter two years after the designation, "I wish the Bald Eagle had not been chosen as the representative of our country. He is a bird of bad moral character; he does not get his living honestly... besides, he is a rank coward."

Others, it seems, agreed with Ben Franklin and expressed their opinions with more deadly tools than the pen. For all its honors and symbolism, the bird has suffered at the hand of man. Fishermen have shot it on sight, fearing it would deplete sport fisheries. Sheep ranchers have shot both bald and golden eagles to keep them from taking lambs—a deed unlikely for the bald eagle. Poachers looking to sell the feathers or the carcasses for mounts have taken many birds. Today, shooting or trapping any bald eagle is illegal, but ironically the bird was not protected by law until 1940, 158 years after we took it as our national symbol.

Even more than from guns and traps, the bald eagle has suffered from a silent killer: DDT. The pesticide has washed into waterways and accumulated in fish populations preyed upon by the eagle. The result has been a thinning of egg shells and lower fledgling survival rates.

Pesticide use, habitat loss, interference with nesting sites, and continued illegal shooting all have decimated the bald eagle population. In 1976, the U.S. Fish and Wildlife Service placed the bird on its threatened and endangered lists in the lower 48 states.

In Colorado, the bald eagle is mostly a winter visitor. In recent times, more nests and wintering birds have been observed along open waterways such as the Colorado, Green, and South Platte rivers. The eagles sometimes gather in great numbers along reservoirs that do not freeze. In the winter of 1987-88, more than 50 were counted near Cheesman Reservoir southwest of Denver.

Bald eagles also turn up in some unlikely places. They often winter below the spillways of dams where the water is kept open. In December 1988, a 3,600-acre section of the buffer zone at the Rocky Mountain Arsenal northwest of Denver was designated as a Special Bald Eagle Management Area by the U.S. Fish and Wildlife Service. The area adjacent to arsenal land, where various pesticides and chemical weapons have been produced for more than four decades, is the winter home of as many as 30 eagles.

The greatest concentration of wintering eagles in the state occurs at another seemingly unlikely spot: the San Luis Valley. In this dry, high-altitude valley in one of the coldest winter regions in the nation, 200 to 300 eagles gather each winter within and around the Alamosa and Monte Vista national wildlife refuges. There they find protection, solitude, and a stable, abundant food supply in the form of waterfowl, prairie dogs, and fish, particularly carp.

Back on the Colorado River, the snow is still falling. Calmly, the eagle in the cottonwood turns its head to watch us as we pass downstream. Before we round the bend, it unfurls its wings to take off. The weight of the air against its wings snaps the branch upon which it rested, and the sound echoes through the canyon like a gunshot.

The bald eagle has, for too many years, heard the sounds of real gunshots follow it across its range. But with a better understanding of the bird, the preservation of some of its habitat, and the banning of DDT, the bald eagle is making a comeback in North America.

The bird we are watching floats out over the river and follows the canoes downstream, passing so closely that we can hear the sound of its wingbeats. Against the canyon walls and the winter sky, it looks majestic, a sight at which even Ben Franklin would have marvelled.

River Otter

Scientific name: Lutra canadensis
Historic range: Statewide
Habitat: Streams, rivers
Size: 10 to 30 pounds, three to four feet long including tail
Identifying traits: Sleek body, long and rounded tail
Status: Endangered in Colorado

The canoe drifts quietly in Ponderosa Gorge. A researcher of the Colorado Division of Wildlife lays his paddle down and raises a radio antenna. As the canoe spins in the current, he points the antenna downstream, listening to a faint beeping sound: The river otter has come home to the Dolores River.

Less than 200 years ago, the river otter, a member of

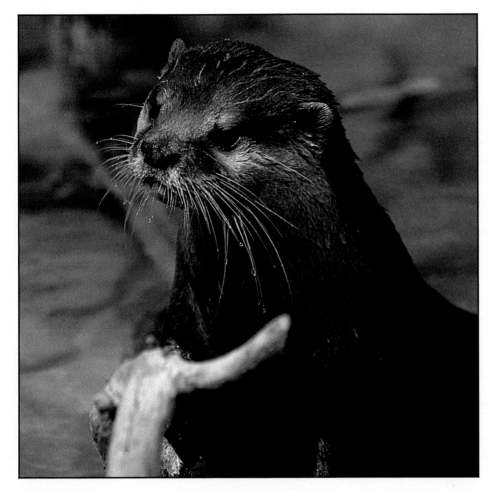

Considered endangered in Colorado, river otters inhabit parts of Rocky Mountain National Park, the Cache la Poudre River, the Piedra River, and the upper reaches of the Colorado River. However, their numbers may increase if an active program to transplant otters to the Delores River in southwestern Colorado is successful. The program, conducted by the Colorado Division of Wildlife, hopes to establish a self-sustaining population of 30 or more animals. SHERM SPOELSTRA

the weasel family, was one of the most widely distributed mammals in North America. Its historic range included almost every major waterway on the continent, including those in Colorado. But for nearly a century, the otter has been only a memory here.

Like a flash of sunlight across the water, the otter is a fast and graceful swimmer. Its short legs, which make it awkward on land, tuck up close to its body in the water as it moves with powerful strokes of its tail. With bursts of speed, it captures fish such as flannelmouth suckers, channel catfish, roundtail chubs, and carp, snagging them on a set of hooklike canine teeth. A stubble of sensitive whiskers helps the otter feel its way along the bottom, as it dislodges rocks in search of crayfish.

Active all year, the otter dives through holes in the ice to fish. It has favorite pullout spots called "landings" that are easily identified by the scat, bones, and tracks that litter the edges. A thick coat of oily, waterproof fur protects the otter from the icy water. This same fur endeared the otter to trappers.

Trapping records in Europe show that a market for otters existed as far back as the 1400s. Almost as soon as Europeans stepped onto this continent, otter trapping began here. Since furs were sold by weight, and beaver, otter, and muskrat pelts were often thrown together, no one knows exactly how many otter pelts were taken. But one thing is clear: the otter began to disappear.

Accelerated by pollution and development, the disappearance did not take long. By the mid-1800s, the river otter was gone from many heartland states. By the early 1900s, it was vanishing throughout the West. The last documented evidence of wild native otters in Colorado is a photograph of two animals trapped on the Yampa River. The date was 1906.

Eventually, trapping was curtailed, and man began to understand the importance of preserving riparian habitat. In 1976, the Colorado Division of Wildlife began reintroducing river otters to the state. Otters from Oregon were first released in Cheesman Reservoir on the South Platte. Others from Newfoundland were released in the Gunnison River. Releases were made in several other locations of historic habitat.

131

Then, on November 4, 1988, the river otter came back to the Dolores. Six otters, obtained from Oregon and Alaska, were released about half a mile above Snaggletooth Rapid. Others will be released as animals become available. The goal is to establish a self-sustaining population of 30 animals. Fitted with tiny radio transmitters, they will be tracked and monitored.

The Dolores River offers the otters an abundant food supply, good bank cover, and remoteness. It flows through one of the last long stretches of undeveloped low-elevation river canyon—so undeveloped that of the 179 miles along which otters will be released, 140 have been recommended for Wild and Scenic River designation.

Once a victim of overtrapping and the degradation of its river habitat, the otter may now benefit from another human development on the Dolores River. The construction of McPhee Dam promises to stop erratic flows that, during dry summers, left major stretches completely dried up. An agreement with the Bureau of Reclamation, which operates the dam, will now ensure a minimum flow even in the dry years, giving the otters a better chance for survival.

Otters are secretive, elusive animals. Their trackers will more often hear their radio signals than see them. Still, the signals are proof enough. The sounds are like heartbeats ensuring that the river otter is alive and well in Colorado.

Peregrine Falcon

Scientific name: Falco peregrinus
Range: Statewide
Habitat: Cliffs, river canyons, gorges
Size: 15 to 25 inches long, up to 46-inch wingspan
Identifying traits: Slate-blue wings, long pointed wings,
  horizontal bars on underbelly
Status: Endangered in Colorado and nationally

The sound is like the whiz of a rock past the ear. High above the Gunnison River, just below the Black Canyon, a peregrine falcon cuts through the still morning air. It comes out of a side canyon and floats out over the river. With a flick of its wings, it searches the air for the angle that will slip it downstream. Then it is gone.

The peregrine falcon is a skilled flier, and its speed kills. When it spots prey, it tucks its wings and drops like a stone in what is called a "stoop," approaching speeds of 220 miles an hour. Like jagged lightning, it strikes its victim with its talons as it passes, often killing it outright. Then it loops back and picks the prey out of mid-air amidst a shower of feathers. The peregrine feeds on small birds such as flickers, jays, magpies, pigeons, and even fast-flying white-throated swifts. It often hunts canyons or rocky cliffs, which funnel flying birds into constricted spots.

For all its dramatics, the peregrine is successful on only 10 to 40 percent of its stoops. Younger birds increase their kill ratio with experience. To fill its stomach, the peregrine hunts over a wide area, as much as 18 miles from its nest.

The peregrine also uses its grace and acrobatics in flight during its mating rituals and in defense of its nest. The male will make wide loops in the sky, calling to its prospective mate, and then dive headlong toward the ground. Soon, the female joins in. The two birds dance with the sky and with each other. Birds defending their territories have been seen to lock talons with their intruders, plunge toward earth, and unfurl their wings at the last moment to alight on a cliff.

The peregrine builds no nest. Instead, the female lays two to six mahogany colored, splotched eggs in a scrape high on a cliff. Both parents help with incubation. The eggs hatch in 33 to 35 days, and the young remain in the nest another seven weeks.

Peregrines have never been abundant in Colorado. The state has two subspecies. The threatened Arctic peregrine is migrant, but historic references point to a small but stable nesting population of the American subspecies. In 1944, an ornithologist commented that it was "not at all uncommon to see 20 to 30 Duck Hawks (peregrine falcons) during the fall and spring migration." In 1962, Robert Wright observed seven in the air at one time over Doudy Lake in Larimer County. Historically, successful aeries were used year after year in places such as Chimney Rock, the Flatirons, Garden of the Gods, and the Yampa River canyon. Over 50 historic nesting sites have been identified in the state.

In the 1950s, the peregrine population across the continent began an alarming decline. The number of pairs known to be nesting in the West dropped from 350 in 1950 to fewer than 50 by 1965. Studies revealed that a major reason for the decline was the widespread use of the pesticide DDT, which builds up in the body tissue of the peregrine and causes a thinning of its eggshells. The thin eggs break under the stress of incubation.

DDT was banned in the United States in 1972, but the damage had already been done. The peregrine falcon

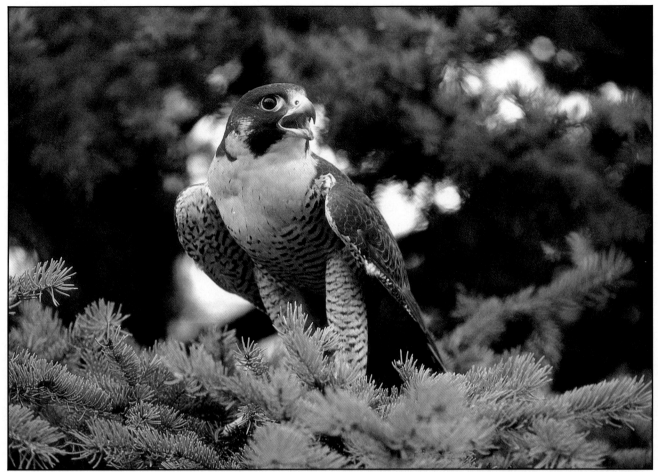

The number of peregrine falcons flashing through the Colorado sky has increased dramatically in recent years, thanks to a highly successful reintroduction program conducted by the Colorado Division of Wildlife and several other public and private groups. Diligent observers may spot peregrines near cliffs west of the foothills and throughout western Colorado, and a few birds may be seen in downtown Denver, where they nest on skyscrapers. Peregrines migrate out of Colorado in the winter, so look for these birds from late March through early October. TOM ULRICH

had vanished from the East, and the populations were dangerously low in the West. That year, only eight aeries were known to be occupied in Colorado, and none of their occupants successfully reared young.

Despite the U.S. ban, DDT use continues in many Latin American countries, where the peregrine and many of the birds it preys upon winter. The pesticide problems, coupled with a naturally low survival rate among fledglings (as many as 60 percent do not survive the first year), meant trouble for the Colorado peregrine.

In 1974, the Colorado Division of Wildlife, in conjunction with other state and federal agencies as well as private groups, began its most expensive and successful recovery program. Eggs were removed from nests by researchers and hatched in laboratories. The young were then either returned to the nests or "hacked," a process by which the chicks are reared in a wild setting until they learn to hunt. Since that time, more than 500 peregrines

have been released into the Colorado wilds.

The recovery program included the release of five birds atop the 23-story Civic Center Plaza in downtown Denver on July 13, 1988. Five more birds were released in 1989. Peregrines released in urban settings are less likely to be preyed upon by golden eagles and great horned owls. They also have access to a resident food supply of pigeons and other small birds, such as starlings, finches, and sparrows. But they do face new hazards, such as flying into traffic, power lines, and mirror glass on office buildings.

Slowly, the peregrine has made the first steps toward a comeback. In 1980, there was still just one successful wild breeding pair in Colorado. But with the foster rearing program and the hack sites, a total of 27 young were fledged. In 1984, the number jumped to 56. In 1990, there were 31 known occupied nests in the state which fledged 62 young, the most since pre-DDT days.

But the peregrine still faces many tests. DDT is still

widely used in many countries, and its effect upon eggshell thickness is still detectable in a large percentage of nests. Clearcutting of rain forests in Central and South America threatens many birds that make up the peregrine's prey base. And a significant portion of the breeding population of peregrine falcons in Colorado is made up of birds reared in captivity and released. It has yet to be proven that the peregrine can sustain its numbers without human intervention.

For now, the peregrine is still a part of the Colorado skies. Like the flash of lightning during a prairie thunderstorm and the red-tinged clouds of a mountain sunset, the peregrine adds beauty and power to the air.

Wolverine

Scientific name: Gulo gulo
Range: Northern to central Colorado
Habitat: Remote forests to timberline
Size: 35 to 50 inches long, 25 to 60 pounds, 12 inches tall at shoulder
Identifying traits: Brown fur with yellowish stipes, bushy tail
Status: Endangered in Colorado

The glimpses are fleeting. One hiker in the Flattops caught a "five-second" look in July 1968. A hunting party near Chimney Rock watched one for about 30 seconds in 1971. Others watched for four minutes as one approached bear bait near Parshall. Here and gone. The wolverine is like that.

The wolverine has never been considered numerous in the state. The Colorado mountains make up the southern extent of its range, and it is a secretive, elusive creature. Between 1871 and 1919, when the last confirmed kill of a wild wolverine occurred in Colorado, there were only 22 recorded sightings.

In 1978, the Colorado Division of Wildlife began a two-year project that included the posting of more than 3,000 "wanted posters" soliciting information about the wolverine. The division also set up hair-snag traps and traveled miles and miles on snowmobiles and skis. The result was one skull estimated to be 10 years old found along the Cimarron River, a pair of fuzzy photographs showing what could be wolverines, the carcass of an animal said to have been killed less than two miles across the Utah border, and 265 personal reports of which only 57 were given enough credibility to be rated as "positive," "probable," or "possible." The status of the wolverine

in Colorado remains unknown.

The wolverine is a short, stout creature, the largest member of the weasel family and the least-known large mammal on the continent. It requires huge tracts of land in order to maintain its solitary habits. A single male can have a range as large as 600 square miles; the range will overlap that of several females but no other males.

For its size, the wolverine is a fierce fighter; it has been known to attack deer and elk almost 10 times its size and will even run a black bear or mountain lion off a kill. But for all its fierceness, the wolverine is not well-equipped to be a predator. Its short legs give it too slow a gait to overtake prey. Instead, the wolverine relies more upon scavenging.

In fact, it is this taste for carrion that has led to the wolverine's decline in many areas. It has eaten poisoned carcasses put out in attempts to control the numbers of wolves, bears, coyotes, and mountain lions. In some parts of its range outside Colorado, it also has been trapped heavily. Although wolverine fur is not considered valuable by furriers, it was widely used to fringe parka hoods because it sheds frost.

The wolverine is mostly nocturnal, although its habits seem tied more to hunger than anything else. And the wolverine's hunger is legendary. Its Latin name translates loosely to "gluttonous glutton." Such hunger keeps it foraging throughout the year; it does not hibernate.

Breeding occurs in summer, and one to four young are born in a den the next April or May. The young stay with their mother for up to two years.

For many years, the wolverine was classified as a furbearer in Colorado. The season was closed in 1965, and it was placed on the Colorado Threatened and Endangered Species list in 1973.

The 1978 study did not verify the existence of a viable population of wolverines in the state, but it did not rule out such a population either. Some people have suggested that the animal may actually be on the increase. Sightings have occurred in similar areas many years apart. Abner Sprague wrote of a sighting in 1878 on the south side of Moraine Park in what would become Rocky Mountain National Park. Almost a hundred years later, another wolverine was sighted in a nearby section of the park.

Too little hard evidence exists to verify or refute any theory. Reports from hikers and skiers continue to trickle in. In March 1988, a pair of tracks was photographed on Guannella Pass near Georgetown, "probable" evidence of wolverine according to Dr. Jim Halfpenny of the Institute of Arctic and Alpine Research. Most biologists agree that likely wolverine habitat can be found in the San Juan

Mountains, the Flattops Wilderness, the Mount Zirkel Wilderness, Rocky Mountain National Park, and the wild lands north and west of the park. That is a lot of land. Trying to find a wolverine in all that rugged country is like searching for a shadow at night. And that is just the way the wolverine would like it.

Wood Frog

Scientific name: Rana sylvatica
Historic range: Between 8,000 and 10,000 feet, North Park, upper Colorado and Laramie rivers.
Habitat: Ponds without permanent inlets or outlets in montane zone
Size: Up to 3.25 inches long
Identifying traits: Black stripe across the eyes, and light stripe along the midline
Status: Threatened in Colorado

Mountain ranges wear away. Glaciers quietly pull back. The land changes slowly, giving wildlife a chance to evolve and adapt to new conditions. But when humans cause rapid changes, even inadvertently, they can throw the system out of balance. The plight of the wood frog is a case in point.

This small, black-masked frog has inhabited the cold

Wood frogs inhabit cold ponds in the mountains, but their numbers have declined because of human activities. In 1979, it became the first amphibian to be placed on the Colorado Threatened and Endangered Species list. JEFF MARCH

glacial ponds of northern Colorado at least since the end of the Ice Age. Near the turn of the century, zoologist Arthur Beardsley collected a specimen near Chambers Lake, but a record of the event was never published. The first published record comes from 1947, when Dr. T. Paul Maslin identified the species and mapped its range along the margins of North Park and at the headwaters of the Colorado and Laramie rivers.

Wood frogs emerge from wintering sites beneath logs and rocks in May and move to breeding ponds while there is still ice on the waters at night. Males begin to call from the margins of ponds or pools without permanent inlets or outlets. During a single night, a mating wood frog pair may attach up to 1,250 eggs to underwater sedges.

Soon after breeding, adult wood frogs migrate to their summer feeding grounds in willow thickets, wet meadows, and along streams. There, they hunt worms, insects, and spiders. Meanwhile, the eggs hatch into tadpoles that metamorphose into juveniles by late August. Some of the young may winter in the larval stage.

The cycle has played itself out for thousands of springs. But, as humans remove brush and trees from the edges of ponds, more spring sun shines on the wood frog's breeding pools, increasing the water temperature. Few wood frog eggs survive in warm water. Those that do are preyed upon by fish species such as trout and small-mouth bass, previously introduced into the ponds by humans. Siltation caused by such disturbances as logging and agriculture also has adversely affected the frog.

The result has been a decline in the number of wood frogs. In 1979, it became the first amphibian to be placed on the Colorado Threatened and Endangered Species list. The Colorado Division of Wildlife has initiated a program to try to stabilize the wood frog's population.

Other Threatened or Engangered Wildlife in Colorado

BIRDS: whooping crane, greater prairie chicken, lesser prairie chicken, plains sharp-tailed grouse, greater sandhill crane, piping plover, and least tern.

MAMMALS: black-footed ferret, grizzly bear, and gray wolf.

FISH: Colorado squawfish, humpback chub, bonytail chub, razorback sucker, greenback cutthroat trout, and Arkansas River darter.

135

For more information

Colorado Division of Wildlife
(Headquarters)
6060 Broadway
Denver, CO 80216
(303) 297-1192

(Central Region)
6060 Broadway
Denver, CO 80216
(303) 291-7230

(Northeast Region)
317 West Prospect Avenue
Fort Collins, CO 80526
(303) 484-2836

(Northwest Region)
711 Independent Avenue
Grand Junction, CO 81505
(303) 248-7175

(Southeast Region)
2126 North Weber
Colorado Springs, CO 80907
(719) 473-2945

(Southwest Region)
2300 South Townsend Avenue
Montrose, CO 81401
(303) 249-3431

**Colorado Division of Parks and
  Outdoor Recreation**
1313 Sherman Street, Rm. 618
Denver, CO 80203
(303) 866-3437

Colorado Board of Tourism
P.O. Box 38700
Denver, CO 80238
(800) 433-2656 or (303) 592-5410

U.S. Fish and Wildlife Service
Denver Federal Center
P.O. Box 25486
Denver, CO 80225
(303) 236-7920

**National Park Service
Rocky Mountain Region**
Denver Federal Center
P.O. Box 25287
Denver, CO 80225
(303) 969-2000

**USDA Forest Service
Rocky Mountain Region**
11177 W. 8th Avenue
P.O. Box 25127
Lakewood, CO 80225
(303) 236-9431

**Bureau of Land Management
Colorado State Office**
2850 Youngfield Street
Lakewood, CO 80215
(303) 236-2100

Rocky Mountain Bighorn Society
P.O. Box 1086
Denver, CO 80201
(303) 278-2502

**Foundation for North American
  Wild Sheep**
802 Canyon Avenue
Cody, WY 82414
(307) 527-6441

Colorado Outfitters Association
P.O. Box 31438
Aurora, CO 80041
(303) 751-9274

U.S. Geological Survey Map Sales
Location:
  Building 810,
  Denver Federal Center
  Kipling at Alameda, Denver
Mailing address:
  Denver Federal Center
  Box 25286
  Denver, CO 80286
  (303) 236-7477

136

Index to species

Do something wild!
Share your tax refund with wildlife.

Colorado's threatened and endangered wildlife need your support. You can help by contributing to the nongame check-off on your Colorado state income tax return.

The efforts of the Colorado Division of Wildlife to protect our nongame wildlife—animals that are not hunted, fished for, or trapped—depend on your contributions for continued success.

The dollars given through the nongame tax check-off support dozens of programs that ensure the survival of Colorado's threatened and endangered animals, including the peregrine falcon, greenback cutthroat trout, river otter, and black-footed ferret.

By checking the nongame check-off box on your state income tax form, you can make an important contribution to these valuable programs. You may contribute any amount you wish. The contribution is tax deductible the following year.

Thanks to contributions of Colorado's tax-payers through the income tax check-off:

• More than 100 endangered river otters have been reintroduced to the state.

• Peregrine falcons are now breeding in Colorado as a result of the release of several hundred of these endangered birds in remote areas of the state.

• More than 100,000 young greenback cutthroat trout, a species native to Colorado's Front Range, have been

released into Colorado's eastern waterways.

• Colorado's Division of Wildlife is able to coordinate and conduct an intensive survey of bald eagles, organized annually by the National Wildlife Federation.

• Valuable wildlife habitat in the San Luis Valley has been acquired for the benefit of many species of birds and fish.

• An urban wildlife project at Barr Lake State Park has been completed in cooperation with the Division of Parks and Outdoor Recreation which includes a nature center, photographic blinds, wooden walkways, and a wildlife gazebo.

Your support is essential for the survival of the Endangered Wildlife Program and its worthy recipients. You can really make a difference in the future of Colorado's nongame wildlife.

Use the check-off box on your state tax form to contribute all or part of your tax refund to help Colorado's nongame and endangered wildlife. If you don't get a tax refund, you can still contribute by adding to your tax payment or by sending money directly to Colorado Nongame Fund, 6060 Broadway, Denver, CO 80216.

Share your Tax Refund with Wildlife

The Colorado Geographic Series

Colorado Wildlife is the sixth book in the Colorado Geographic Series, published by Falcon Press. The other books are *The Rivers of Colorado* by Jeff Rennicke, *Colorado Mountain Ranges* by Jeff Rennicke, *Colorado Ski Country* by Charlie Meyers, *Pikes Peak Country* by Jim Scott, and *Colorado Parklands* by Stewart M. Green. Each book features easy-to-read, informative text and 100 or more color photographs. Falcon Press also publishes recreational

guidebooks such as *The Hiker's Guide to Colorado* and *The Floater's Guide to Colorado*. For more information on the Colorado Geographic Series and other books and calendars by Falcon Press, please contact your local bookstore or write to Falcon Press, P.O. Box 1718, Helena, MT 59624. You also may call toll-free 1-800-582-BOOK. If you write or call, please ask for a free catalog.